RIG

NEW WRITING FROM
BRITAIN'S OLDEST PUBLISHER

Risk-taking writing for risk-taking readers.

JM Originals was launched in 2015 to champion
distinctive, experimental, genre-defying fiction and
non-fiction. From memoirs and short stories to literary
and speculative fiction, it is a place where readers can
find something, well, *original*.

JM Originals is unlike any other list out there with its
editors having sole say in the books that get published
on the list. The buck stops with them and that is what
makes things so exciting. They can publish from the
heart, on a hunch, or because they just really, really
like the words they've read.

Many Originals authors have gone on to win or be
shortlisted for a whole host of prizes including
the Booker Prize, the Desmond Elliott Award and the
Women's Prize for Fiction. Others have been selected
for promotions such as Indie Book of the Month. Our
hope for our wonderful authors is that JM Originals
will be the first step in their publishing journey and
that they will continue writing books for John Murray
well into the future.

Every JM Original is published with a limited-edition print run. This means every time you buy one of our covetable books, you're not only investing in an author's career but also building a library of (potentially!) valuable first editions. Writers need readers and we'd love for you to become part of our JM Originals community. Get in contact and tell us what you love about our books. We're waiting to hear from you.

Coming from JM Originals in 2021

Penny Baps | Kevin Doherty
A beautifully-told debut about the relationship between brothers and the difference between good and bad.

A Length of Road | Robert Hamberger
A memoir about love and loss, fatherhood and masculinity, and John Clare, by a Polari Prize -shortlisted poet.

We Could Not See the Stars | Elizabeth Wong
To discover the truth about his mother, Han must leave his village and venture to a group of islands which hold the answer to a long-held secret.

A Length of Road

Finding myself in the footsteps of John Clare

JM ORIGINALS

First published in Great Britain in 2021 by JM Originals
An Imprint of John Murray (Publishers)
An Hachette UK company

1

Copyright © Robert Hamberger 2021

The right of Robert Hamberger to be identified as the Author of the Work has been
asserted by him in accordance with the Copyright, Designs and Patents Act 1988.

A CIP catalogue record for this title is available from the British Library

Trade Paperback ISBN 978-1-473-69793-5
eBook ISBN 978-1-473-69794-2

Typeset in Minion Pro 11.5/14.5 pt by Palimpsest Book Production Limited,
Falkirk, Stirlingshire

Printed and bound in Great Britain by Clays Ltd, Elcograf S.p.A.

John Murray policy is to use papers that are natural, renewable and
recyclable products and made from wood grown in sustainable forests.
The logging and manufacturing processes are expected to conform
to the environmental regulations of the country of origin.

John Murray (Publishers)
Carmelite House
50 Victoria Embankment
London EC4Y ODZ

www.johnmurraypress.co.uk

for
Clifford and Andrew, Helen and Ian, Annie and Alf

And every sound that meets the ear is love
John Clare,
from 'A Spring Morning'

Contents

Author's Note

John Clare is presented differently by his various editors. Some publish Clare's work exactly as his manuscripts appear, with his misspelling, idiosyncratic punctuation and gaps in his text to represent pauses. Others standardise his spelling and punctuation. To reflect these approaches my quotations from Clare appear as each editor has published them.

My poems in this book travel back to Clare's experience in July 1841, in order to depict a different approach to his walk. I use quotations from Clare's journal as epigraphs for a series of poems that speak in Clare's imagined voice and in the dramatised voices of people Clare met on his journey.

Preface

Sunday, 14 April 2019

This morning I walk beside my favourite stretch of sea in Brighton's Kemptown, with the pier twenty minutes ahead and the waves on pebbles fifty feet below me. Sky marries sea, while the little metal flowers of the wind farm edge the horizon miles away, and four lanes of sporadic seafront traffic drive towards Shoreham, towards Rottingdean.

Today is the anniversary of the first day of my eighty-five-mile trek from Epping Forest to Northborough over four days. Twenty-four years ago I had this daft idea to retrace the walk John Clare made in 1841, when he escaped from High Beach Asylum to walk home. I think of the man I was then, setting out on my expedition with a head full of troubles, weighed down by a rucksack, speaking into my Dictaphone. What better way to celebrate the changes in my life than this morning's easy stroll along the prom? I feel like shouting with D. H. Lawrence: 'Look! We have come through!' as if the world should see my changes.

A Length of Road

One early morning yacht shows a sail sharp as a cuttlefish bone. There's a stiff breeze. My shadow walks with me in the sun, while a refuse collector trundles his trolley. I must return to my desk soon, explain why it's taken twenty-four years to finish writing this book. What took me so long? Life and exhaustion from my full-time job in social work kept interfering. Self-doubt stuck its oar in repeatedly. This book (which I sometimes dared to imagine might become a real book in my hands) spent various drafts and too many years moving from tabletop to bottom drawer to tabletop again. It wouldn't let me go, nudging forward inch by inch, nagging me to find enough faith in myself to finish it. Stepping away from the manuscript (for five years when I moved to Brighton) helped me return to it with a clearer eye. I learned the value of persistence, like the journey I was describing.

One long bank of cloud is waiting like a train above the pier. A jogger in an orange top pounds towards me. The crazy golf, the playground and the beach volleyball court below are empty, too early for punters. Memoir's a baggy, commodious form and there's chutzpah in using what Clare called *that little personal pronoun 'I' . . . such a presumption ambitious swaggering little fellow.* But if I don't respect my story enough to claim and share it, who else will? I tried to write previous drafts as if I were Adrienne Rich or Mark Doty, until I hit upon the revolutionary idea to write as myself. My hunch is that there are thornier hedges to jump, unique barriers of doubt, questioning and even self-erasure for working-class writers, which is one reason why Clare's example is so remarkable. I feel sure those obstacles added to the twenty-four years, alongside facing the unhappy man I used to be and letting him speak freely. It became a sacred duty to myself, to face the past and find words for it.

The past often feels present, elbows its way through – like the immediacy of grief – so I wanted to honour the man who followed Clare's walk and make his experience present on the page, having Clare as my elusive torch-bearer, guiding my path. With no one setting deadlines, I could choose whatever pace felt right (while juggling other commitments) and write it for myself, almost in secret. Building the house of the book one brick, one word, at a time deepened my understanding of my life and the people in it, as well as giving me longer to consider the meaning of my walk and the significance of Clare's writing. My lines weathered with the years taken to write them. I couldn't have written them any other way.

This morning a few sparrows cheep in the bushes and under occasional benches along the prom, while gulls make their noise on turquoise-and-rust railings. I've already passed the bearded homeless man I've seen here for weeks. He uses a Victorian shelter bench as his bed, and stuffs his sleeping bag under it during the day, when he trudges around Brighton's streets. Coming closer behind my ear a young couple laugh with each other, catch me up, stride past. The waves change colour restlessly, shrugging their shoulders, giving themselves up on the beach below, always ready to be replaced. A Jack Russell trots past with a ball in its mouth. I'll reach the pier in ten minutes, say hello to the tide again and hurry back to my waiting desk. There's work to do, a book to finish.

Preparations

10 February 1995

I spread out four Ordnance Survey maps edge to edge on my front-room carpet. I'm trying to find John Clare's route from the asylum in Epping Forest back to his home in Northborough, near Peterborough. In July 1841 Clare escaped from what he saw as a prison and walked for four days over eighty-five miles to get home, sleeping rough, with little to eat or drink, no money and no map. For the past few months I've been hatching a crazy plan to retrace his walk. My belly's on the maps now. My elbows dent the paper, and my finger's sliding over roads and gradients to find the names mentioned in Clare's account:

Enfield Town
Stevenage
Potton
Buckden
Stilton

Peterborough
Walton
Werrington

They're simply words to me. They don't mean anything yet. I follow a jagged heart-line with my finger, reaching towards Clare's home. I admire his achievement, but I haven't learnt how to read the roads and I'm no seasoned walker.

I fold the maps away, like four paper concertinas. I'm a little dispirited by the challenge I've set myself. Who am I trying to kid? I sit in my home in silence, with my children asleep upstairs and my wife out tonight. Why do I plan to leave them, to walk back to them? Why should I, an unknown poet and social worker from the East End, with three young kids and a marriage in trouble, choose this time to ape John Clare, a great Northamptonshire poet and agricultural labourer? Why does his life and work speak to me, like some sort of kindred spirit, as if I'm lonely for brotherhood across a hundred and fifty years? We both strayed into writing from non-bookish families, misfits hoping poetry might solve our lives, but our circumstances are so different. I've no right to claim kinship. Yet I've got it in my head to copy his walk this Easter, the nearest gap of four days I can find. So far the only thing I'm clear about is wanting to discover some of what Clare went through on his walk by putting myself through a trial of miles, thinking I might capture a tenth of his experience, his shine might rub off on me. What else am I hoping to prove?

9 April

I drive the route of Clare's journey with my friend Ian and my seven-year-old son, Joe: a reconnoitre, as if this odd enterprise has developed into a planned campaign. Ian takes notes of the route in his barbed-wire artist's handwriting: an idiot's guide I'm bound to need because of my problem with maps. 'Left at A112 to Chingford. At A110 junction take right to Enfield across reservoir.'

As we speed through Potter's Bar I notice I LOVE YOU painted on a brick wall. Neat white capitals over two feet high. I imagine a man wrote that message, decided he would paint it carefully, painstakingly, one night to declare his feelings to whoever lives opposite, leaving it unsigned. I imagine a woman woke to read it the next morning, but I can't work out what she thought. I see her opening her bedroom curtains to it today and every morning, until the message loses its novelty, grows stale. Is that always the way with love?

In the late afternoon we reach Glinton near Northborough, and park the car. We want to find the footpath where Clare would have walked a hundred and fifty years ago. Joe is tired and lolls on the backseat chewing toffees. He's had a long day.

Ian and I stroll to the footbridge over a river among fields and go no further. We check the map and stand talking in the air for a while. Ian praises the usual simple sights around us – sights Clare would have known well – elms under a sea-colour sky; celandines by ploughed soil; this idea of eternal England that Ian paints and still believes in, with all its standing stones, morris dancers and ruined abbeys, rounded off by the sharp detail of a scythe leaning against a dry-stone wall and

The Lark Ascending as its soundtrack. He's enthusiastic. I'm feeling sceptical and unsettled, slightly daunted by the task ahead. Walking through six counties next week might at least give me a glimpse of how much this chunk of England has changed since Clare's walk, whether any echoes of Ian's eternal England may still be left.

First Day

Friday, 14 April 1995

It's 11.30 on Good Friday morning. My wife Dee and the kids dropped me off a minute ago and have driven away, wishing me luck and waving from car windows. I murmur into my Dictaphone, keeping track of whatever I see. To help me on my way the kids each said, 'Good luck Dad' into the Dictaphone, with a few excited giggles and my nine-year-old son Isaac saying, 'Hope you make it in about five days.' Dee took a photo before we parted, like I was an adventurer setting out on my grand expedition. Will we all be changed when I get back?

I'm at the edge of Epping Forest, by Lippitts Hill Lodge, the site of Dr Allen's High Beach Asylum. The Lodge is surrounded by a high wooden fence, but I can see the slate roofs of the painted sandstone buildings behind, and assume it's part of the asylum run by Dr Allen when it had 'gardens, pleasure grounds and sixteen acres of fields'. It now appears to be a private house or business, hidden behind tall black gates; a place of privilege.

Opposite the Lodge I imagine I'm seeing the view Clare would have seen. Wide shaggy grass moves towards brambles and cow parsley, ivy, nettles and heathland under a pearly grey sky. I hear bird calls: a cat's cradle of chirrups and whistles, trills and flutes looping between and around each other from hedge to twig to branch. Light flickers on all the leaves: green ovals, hearts, spades and feather-shapes. Clare called it *the green variety.* For a minute no one else walks this tarmac road, its white SLOW signs under my boots. I might almost glimpse Clare here, a man in russet clothes dodging between the trunks, dipping below branches, deciding it was finally time to leave.

After two doctors had signed a certificate to confirm his insanity, Clare was moved from his home in Northborough to High Beach private asylum for four years from 1837 to 1841, until what he calls *my escape from the madhouse.* Clare later told Dr Allen *the greatest annoyance in such places as yours are those servants styled keepers who often assumed as much authority over me as if I had been their prisoner & not likeing to quarrel I put up with it till I was weary of the place altogether so I heard the voice of freedom & started.*

When he first walked away from the Lodge, Clare would probably have tried to appear as casual as possible to avoid suspicion, as if he was merely repeating one of his strolls through the forest. On one of those earlier strolls, when he was feeling *very melancholly* Clare had struck a deal with some Gypsies to be hidden in their camp. But that plan was going to cost him – he promised a Gypsy fifty pounds to help him escape, although of course he had no money to speak of. It's no wonder the Gypsy *did not seem so willing.* When Clare returned to the site of their camp two days later on Sunday 18 July the Gypsies had cleared out, leaving *an*

6

*old wide-awake hat & an old straw bonnet of the plum-pud-
ding sort.*

I pass Lippitts Hill firearms training camp, with its bolted
green-barred gate, chain-link fence, raised white barrier and
a small blue sign saying Lippitts Hill Camp – Metropolitan
Police. It's opposite The Owl pub, which looks as if it was
rebuilt in the seventies, so has only retained the name from
when Clare lent Miss Fish at The Owl his copy of Byron's *Don
Juan*. On the pub sign above, an owl's moony eyes follow me.
On the grass below a robin dips for a worm. A white horse
gallops free in the riding school, no saddle or rider on its
back. I think how it would feel to be that horse, let loose at
last, to jump whatever fences are placed before me.

Bluebells uncurl while daffodils fade. A tortoiseshell cat
under a hedge watches as I walk past. Nettles are rising six
inches now, a blackbird flickering from branch to branch. A
smashed television is dumped beside the knotty feet of trees
with the usual Coke cans, and a scrappy porn magazine spreads
itself under the hedge.

Is it Clare's voice of freedom in my head or mine in my
own? The mad poet sent to save or ruin me. Clare's voice of
freedom must have felt instinctive. He couldn't stop himself
from escaping the identity of a patient, where *madhouse traps
still take me by the collar.* I admire the way he snatched control
of his future back into his own hands, decided he was going
to write it himself rather than have his life story written for
him: another mythic story of a man going home. Walking
away from the forest feels like a moment when his body
understood it was no longer necessary to stay where he'd been
put. He wasn't doing as he was told.

*

If Clare was walking home, can I say the same? These past six weeks have shaken my foundations. I'm forced to re-examine them while they crumble round my ears, but what better way to test where home is than against my skin?

After sixteen years my marriage is collapsing. I moved out of Holly House in our Northamptonshire village six weeks ago, only a fortnight or so after I opened those maps on our front-room carpet. Our separation has been years in the making. It's a ten-a-penny tale: initial happiness gradually replaced by increasing arguments, distance and differences, until we barely knew each other – or ourselves – any more. It wasn't a happy place to bring up children. Despite occasional good times, there was (for both of us I imagine) an unappeased sense of disappointment about the direction our marriage had been taking. The two-hundredth crisis one night in late February led to our agreement that I should move out, at least for a while.

After an unsuccessful session at Relate, Dee was advised it would be a good idea to make it clear to the children that our separation was now a permanent arrangement. So, on the journey down, we stopped the car at Epping to say as clearly as we could to the children that we wouldn't be living together again. The three of them in the backseat of the car – Isaac nine, Joe seven and Amy two and a half – watched our faces intently, warily, for unspoken clues. They didn't say much. I tried to explain that we loved them, but this was the best solution, because it was silly us being unhappy together, and I'd always be seeing them.

They'd already experienced six weeks of me not living at Holly House and seeing me every other day. I hoped they might be starting to get used to staying with me some weekends and

Wednesday nights in my rented room in Rothwell, ten miles away. Every time I tried to make spreading the sleeping bags on the carpet an adventure for the boys.

This morning, as I stride purposefully past forget-me-nots and a fallen silver birch, I flinch at our crass timing: confirming our separation to the children an hour before I disappear for four days. I've thrown a bomb into their lives and walked away.

When I was six – younger than Joe is now – my mother's husband Tommy (the man I saw as my father) sat in our bedroom after school, quietly explaining he was going to leave and take our older adopted brother Peter with him. This felt like something big and desolate that the grown-ups had decided. Things would be different and we couldn't change them back. I understood enough to cry as I stared through the first-floor landing railings at his Ford Anglia, watching them drive away. Now Dee has driven away, taking my kids with her.

The houses I pass in the forest ooze money, set back from the road behind hedges, narcissus and imposing fences. Occasional walkers and plodding horses with placid riders cross my path. I avoid a sloppy pyramid of horse dung in the road. The flowers of a horse chestnut sway like a host of candles. I'm plucking petals by the roadside: she loves me – loves me not – loves me. Stuck with she loves me not.

This morning, in the early hours, I woke alone again in my rented room and understood there was no going back. I'm facing this unfamiliar new fact in my life, with no moral associations of *bad* or *good*; a certainty as simple as my two legs. I'm learning what I should have always known. We've been separate from each other since the night we met twenty years ago, as individual and different as each other's bodies. Now, living apart from her, I'm starting to recognise those differences more clearly, as if the river between our two countries has begun widening into a sea.

One of Clare's delusions was that he'd been imprisoned at High Beach Asylum for bigamy, mistakenly believing he'd married his first love Mary Joyce before his actual wife Patty Turner. Part of the motivation for Clare's journey in 1841 was to return to his first love, but the reality was that Mary was no longer there, having died three years earlier in an accidental fire. I can find no evidence that Clare had been informed of Mary's death while he was at High Beach. So he walked back to her and returned home to news of her death. Years earlier he wrote: *my first feelings of love was created at school even while a boy   a young girl, I may say a child, won my affections not only by her face which I still think very handsome but by her meek modest and quiet disposition . . . her name was Mary and my regard for her last(ed) a long time after school days was over but it was platonic affection, nothing else but love in idea.*

I met Dee when I was eighteen, on our first night at university. Her first words to me were: 'Can I say hello to you?' She stood smiling before me at a freshers' party, with her long straight hair, gold wire-rimmed glasses and shabby but glamorous black astrakhan coat. In a room full of strangers hers was the first friendly face.

I tell myself I'm not returning to her. I'm walking back to the East Midlands where she and our children live, but I expect her to be where I left her, as if I could fantasise that she's waiting for my return, still wanting to say hello. Are Clare and I both returning to women who are no longer there? Perhaps I can use this walk to unravel the knots of *love in idea*, this danger of romantic love, mixing up the woman I love with myself, until I can't imagine how my life might continue without her, can't conceive of my life outside of being her husband. Clare made up a marriage to Mary in his head, while his real wife Patty had to suffer that humiliation. Why do men create fantasies of living women and confuse the two? How much of the woman I loved, in this useless romantic way, was a fantasy I moulded onto my wife's real skin?

If T. S. Eliot thought April was 'the cruellest month', Clare saw it in *The Shepherd's Calendar* as

> *The fairest child of spring*
> *And every hour that comes with thee*
> *Comes some new joy to bring*
> *The trees still deepen in their bloom*
> *Grass greens the meadow lands*

This walk might help me find out if Eliot or Clare's version of April is more accurate, if coming alive again after winter means cruelty or celebration. It could be both.

An orange butterfly settles momentarily near my boots. Towards Sewardstone, facing me, a field of oil-seed rape trembles yellow heads. Blackthorn blossom is out, white sprigs flowering next to thorns. Leaving the forest, I say farewell to birdsong and brambles, to what Clare called being *hid in a palace green.* I walk facing the traffic now, bowed under my rucksack's weight. Cars will be my companions for some time. I turn left on the A112 towards Chingford, no music in head-phones to distract me. I want to test myself against the discipline of solitude, as if I've slipped under webs and nets by leaving this century's trappings behind, as if that could bring me closer to something more 'authentic', The Clare Experience. It'll only brush the edge of what he went through, yet paying attention to my senses – to what I see around me, a commentary walking through my head – might almost bring me closer to him.

Why has Clare hooked me? Why does he seem sometimes to talk directly to me? It's the intimacy of his voice, but I also feel he's flitted through aspects of my life, so it's high time to face him. When I was fifteen, I began writing the journal I've kept until now. Within a week of starting it there was an entry about my art teacher lending me a book of Clare's poems. I wrote: 'I must admit I have never heard of him before. I read them and realise that this is true poetry, and how much I would like to write like that.'

What did I mean then by true poetry, wanting to write like that? Clare called it *real simple soul-moving poetry* and compared it to childhood. I was a bookish teenager in a Whitechapel council flat, with ambitions to become a writer. Apart from the notable exception of D. H. Lawrence, I had no example of working-class writers before me, until Clare arrived with the 'peasant poet' publicity that still hangs around him. If Clare could manage it against all those odds – to publish true poetry, make a name for himself – I might have a chance of doing the same. But the other publicity hanging around Clare was his madness. It felt like a warning to any working-class teenager with arty aspirations, ideas above his station, as if the peasant poet and madness were indelibly connected, and madness became a punishment for trying to step outside his class with his writing. 'If you're not careful this is where writing gets you, Mr Arty Teenager.' In my journal I said Clare was 'betrayed', but didn't go into detail about who or what I thought might have betrayed him. I was probably too confused about his biography then, as if ending up in a madhouse must surely be someone's fault, the result of forces stacked against him.

In a neat front garden, a woman in her sixties in a black top and dark blue skirt fills a black dustbin-liner with grass cuttings. I imagine she's recently widowed, hence the sombre clothes, and that filling a dustbin-liner might be part of her resolve to survive.

When I walk past the garden I admit I've no idea what's happened to her. All I know is my own resolve to survive includes a four-day walk over Easter that's as meaningful as filling a bag with grass cuttings. Anything that gets me or the woman in the garden up in the morning gives us a reason to live.

As a working-class teenager with writerly aspirations, I was lucky enough to have an ally. My schoolfriend Clifford crowds my teenage journals with his opinions, his jokes, the books he read, the artists he liked and his anxieties. We felt easy in each other's company. We discovered and explored an incredible new landscape together, peopled by exotic creatures like

13

Virginia Woolf, T. S. Eliot, Katherine Mansfield, Matisse, Henri Gaudier-Brzeska and Rembrandt. Our plan was that Clifford would be the artist and I would be the writer and we would both make a splash in our respective worlds, show middle-class wankers who occupy art and literature what 'true' art looked like. We would shake them up. We clubbed together and felt stronger, less isolated by doing so.

Clare was less fortunate. Although he enjoyed friendships, his writings about his early life show few allies in poetry to keep him going. He wrote *I made but few close friendships for I found few with the like tastes inclinations and feelings.* When he walked with his friends in the fields *I often try'd their taste by pointing out some striking beauty in a wild flower or object in the surrounding senery to which they woud seldom make an answer, and if they did twas such as 'they could see nothing worth looking at' . . . I thought somtimes that I surely had a taste peculialy by myself and that nobody else thought or saw things as I did.*

Clare's right that nobody thought or saw things as he did. Isolation for him becomes celebration for his readers. Education cost money. Edward Storey notes that Clare's parents (particularly his mother, who was illiterate) were keen on Clare's schooling: 'It cost Mrs Clare a few pence each week out of her own purse to keep her son at school...seldom a year passed without Clare getting ten or eleven weeks' schooling each year until he was nearly twelve.' So, following his meagre formal education, Clare was largely self-taught. This also set him apart. He writes powerfully about feeling different from his fellow villagers, being part of a class where writing poetry was not meant to have any place, *chilling damp with fear whenever I thought of it, the laughs and jeers of those around me when they found out I was a poet was present death to my ambitious apprehensions for in our unlettered villages the best of the inhabitents have little more knowledge in reading than what can be gleaned from a weekly Newspaper.*

As teenagers Clifford and I wanted to be connected to that arty world from which we felt excluded. We met as eleven-year-olds, on our first morning at Parmiter's, one of the last grammar schools in Bethnal Green; a couple of hand-picked working-class boys who'd been offered a chance to use selective education to climb away from our background, if we wanted to take it. Of course, we didn't understand that possibility then. We were simply two bright boys from fatherless families, who felt we'd pleased our mothers by being chosen.

The register had just been called before lessons started, and Mr Robinson, our squat, balding form teacher, had temporarily left the classroom. Boys around us began to whisper and snigger at first, talking more boldly as the minutes dragged, eventually squabbling and lobbing paper aeroplanes, pencils or rulers across the room. We'd been seated alphabetically beside each other at two scarred and scribbled desks, with empty holes for thimble-like white china inkwells in the top right-hand corners. Among the chaos, the silence between us grew more awkward the longer it progressed, but I was too embarrassed to break it. Clifford cracked first.

'What's your name then?' he asked.

Before I could answer, Mr Robinson barged back into the class shouting, 'Right, shut up you lot. Let's get down to work.'

During school holidays we would often catch a bus from the East End to the West End, and wander round Foyles and the Charing Cross Road second-hand bookshops, the National Gallery and the National Portrait Gallery, where we saw

William Hilton's portrait of Clare, in his brown jacket, his leafy gold and steel-blue cravat, dull yellow waistcoat. That luminous expression on his face, staring past us slightly upwards towards inspiration in the distance, lips parted and tousled auburn hair, every inch the starry young poet. It was painted on his first trip to London, commissioned by his publisher to boost publicity for this peasant poet making his name in the capital. It's no wonder he's looking inspired. The world's eyes are on him.

Clifford loved opera, so we improvised and recorded a sung version of *The Waste Land* on cassette, using his battered red-painted piano and my voice. On his bedroom wall he painted Don Quixote and Sancho Panza. Once at the Tate we saw Henry Moore with his walking stick gradually circling Rodin's *The Kiss*, admiring it with a few hangers-on. It seemed to us like an ageing hero had descended from some higher place of art to breathe our air. One morning beside St James's Park we slipped unnoticed into an ICA exhibition of Picasso's erotic etchings. We must have arrived before the exhibition opened, as we had the gallery to ourselves. All those finely drawn etchings of the artist and his nude models, minotaurs and nymphs, flourishing intricate penises and vaginas looked thrilling to a couple of teenage boys, however artistic our inclinations, as if they represented another magical world from which we were – at that moment – excluded.

A man sponges his car, suds dribbling across the roof and on to the windscreen. Couples pull out from driveways into queues of stalled traffic. I wonder where everyone's going, to which good place. I imagine what it might be like to live inside a routine again: to plan to wash your car on Good Friday morning, before taking your wife and kids out for a drive.

I'm miles from how my kids are spending the rest of their day, feel sorry for them having a father who's left and appears to be walking away.

It felt as if I met Clare again when I met Dee at eighteen, and I associate Clare with her. When we were falling in love as English Literature students, she told me about reciting his sonnet 'First Sight of Spring' in a local elocution competition as a child:

> *The squirrel sputters up the powdered oak*
> *With tail cocked o'er his head and ears errect*
> *Startled to hear the woodman's understroke*
> *And with the courage that his fears collect*
> *He hisses fierce, half malice and half glee . . .*

She dramatised her reading to me, wide-eyed, showed me how as a girl she would have relished that lovely dialect word 'sputters' to describe a squirrel skittering up a trunk. I was *over head and ears in love*, as Clare describes it. I'd never met anyone like her. I was a city boy swept away by the thought of squirrels sputtering up trunks; by her teaching me how dead-nettles don't sting if you look out for their creamy flowers; how goose-grass clings to the shins of your jeans if you walk through it; how cuckoo-spit hung on the intersections between stems and leaves like clusters of caught snow. I'd never noticed before.

When we travelled to her home in Northamptonshire I

remember her poking a grass-spear into cuckoo-spit, though the insect hidden inside had already disappeared. She found little yolk-yellow flowers tinged with red she called 'eggs and bacon', and low-lying tiny blue flowers she called 'grandmother's eyes'. The roadside and meadow flowers had names that sounded like poetry: campion, bird's-foot-trefoil, cranesbill, periwinkle, vetch, herb Robert, shepherd's purse, where she split open the heart-shaped purse and showed me money-seeds inside. She taught me the proper way to use a kissing gate, with a kiss over the slats to allow you through. Once she taught me about peeling back the dirty pennies of honesty after flowering, to unwrap their ghostly coins. There was a wider world than London, a different England, and I was discovering it through her.

King George's Reservoir stretches along my right, with four tower blocks, a line of pylons and a gasometer behind it. There's barely a flicker of any rural views that Clare might have seen, apart from a donkey nipping grass on the slopes up to the reservoir and a chaffinch flying from bush to tree singing as it flies. Three young men ride past on bicycles baa'ing at sheep. They get one reply.

Before it disappears behind the slope, the surface of the reservoir's calm as linen, with Pick's Cottage Carp Lake on its opposite side: two slabs of grey water. Men sit for hours beside their rods, staring into reflections, where they can't see carp flicking lazy tails, ignoring the maggot, avoiding the hook.

Describing the start of the first day of his walk on 20 July 1841, Clare wrote in his journal *Reconnitred the route the Gipsey pointed out & found it a legible one to make a*

*movement & having only honest courage & myself in my army
I led the way & my troops soon followed.* No one followed Clare
from Epping Forest, even if he felt he was setting out to battle,
captain of an army in his head.

The five pages of Clare's journal are, in Iain Sinclair's words,
'one of the wonders of English prose', describing 'one of the
great English journeys'. When I first read it last autumn I was
stunned by its pathos and exhaustion. Last week I visited
Northampton Library to study the microfiche of Clare's manuscript. His looped and twirly handwriting is close-packed on
the pages. Brown ink blotches over three-and-a-half sides of
crowded lines, sloping down without punctuation towards the
right and narrowing as his account progresses, like there's a
rush to express his escape: get the words written and journey
done, taking gulps of breath as he goes.

I've been walking for an hour and it feels much longer. Sweat
presses cold on my back against the rucksack. A magpie flies
uphill.

I'm in a residential street approaching Enfield Town. Clare
got lost around here. His journal says, *I missed the lane to
Enfield Town & was going down Enfield Highway till I passed
the Labour in vain Public-house where a person I knew coming
out of the door told me the way.*

I pass bay-window houses with stucco ivy leaves over their
doors and a few satellite dishes on their walls. A young woman
watches her boyfriend vacuum the car. Daffodils are browned
off beside wheelie-bins in scuffed front gardens, a few with
For Sale or Sold hoardings on posts by their fences. I count
endless cars, white vans and double-decker buses. I'm walking

no faster than an old woman in a turquoise knitted cardigan lugging shopping on the other side of the road. If it's meant to be a race, she's winning.

Clare's sense of home was enshrined in the fact that his birth-place, childhood and adult home were the same building. He called the cottage of his birth *my own old home of homes* and didn't leave his birthplace – moving four miles from Helpston to Northborough – until shortly before his thirty-ninth birthday. Staying where you've been born was common enough for Clare's class. What does that continuity do for a poet? It must have given him focus and precision, time to notice. In an early poem 'Helpstone' he writes of *lost roads leading every where but home*; yet he turns the end of that poem towards home, as if it's a divining rod twitching his pen:

> *Each hated track so slowly left behind*
> *Makes for the home which night denies to find*
> *And every wish that leaves the aching breast*
> *Flies to the spot where all its wishes rest*

He became a homing pigeon loosed from his cage of twigs in Epping Forest, flying back to Helpston, his birthplace, or Northborough, his recent home, or even Glinton, Mary's home, two miles from Helpston. Those three villages and surrounding heaths and fields enclosed his emotional terrain, his homeland.

Copying Clare's journey means I'm walking past my child-hood flat towards the house of my adulthood. Yet I walked away from that flat in Whitechapel years ago. I admitted to

Dee when we married that I wanted a change from London. The move was a shift from city to country, and I relished the rooms of my marriage nestled in the dip of a hill: fields, trees and hedges outside my writing window at Holly House. I don't belong in London any more, yet as a child and adolescent I thought London was the centre of the world. When Clifford and I imagined storming the ramparts of the writing and painting fortresses, we assumed they were built in London.

Clare's two-up two-down childhood cottage – occupied by his parents, his maternal grandmother, he and his younger sister Sophy – became *my happy spot*. In 'To My Cottage' he writes:

> *While the fond parent wound her whirring spool*
> *And spared a sigh for the poor wanderer's lot.*

My childhood home meant my parents, my two brothers and our two-bedroom first-floor council flat at Gascoyne House in Hackney, with me – the middle child – literally feeling safe in the centre of it, unassailable. But after Tommy left when I was six, taking my adopted older brother Peter with him, it felt like a room with the wall ripped away, as if we were exposed to the elements now, yellow curtains flapping in the wind, boats on our blue bedroom wallpaper tossed on an uncertain sea. We were exposed to the weather of my mother's moods, as if one evening after school she might follow her husband to a mysterious place miles away where we'd never find her, if I didn't behave myself, if I and my younger brother Stephen weren't good boys. My mother never made such threats (it was probably the last thing on her mind)

21

but trying to be a good boy to please her, to stop her leaving, became my secret ambition as a child.

In Gascoyne House our elderly neighbour was May, I think, or Mary or Molly. A thin proud woman, with winged glasses and soft white hair. She liked chatting to me as she moved about her housework, peeling carrots and potatoes, shelling peas, ironing sheets with an old flat iron that fascinated me. She heated its heavy black boat shape on a dangerous metal plate. I steered clear of it, but loved the smell of steamed sheets drifting through her front room, as she sailed the flat iron over white linen, smoothing every wrinkle. She taught me a strange silly song I can still sing:

> I went down the lane
> to buy a penny whistle.
> The copper come along
> and took me penny whistle.
> I asked him for it back.
> He said 'I haven't got it.'
> Oy Oy Curly Locks
> You got it in y'pocket!

It might have been an old street song, or something from the music hall. I had no idea what it meant, but I loved sing-shouting the last two lines along with her. They made me happy.

When she died, a family with four children younger than me moved in next door. The father had black greased hair and a quiff like Elvis. They told us they'd lived in a caravan before. I couldn't imagine that, though it sounded exciting. When we visited their flat it felt barer – with floorboards and no carpets – but more relaxed than being at home, so casual that the little girls wore no knickers when they cuddled up to their fat laughing mother on the settee, twirling their side-curls sleepily as they sucked on bedtime bottles.

A wailing police car attempts to weave through traffic. People step outside their houses to stare: women jutting toddlers or babies on their hips, while the blue light slurs over them. A car's across the centre of the road, windscreen cracked and dented as if a weight has fallen against it. The wiper has snapped, and what I assume to be a man lies under a blanket in the road, with people clustered round him. A black shoe stands by itself on the tarmac.

Police and witnesses point in different directions. Drivers are manoeuvring their wheels to turn the other way and escape the traffic jam. An ambulance nudges forward. It's all going on quietly – almost respectfully – centred round that blanketed figure lying in the road.

Clare writes of *seeing when I was younger a man name Thomas Drake after he had fell off a load of hay and broke his neck   the gastly palness of death struck such a terror on me that I could not forget it for years.*

Five minutes later I'm leaving the scene past Ladysmith Road, and it might be easier to let the 'ghastly paleness of death' slide away as swiftly as those streets. The further I walk from the accident the more I begin to think about lunch. Unlike Clare not forgetting it for years, my reaction's as careless as walking past a stranger whose face I've no risk of remembering, having never seen him.

*

When my mother moved with us to Collingwood House from Hackney several months after the break-up to live nearer her own mother and three sisters in Whitechapel, the experience of family widened. My aunts Suzie, Nettie and Hannah and my nan Jane Braithwaite each lived five minutes away in neighbouring blocks of flats. From then on, we saw these women, and seven of my cousins, virtually every day. Their brothers Charlie and Joey had moved up in the world in their jobs, and were already living in Essex, bringing up their families away from us. (In the East End in those days a move to Essex was seen as a mark of success – getting out and getting on – buying your own house, your own car.)

So the African proverb 'It takes a village to raise a child' came true for me. My aunts, uncles, cousins and nan became my village. Their powerful personalities crowded my days. They were a support to my mother as she embarked on her new lone parenthood. My actions were on show; these adults could talk about them, laugh at things I did, or tell me off, make judgements, if I squabbled too much with my cousins. But I liked being around them. They dug themselves into my landscape from then on: solid, familiar and reliable, surrounding me like standing stones.

Years later, Aunt Nettie told me that she remembered walking past our flats when, seeing her through the black landing railings where I knelt, I started shouting 'Arm in! Arm in!' and she couldn't work out what I meant. I was using the phrase my mother said to get me into my coat when we were going out, and I was telling my aunt I wanted to go out with her. Wherever she was going was bound to be more exciting than staring through landing railings.

Another song from childhood comes to me, even stranger

than the first. We often visited Aunt Suzie and Uncle Laurie in Redmill House, one block of flats away. When she was absorbed in housework, Aunt Suzie sang in a high lilting voice that sounded carefree. She sang one song that was perhaps nonsense, or an obscure dialect, or a language I couldn't understand. The peculiar words intrigued me. I learnt to sing them, and sing them now into my Dictaphone:

> Kaka-di-roon and kany-enta
> Shopa-di-aysh, kazamakazee

After that she'd sing variations of the tune in a weird and joyful improvisation, to the rhythm of polishing knick-knacks or buttering bread.

On the other side of Enfield Town, I find a park with a fifteen-foot-high grey stone memorial to OUR GLORIOUS DEAD, a wreath carved above the sombre capitals and a sarcophagus at its summit. A black chain is looped around flagstones, and three steps lead to it, with the dates of both wars, stone laurel leaves, and a half-circle of tightly budded rhododendrons facing the crossroads traffic-lights.

A poplar flickers in the breeze. Beside the bus stop a grey-bearded Asian man sits on a plastic stool playing an accordion, a tin can in front of him for coins. His music sounds jaunty and melancholy in the same notes and no one seems to throw him money. I unload my rucksack, unwrap sandwiches on grass spattered with daisies and dandelions. A magpie scares a rook from its territory. It's two o'clock and, according to the pedometer, I've walked six miles, although I'm not convinced.

I unlace my boots, ease myself out of their creaky leather. I pull off thick socks to give my feet an airing, while the accordion changes its tune.

From the age of six to twenty-two I lived with my mother and younger brother Stephen in a two-bedroom council flat on the third floor of Collingwood House. It's a block of post-war flats, with khaki-coloured bricks and cramped verandahs overlooking Cambridge Heath Road, five minutes' walk from Whitechapel Road market. Like Clare's Helpston cottage, that home's the bedrock to my early life, the template I've moved on from, compared with the six others I've lived in so far.

My elder brother Peter came back to live with us, intermittently, for some of his teenage years, after his relationship with Tommy became strained, and Tommy and his new wife, Dorothy, chucked him out.

Our building formed part of Collingwood Estate, which was made up of eight or so blocks of four-storey flats, most of them post-war, although Harvey House and Bullen House (where my nan lived) were pre-war red-brick. In the sixties Eagle House (where my nan moved in her later years) and Orion House (our version of high-rise) were built nearby.

Collingwood House was designed in the shape of a massive hook, or an inverted question mark. Four straight storeys turned on themselves at the end. Until a few tenants began buying their council flats after Thatcher's policy change in the eighties, there was a deliberate uniformity. All third-storey front doors were red because all fourth-storey doors were blue. All second-storey doors were blue because all first-storey doors were red. Some tenants' window boxes, overhanging the landing walls, stayed bare whatever the season, while others blossomed with geraniums or busy Lizzies. Ours held ice plants, because they were easy to tend and gave a splash of chill-pink blooms late every summer.

The landings ran around each storey. Kids could race along them, and annoy grown-ups by playing knock down ginger, rapping on door knockers and running away. Our landing overlooked an asphalt playground about half the length and width of a football pitch. At the other end of the playground, Grindall House's identical doors faced us. Berry House and Redmill House (where Aunt Suzie and Uncle Laurie lived) stood on my right and backed onto this playground I saw every time I opened my front door. Their landings faced Headlam Street, where parked cars narrowed the road all day, and where my Uncle George's motorbike sidecar caught fire, flames flapping their torn orange flag in the wind.

At the end of every landing smelly black iron rubbish-chutes stood in porches, by the head of each iron-railing staircase. My mother would splash Dettol into ours occasionally to improve the whiff that rose whenever its mouth opened. Milky-green tiles covered the bottom half of every stairwell, while cream paint made an attempt to brighten the top half of staircase walls.

Some images from childhood stay in close-up, and the stairs was one of them. The staircase of Collingwood House had a different atmosphere from Gascoyne House in Hackney. Our move of a few miles dragged me away from my familiar world. I sat for hours on the staircase, with my shorts and snake-clasp belt and scabby knees, playing and oblivious, or feeling sorry for myself, my finger smearing a tiny puddle of spit over grey stone that seemed to be mixed with infinitesimal sparks like black stars, the same dark glitter as pencils. My stairs held the sandpaper sound of writing with a pencil. Strokes of shoe soles against stone when someone climbed ahead of me, or followed me upstairs, were my daily music. Like matches scraped along the edge of a matchbox, failing to flame, until those steps became mine coming home, leaving home.

Half an hour later my sandwiches are eaten, and a crust is chucked to the lucky magpie. A blackboard sign outside the Old Wheatsheaf pub tells me *Education Is Important – But Beer is Importanter.*

At the crest of the hill beside a mini-roundabout, where I turn right onto the Ridgeway towards Enfield Chase, an elderly couple sit on a bench. He's spruce, with his neat red tie, and palms cupped over the crook of a walking stick standing between his knees. Her liver-spotted thick-veined hands rest in her lap. Both stare ahead at me and the traffic, not saying a word to each other. I wonder what their silence means. Contentment or apathy, or such ease in each other's company that words are no longer required? I feel an ache of envy that this marriage, whatever its content, has lasted more years than Dee and I could manage. The possibility of a lifelong marriage fades a little more every morning. This old couple aren't competing with anyone. They live in the moment of their marriage, watching the world and whatever unrolls in it, separately and together. Dee and I won't grow old together. We could have torn each other to shreds before a golden anniversary, so it's better to let the years without each other take care of themselves. Walk your way out of this. Find a way clear.

*

Clare writes of *wandering about the fields watching the habits of birds* as a child, *playing at marbles on the smooth beaten sheep tracks or leap frog among the thimey molehills somtimes ranging among the corn to get the red and blue flowers for cockades to play at soldiers or runing into the woods to hunt strawberrys or stealing peas.* Our playground was the centre of the estate, a grey rectangle with twelve-foot-high chain-link fences running along the sides, to protect windows from footballs. The playground was big enough for boys from the flats to team up for football matches, and occasional cricket or rounders or, during Wimbledon fortnight, doubles for tennis with an imaginary net. Girls and boys played tin tan Tommy: whoever was 'it' had to rap a tin can and shout, 'Tin tan Tommy – I see Tracey behind the pram-shed.' If you were right, Tracey was out. A broken roundabout at the Collingwood House end was often the place to get 'home' to without being caught. Three rusted swings swayed nearby on a metal frame, until they were vandalised and never repaired.

Clare writes of noticing as a boy *the different greens of the woodland trees the dark oak the paler ash the mellow lime the white poplar peeping above the rest like leafy steeples the grey willow shining chilly in the sun as if the morning mist still lingered on its cool green.* The trunks of our young trees stood corseted in wire cages, on strips of grass along the backs of Berry House and Redmill House, where you weren't supposed to play. On either side of the entrance to the playground rosebushes and fuchsia flowered behind waist-high black-painted railings, near a row of half-a-dozen locked pram-sheds with grey doors.

Clare sees around his childhood's horizon *the little ups and downs and roly poly child mountains of the broken heath with*

29

their brown messy crowns and little green bottoms where the sheep feed and hide from the sun   the stone quarry with its magnified precipices   the wind mills sweeing idly to the summer wind. Across the road from Collingwood House, down Darling Row, the Albion Brewery worked for years, until it closed and was pulled down after I moved away, replaced by a shiny new Sainsbury's and car park. Through my childhood and adolescence, the brewery was a site of clatter and industry, with that raw, sharp tang of hops in the air and up the nose most afternoons. Grey smoke foamed from the brewery chimney, giving a rainbow to the nearest street lights in the early evenings. I remember reading brewery slogans on walls in my childhood and adolescence, like advice in gold letters, telling me to TAKE COURAGE.

Metal barrels clanged a weird bell-like melody as they were rolled and stacked onto carts by shouting brewery men. Throughout the day teams of dray horses pulled carts loaded with barrels. Some Saturday mornings Uncle Laurie took us to feed carrots to the dray horses: their enormous shaggy fetlocks, straggly fringes and deep nostrils; their uneven yellow teeth, which never nipped if you held your palm steady and weren't afraid. I felt the wet slip of lips against my open hand when a carrot disappeared.

Along the Ridgeway a plump middle-aged woman in her electric wheelchair trundles up and down the stretch of pavement outside Arnold House, a gabled white-painted Leonard Cheshire Home. She manoeuvres the wheelchair full circle to ride back the way she came: the same thirty yards of pavement. She's a lioness pacing behind bars. I wonder if she wants to escape; if she hears Clare's *voice of freedom* and wants to be gone from having to retrace her path again and again.

If she chooses to leave, how far will her wheelchair carry her before the power runs out? I only know she needs to repeat her ride, and I watch her do it without understanding. She might stop the minute I'm gone.

Clare writes of his neighbours in Helpston village, *most of them have known me from childhood & coud never find that I had any faults till now – I possesd their good word 18 years & it did me no service – & if I shoud live to wear their bad one as long it will do me no harm.* The public aspects of living in the flats were my urban version of Clare's village. Neighbours watched me grow up for years, even if they didn't often acknowledge or particularly approve of me. The flats housed a range of characters, tribal loyalties, alliances, love affairs, secrets and feuds between neighbours and extended families who, like us, had many relatives living on the same estate. I often entered or left the flats while a cluster of neighbours were talking or laughing near the downstairs dust-chute. A door-entry system was added for security after I moved out, but when I lived there you could come and go as you pleased.

After work on spring and summer evenings, middle-aged men in vests rested their forearms on landing walls by half-open doors; smoking sometimes, staring out into the street or playground as if they were quiet guardians, lifting their hand to anyone they knew. When I opened our front door pigeons often flew up at me, to rest on window boxes or the mess-whitened wall. They mistook any movement along our landing for the arrival of our next-door neighbour, a Jewish widower, who fed them monkey-nuts from his jacket pocket.

In my teens the Jewish widower died, and an Asian family moved in with two small children and a baby. My mother said they caused no trouble, though she complained about spicy cooking smells along the landing, as other Asian neighbours moved in. She started giving next-door's children boiled sweets and grew close to the couple, who would always smile shyly when we met on the stairs or landing, though the woman spoke few English words. As I became a teenager the settling of Asian families altered the estate's ethnic mix, which had been mainly Jewish and white working class, with a few black families. Neighbours who lived there for years started talking about 'the Pakis', sometimes affectionately, often with contempt. Painted slogans appeared on brick walls:

JEWS & PAKIS OUT
WHITE SLAGS GO WITH WOGS
KILL WHITE TRASH

One Sunday the Anti-Nazi League marched along Cambridge Heath Road towards Brick Lane, chanting 'Black and White Unite and Fight' and hoisting placards into the air. We watched them from our verandah. Chants and whistles took over the road below us for ten noisy minutes.

The atmosphere in the estate began to feel less safe. My brother remembers my mother shouting '*Stee*-ven *Stee*-ven' from our third-floor landing when it grew dark on summer evenings, calling him home from where he chatted with other teenagers by the gate near Redmill House and the Barley Mow. I'd hear other names called occasionally, usually by women, when it was time for tea or they felt it had grown too dark.

In my teenage years, when I imagined I'd write the Great British Novel, I planned a book of linked short stories called 'The Flats'. I wrote 'Whitechapel Notes', a prose piece about the estate, but I never wrote any more.

I pass a magnolia tree, petals curled like Art Nouveau teacups. A laburnum decorates another garden, with strings of lemon flowers. A man in a black T-shirt hoses his shiny black Mercedes in the driveway. Outside Chase Farm Ambulance Station, with its fleet of ambulances, four Chase Farm Hospital nurses wait for their bus, joking to each other, puffing fags.

A smartly dressed young woman with a floppy fringe walks towards me as I talk into my Dictaphone. She looks at me anxiously. For three seconds her vanilla perfume wins the contest against cigarette smoke when our paths cross.

Leaving the Royal Chace Hotel, along the Ridgeway, the landscape opens to fields on either side and wisps of cloud like combed white hair. A subtle breeze tickles my skin. It's perfect walking weather. Perhaps this is where, on his first day, Clare started to feel more optimistic, *bye & bye on the great York Road where it was all plain sailing*. I even hear birdsong again beyond the traffic, and see cows clumped under the shade of a tree. Two yellow fields of oil-seed rape stink in the sun, like a smell of old furniture shut inside rooms. Leaves are easing themselves from tight buds, jutting green elbows as if they've lived in straitjackets too long.

Shapes of horses' hooves have been imprinted into tarmac under my boots. Dee was handed a cardboard silver horseshoe by a blonde girl as we stood on the steps of the church after our wedding sixteen years ago. We propped a black painted horseshoe in the porch of Holly House, where our son Joe was born nine years later. I'm striding over a path of good-luck charms.

The two men missing from my landscape were my father and maternal grandfather. They left gaps in my circle of standing stones. Clare's grandfather had also disappeared; in his case he was *a Scotchman by birth and a schoolmaster by profession,* who *left the village and my grandmother soon after the deplorable accident of misplaced love was revealed to him.*

My mother adored her father. Her love for him was still shining from the words she used to talk about him. He worked in the docks at Wapping as a crane driver on the Thames, by all accounts a proud independent man who once walked through a picket of striking dockers, telling them he was going to work because he believed by striking they'd cut their own throats. My grandmother was Jewish, from Portuguese Jews who'd emigrated to England from the Netherlands sometime during the 1830s and settled in the East End. I have an ancestor with the amazing name of Hana Ribca Rodrigues De Marcado – born in the Netherlands in 1793, the same year as Clare – and my grandmother's parents were Hannah Ereira and Joseph Van Den Bogaert, a cigar-maker. I recently discovered that my grandmother's elder brother Isaac (who I never met) was once a pimp and gangster who dressed as a cowboy. He was given the local nickname 'Darkie the Coon' because of his swarthy complexion, but reformed after a glass attack that made his face 'like the map of England' (as his attacker said). He went on to be awarded the Military Medal in the First

World War. My grandad was a Gentile, so he and my nan both married outside their faiths. I don't know whether they shamed their families by doing so, or whether having a former pimp as a brother caused problems. Nobody told me; those stories are already lost.

My grandad died from cancer a few years before my parents' separation. One of my earliest memories – before I was three years old – is walking towards him in the front room of Bullen House. He was lying on my nan's settee during his last illness, in blue- and white-striped pyjamas, a few buttons of the jacket undone and wisps of grey chest-hair showing. I couldn't work out why he lay in pyjamas in the front room during the day, because pyjamas were for night. No one explained why it was allowed. He was ready to welcome me as I hesitantly approached. I'm always walking towards him, his arms opening in slow motion to greet me, although I never manage to reach his thin embrace.

When we first moved to the estate there were still wild uncultivated places where children could play, where hillocks and troughs of earth had been left to themselves among the buildings. We called each of them the Dump. Weeds and ragwort and occasional poppies swayed there. I thought they were the craters left by bombs across Bethnal Green from the war, with no money to build on them. My nan was psychic and once said my dead grandad told her I mustn't play there. It was dangerous in the Dump near the church. I was forbidden to enter. A week later a man was found murdered in the mud, and my mother and aunts talked in hushed admiring tones about how their father saved my life from beyond the grave. Years afterwards a neat play area was built there, railings and a path taking the place of bindweed and brambles.

This extended family, with its strong women and shadowy men, became secure if we behaved ourselves, but ran the risk of stifling us. My brothers and most of my cousins have moved away from East London now. Apart from the exception of his escape, Clare did his best to prove there's beauty in staying put; but I wonder how else me, my brothers and cousins might have become ourselves, without moving away.

After those teenage years of arty exploration with Clifford, my chance to branch out came when I moved at eighteen to Sussex University near Brighton, my first long period far from home. A year earlier Clifford had travelled with me from London to Brighton for my interview for an English degree course, to offer moral support with my pre-interview nerves. I was stepping outside the East End, the first in my family to consider university. When we returned to Brighton station after my interview, we had fifty minutes or so before our Victoria train. Outside the station forecourt we saw straight down the road to the sea, glinting ahead in early evening sun. We felt starved of the sea in London, so dared each other to run down Queen's Road in the time left between trains. In my journal as a seventeen-year-old I wrote: 'We ran all the way from the station, down to the sea, looked at the waves, violet in the evening light, and ran all the way back up to the station in time to catch our train.'

On that first night at university I said 'Yes' when Dee appeared from nowhere in her astrakhan coat and asked if she could say hello. I don't regret that yes. She makes me laugh like no one else, though the laughter's dwindled lately. She's bright to the brim with ideas, capable and scatty, artistic and clumsy, and I can't believe I'm losing her from my side. I assume this is how love feels when it's breaking from behind my ribs. Walking away becomes a necessity, running back its noisy twin.

As we grew closer during our first term together, Dee took me to visit her home in Northamptonshire. She lived with her maternal grandparents after her mother had died. They were Northants people born and bred, her lanky jokey grandfather Bill, a retired stonemason, her short sparky grandmother Nell making the best scones and dumplings I've tasted. In my first weekend at their bungalow in Kettering, Dee's gran asked if I'd heard of John Clare. She looked impressed when I said I had and spilled her some know-it-all facts, hoping they might give me a bigger tick on her 'is-this-boyfriend-worth-it' list. They saw Clare as 'their' poet, with a sense of fond possession – the poet of Northamptonshire – so much so that I mistakenly assumed he must have lived a few miles from their home; until we drove some months later with Dee's brother for over an hour to Helpston near Peterborough. We photographed him perched on a millstone-post beside Clare's green front door, its little thatched roof bristling like a buzzard's nest above the threshold.

While I was busy falling in love in Brighton, Clifford had been attending a psychiatric day hospital near Hackney Marshes a few days every week, to help him deal with anxieties and panic attacks that had been plaguing him since late adolescence. He took part in hours of group therapy, and several months there helped him face his demons. Greater understanding about himself probably led him to tell me, one sun-spilt afternoon in Victoria Park, that he was gay. He was surprised I hadn't realised, though I never could see what was two inches from my nose. When he finished at the day hospital, he met John, his first boyfriend, who introduced him to drag queens and drama queens, gay clubs and charming young men who swerved into dark moods and drank too much.

After a Foundation year at Hornsey, Clifford studied for his fine arts degree at St Martin's in Charing Cross Road. It was a liberating time for him and he celebrated with an Abstract Expressionist phase: six-foot canvases splashed and scored by reds and oranges, purple patches, waves of blue, jungle greens. He holidayed in Paris with his student friend Jenny, who sewed him cream trousers with occasional six-inch black piano keys in jagged patterns across his thighs and shins, the back of his knees. They were the clothes art students wore. He bought me a diamanté letter 'R' tiepin from a Parisian flea market that I still wear in my jacket lapel. He hand-painted a narrow tie for my birthday, with blocks of pastel colours. It hangs in the wardrobe of my rented room, one of the precious things I took with me when I moved out.

I'm standing by a tree near Enfield Chase. Red and violet plastic flowers, grimed by dust, poke from a basket nailed to the trunk that reads: 'In Memory of John T. Cod who died tragically at this tree on 9/9/89 aged 29. R.I.P.'

A dead chaffinch lies scrunched in nettles. Daffodils droop shrivelled heads and tin cans and plastic bags fritter away in the ditch. For half a minute there's a hush in traffic: just me and the cows in the sun. Here comes the ghastly paleness of death again, that blanketed figure in the road. A young man makes a wanker sign to me as he speeds past in his swanky car. Drum and bass thumps from speakers inside, as if the car has a heartbeat. He disappears in an exhaust cloud round the bend.

As I stand under this tree, leaves pattering above me, an afternoon years before I married comes back. I step into Clifford's first-floor front room at 103 Lauriston Road in Hackney. I expect to find him there, but he's gone. The room's shimmering with shadows of plane-tree leaves through three sash-windows in the sun. Dancing shapes, like tethered birds, flicker across his walls, as if the room's alive with leaves and I only had to open his door to discover it.

Near Plumridge Hill a crow makes its black mark in a field sharp with barley, and I scare two rabbits into their burrow. A bird in the hedge shoots out a single note over and over at the height of my chest. I can't find it, but Clare would have recognised its insistent call. It reminds me of him as it sings behind a thicket, although his were a range of notes in all their colours. His poem 'The Progress of Rhyme' tries to reproduce the sounds of a nightingale in a wood:

> *And aye so different was the strain*
> *She'd scarce repeat the note again:*
> *'Chew-chew chew-chew' and higher still,*
> *'Cheer-cheer cheer-cheer' more loud and shrill,*
> *'Cheer-up cheer-up cheer-up' – and dropped*
> *Low – 'Tweet tweet jug jug jug' – and stopped*
> *One moment just to drink the sound*
> *Her music made, and then a round*
> *Of stranger witching notes was heard*
> *As if it was a stranger bird:*

> '*Wew-wew wew-wew chur-chur chur-chur*
> *Woo-it woo-it*' – *could this be her?*
> '*Tee-rew tee-rew tee-rew tee-rew*
> *Chew-rit chew-rit*' – *and ever new* –
> '*Will-will will-will grig-grig grig-grig.*'

It's astonishing that this was written around 1824. Its experiment with sound-poetry, with bending words so they mimic bird noises, feels so radical – so Gertrude Stein – yet when read aloud the nightingale's calling from my mouth. This fascination with how it sounds makes Clare ready to run the risk of gibberish, instructing us to listen carefully, without prejudice:

> *The more I listened and the more*
> *Each note seemed sweeter than before.*

He wants to lead us deeper into the wood, where words become abstract noise again if we throw away our preconceptions, stay attentive.

In Keats's 'Ode to a Nightingale' (written about five years before 'The Progress of Rhyme') the nightingale moves through the poet's love of his lines, following Keats's feelings about himself and death. Although Keats and Clare admired each other and came within a whisker of meeting, they were absorbed in subtly different fields of enquiry. Their critique of each other is illuminating. Keats told their mutual publisher Taylor: 'Images from Nature are too much introduced without being called for by a particular Sentiment . . . the Description overlaid and stifled that which ought to be the prevailing Idea.' Clare's criticism is equally astute, *his*

descriptions of senery are often very fine but as it is the case
with other inhabitants of great citys he often described nature
as she appeared to his fancys and not as he would have
described her had he witnessed the things he describes. They're
basically mirroring each other's advice: less description please
from Mr Clare, fewer 'fancys' please from Mr Keats. So Keats
says to Clare 'Write more like me' and Clare says to Keats
'Write more like me.' Yet Clare's description *becomes* the idea
in this poem, slaps the nightingale's music onto paper before
our eyes, into our tongues and ears if we speak his lines
aloud. He allows the nightingale to take over his poem, steps
back as an act of reverence, a gesture towards wordlessness,
while he follows the song through the wood.

My bird in the hedge is probably warning me off its territory. I don't share Clare's knowledge, his fascinated sympathy
for nightingales and spiders, badgers and foxes. He respects
their 'stranger' otherness, watching and listening in awe,
making notes. Like Keats, I've lived too long in the city. I
stay an ignorant town-mouse stumbling in Clare's country
shadow.

At 3.30 p.m. I cross the border into Hertfordshire, a 'County
of Opportunity' according to its sign. It's taken four hours.
I walk over a bridge above the M25. An island of trees rustles
at the centre of the roundabout. Eight lanes of traffic race
under my boots. I glance down through grids and railings
at the speed and noise below, momentarily consider jumping,
as if meeting those wheels would be welcome. Just jump. It'll
all be over. Pain gone. I instantly dismiss the idea, but
thinking it shows I'm more strung out than I realised. I'm

fixed to the road, *Keep walking* a mantra to protect me, carry me to a place that may be kinder, because the things I see don't care. Their indifference to my welfare proves the only thing saving me is myself.

Shall I count ten ferns by the roadside? Blackthorn buds move their white speckles above dented lager cans, a soiled cardigan. Dock leaves cheek by jowl with nettles; beside the yellow shreds of ragwort, which we called wet-the-beds when we were children. Clare's sonnet 'The Ragwort' pays homage to this disregarded flower:

> *I love to see thee come and litter gold . . .*
> *Decking rude spots in beautys marigold*
> *That without thee were dreary to behold*
> *Sun burnt and bare – . . .*

It's like he's smuggling a polemic between his lines: *thou humble flower with tattered leaves* deserves praise as much as any more traditionally 'poetic' rose, because there's no hierarchy. It's as if Clare took the dictum 'Write about what you know' to heart, so even the wet-the-beds of childhood can be celebrated as a *waste of shining blossoms*. Everything in nature noticed by Clare, however mundane, becomes a cause of wonder.

A few months after we met, Dee and I danced close together in a student club to 'No Woman, No Cry', with its lines about a future where you can't forget your past. I think we realised then we were falling in love. During our first half-term break before Christmas, when we travelled back to our respective homes eighty miles apart, Dee said to me one night on the phone: 'I'm going to ask you something you must ignore. Will you marry me?'

Four years after her question, at our wedding in the church of St John at Bethnal Green, we repeated our vows to each other: 'All that I am I give to you.' We asked the priest to read from one of D. H. Lawrence's letters, as if it was our credo:

> One must learn to love, and go through a great deal of suffering to get to it, like any knight of the grail, and the journey is always *towards* the other soul, not away from it. Do you think love is an accomplished thing, the day it is recognized? It isn't. To love, you have to learn to understand the other, more than she understands herself, and to submit to her understanding of you. It is damnably difficult and painful, but it is the only thing which endures.

Am I walking away from Dee's soul today, no longer towards it? I spent twenty years enmeshed with her, loving that entanglement, walking willingly towards Lawrence's submission, until roses turned to briars that cut my hands and nipped my ankles, and the only path left was retreating, admitting defeat. Has it been the same for her – petals and thorns, blood on the finger? Giving all that I am, and it's no longer wanted.

The traffic light leading up from the M25 slip road has a sticker that says it's a crash-friendly pole. Leaving the roundabout, early tulips and laurel hedges brighten the front gardens of 1930s houses towards Potters Bar. I pass a purple lilac, as if its turrets savour the sun.

Two months after his first poetry collection was published to great acclaim, Clare married Patty Turner on 16 March 1820. She was seven months pregnant, given away by her uncle rather than her father, who had told her *as she had made her bed hard she shoud lie on it.* Her parents didn't rate Clare, who had been an impoverished lime-burner with no prospects when the couple first met two years earlier, and her pregnancy didn't help matters. Clare claimed when he first saw Patty walking across the fields *I was in love at first sight & not knowing who she was or were she came from I felt very ill at rest I clomb on the top of a dotterel to see which way she went till she was out of sight.* Our love-struck lime-burner sways in the spiky branches of a pollard tree, all the better to see her. He might even recall being stuck in those branches at the end of his oozy love poem 'Patty', published in that first collection:

> *And brush the weaving branches by*
> *Of briars and thorns so matty,*
> *So oft reflection warms a sigh,*
> *'Here first I met my Patty.'*

Yet Clare's prose accounts of his marriage sound more ambivalent. In his *Sketches in the Life of John Clare*, written for his publisher John Taylor a year after his wedding, he states: *I was little fit or inclined for marrying but my thoughtless and ram headed proceedings, as I was never anything else but a fool, commiting rashly and repenting too late having injured her character as well as my own . . . the wide mouth of the world was open against her, swallowing every thing that started to discredit her . . . hurt and vex me it did, but I felt more affection for her then ever and I determind to support her.* Later he writes (although who's to say which may be the more honest version?) *I held out as long as I coud & then married her.* A month after his daughter was born he conceded to a friend, *I think (Patty) will prove a better bargain then I expected.*

Like all couples, they took a gamble on each other, blew on the dice in each other's fist. For Clare, the gamble paid off. Patty stayed committed to him throughout their long marriage, despite shared years of poverty, his diminishing publications and increasing mental illness. When they married Patty was illiterate; a wobbly cross marks her name in the parish register. Later she gave a brief, poignant glimpse of their happy court-ship, gathering lily-of-the-valley together: 'When John came I'd run and get my gingham dress from the hedge where it was airing, and put it on whether dry or not.' A little breath-less and over the moon for his footstep, Patty waits for his kiss again, the checks on her best dress still slightly damp against her shins and shoulders.

After our wedding reception, tin cans had been tied to our car's exhaust by Clifford (my best man) and our cousins. Their clatter was thrilling and disconcerting as we drove, waving and noisy, from the reception past all our cheering guests. Dee was scared we'd crash, and insisted that we untie the cans as soon as we drove round the corner, out of sight. I swore at her, because I thought she was a spoilsport. Mine was the first cross word in a marriage a few hours old.

A cardboard felt-tipped 'Just Married' sign was lodged by the car's back window when we drove through London's crazy centre on Saturday evening towards Salisbury, on the journey to our honeymoon in Cornwall. When we sped past Marble Arch, desperately trying to swerve into the right lane of traffic, a car crammed with young men pulled alongside us for thirty seconds. One passenger pointed his fingers at me like a gun, cocked an invisible trigger and, from one car window to another, blew me away. He mouthed the bullet designed for me, with a slow-motion puff of his lips, aiming (of course) for the heart.

Potters Bar Theatre Company is showing *We'll Meet Again*. When I approach the town a couple with children in their car drive away from a furniture store with a child's mattress and flat-pack bed on the roof rack. I envy them and their destination.

Starting our married life together, I assumed my adult home would be rooted in Dee and, later, our children; but experience has proved otherwise. So where's my home now? Am I walking there this afternoon by slogging back to my children? Or am I temporarily without a home, a lodger in one room in Rothwell? Clare called himself *homeless at home* when he finished writing his account of his walk. That echoes for me, though I tell myself walking roads won't define me.

Where will I sleep tonight? The question jolts, but I can escape it in a few days, return after this weary interlude to my rented bed. I consider what it would be like if this question defined me, if, hour after hour, night after night, I never knew where I'd be sleeping or how I'd eat. To live with that uncertainty when light wakes me, and I must move on.

Is home in the people I love, familiar bricks and mortar, a set of streets? Last week my friend Brenda tapped her forehead and said, 'It's in here.' For me, home is rooted in my children, but also in the room I rent; dispersed between Holly House (home of my marriage) and Jubilee Street (where I lodge). An old line from my 'Dancing Bear' poem a few years ago says, 'My home is my self.' Perhaps I'll carry the idea of home on my back for months, with its lamps and rugs and wallpaper.

Outside the Green Man pub a stall sells jellied eels. Years ago, a stall outside Kelly's pie-and-mash shop along Bethnal Green Road sold them. Live eels writhed in a metal tray of water, their shiny skin the shade of rotten bananas. I remember the vendor scooping one out to chop it into inch-size pieces on a butcher's slab.

Over the road a man hawks up phlegm and spits into his flowerbed. Beside Oakmere Park on my right a sprayed sign assures me POTTERS BAR STINKS, though it looks like anywhere else to me, with its modest rows of shops.

The pedometer says I've walked eleven miles. I read a white shin-high pillar before the Little Heath traffic lights. A St George's Cross with a sword in the top left-hand corner has '24 Vict.' moulded into it, commemorating the twenty-fourth year of Victoria's reign in 1861 – twenty years after Clare's walk – as if I carve a path through history. On a roof a male pigeon parades his puffed-chest desire dance, while the female bobs to and fro, deciding whether to fly.

A teenage couple smooch beside the Church Road bus stop, as if they're fascinated by each other's hair and cheeks and eyelashes, probing more ingenious ways to make each other laugh, to make their twentieth kiss last a minute longer.

I try the compass to check if I'm walking roughly north. A

sign ahead says Hatfield Road (Great North Road), so I'm on the right track.

By Hawkshead Road at a quarter to five I pass the I LOVE YOU message, close up and slow motion this time. The first time I told Dee I loved her, in my student room on campus, it felt exposed, unalterable, like a declaration to myself as well as her. We add that statement to the air, hoping to hear the same. If we're lucky we echo each other. I walk away from I LOVE YOU, leave it standing, want to decipher white words on red brick. Whoever painted them knew what they meant.

Loving Dee and being unable to live with her look like facts as simple as the letters on that wall. I blunder across a moor where love's helicopter dropped me six weeks ago, hoping I won't end up in flames, the match between my own singed fingers.

I cover a prolonged stretch of speeding cars over-shaded by trees and hemmed by brambles, cow parsley, elderflower and campion. I scare a squirrel that runs up the nearest trunk. When my son Isaac was four and excited he said, 'There's a squirrel running all over my body,' as if his body had turned into a tree.

Separation's broken my coupledom. I've slouched into singleness again, although neither Dee nor I felt comfortable in that purposeful way of living. We were imposters, who sometimes made fun of the carefully coordinated living rooms of married friends in Market Harborough. Our children were never as colour-coordinated as theirs; our cars always the wrong make or registration. When we told one of those acquaintances that we'd separated a few weeks ago he looked scared, nearly backed away, as if separation might be contagious. I'm haunted by Samuel Beckett's lines: 'you must go on, I can't go on, I'll go on.' Tiredness makes me heavy, dragging myself through miles of trudging, that battle of phrases beating my temples: 'you must go on, I can't go on, I'll go on.'

The place I paused a minute ago ceases to exist once I move forward. It's like Clare's struggle between staying put or changing, and changing anyway, even if you stay put. Six months ago, I expected my life to be mapped out. I would stay in my marriage, despite its increasing unhappiness. I would live with my children, make the best of it. I thought I knew what was going to happen, but I'm on a road I've never seen before. This uncertainty's edged with anticipation. I fought so long to shore up the walls of my house that their crumbling brings a chance for change.

One evening after tea at our circular dining table in Whitechapel, a few days before I caught my train to Brighton, my mother suddenly said, 'They say people change when they go to university. Don't change.' She rarely expressed emotion, buttoned her lip, did her best to work hard and stay strong. I felt embarrassed, a little flattered, and under subtle pressure. I probably told her not to worry. We didn't go in for deep conversations in our house. 'Don't change' sounded like an order and a plea.

I disobeyed her the minute her back was turned. I met Dee on my first night, and over those early few months we fell in love. My mother was probably scared she'd lose me to strange middle-class ways, that I'd zoom up in the world away from her, but how can we breathe without changing?

49

A Length of Road

Let me open myself like a door today, surrender instead of resist. Change dances the way two lapwings succumb to the slightest breeze. They soar together momentarily, before one dips over low crops. Its mate dive-bombs and lifts again, rising on whatever current plays with it, scooting down in an arc, until it settles in grass yards from its companion.

The Cock o' the North pub is followed by a swathe of fields, two lanes of fast traffic, a pylon on the left and the blue and white hoarding of Rookery Café ahead. Its dingy pebbledash shows parked cars and a few customers eating outside in trainers and caps. They notice and ignore me with the same flick of the eyes. My thighs and hips are aching; the back of my right shin and soles of both feet twinge. Three young women in black walk towards the café. The men chew and watch, as if they're assessing them with a proprietorial air, giving them marks.

I see a birch-tree wood behind a stone wall. Perhaps I could get lost there, if I choose. Give up this walk; let it go like water through my fingers. My purpose has gone. I never needed it. I'll crack branches underfoot, swish leaves by moving through them, unstrap my rucksack and lie down at last among skinny birches. I could find another purpose tomorrow. I set myself a task when I thought I needed an aim. I play with the fantasy of stopping, looking up through a shimmer of leaves, until my eyes close and the noise of rooks fades to sleep.

I enter Hatfield at six o'clock, facing three grey warehouses of Safeway, Tesco and Mitsubishi. The inter-city train judders nearby for thirty seconds until it's gone. Catkin buds on the pavement curl like dead bees. Pigeons coo and roost under this bridge, with a few broken eggshells and spatterings of bird-shit. Their grey wings shuffle above me.

In Clare's day the Great North Road (or the Great York Road as he called it) would have seen mail coaches rattling postbags, passengers and luggage north and south. He'd have been one of a number of pedestrians along this road, no one worthy of a second look, unless his haunted expression singled him out. Clare makes no mention of the miles between Enfield Town and Stevenage in his account. He says he was *meeting no enemy & fearing none*, so he must have realised the asylum was safely behind him, no search party combing the roads to sniff him out, drag him back. Do I look like I've escaped from an asylum to these drivers? Walking along muttering into a Dictaphone, rucksack slung across my back, lugging my bag, jacket round my shoulders. Walking when any sensible man would be driving, at a time like this, on a road like this. I think of families in cosy kitchens, buttering hot cross buns for Good Friday teas. Can I knock on your door and be let in? Give me a plate of food please, a cup of tea – pretend I'm not here.

I eat my own tea perched on a white plastic chair outside a café-trailer called The Snack Bar, in a corner by the train station, opposite the black curls of Hatfield House gates. The statue of a bearded Victorian sits on a plinth, as if he's a concierge, with lions on pillars holding shields either side, posing as guard dogs. Pine trees tower behind the gates, where over four hundred years ago a scared red-headed young woman stood under an oak to be told she was queen. Taxis queue for passengers from the next train. A driver dozes with his engine running: head lolling and mouth ajar.

51

It's £1.35p for a large tea in a polystyrene cup and a jacket potato with coleslaw on a paper plate. I savour every bite with my plastic cutlery. Pat and Mo run the show; one wiry, the other stocky; the two women are probably in their late forties, baggy T-shirts and black leggings, hair scraped back into tight ponytails. They look tired and capable, keeping an eye out for every nuance around them: which taxis are pulling in; which trains are late; which passengers are their regulars. Bringing my potato, Pat told me they stay open until two in the morning. I'm impressed by their energy: late finishes and early rises, keeping their show on the road, proud of how they work as a team, build a careful profit, stay afloat.

Buckling on my rucksack again, I trudge through another housing estate in Hatfield. I've clearly gone wrong, in the same way that Clare took a wrong turning when he first left the forest, *being careless in mapping down the route as the Gipsey told me.* I've no Gypsy to point out the road, but realise I should have turned before reaching Hatfield House. I was seduced by the prospect of seeing it, even from afar. I should have been tipped off by Clare's silence on the matter. I couldn't believe the Great North Road temporarily disappears at a Safeway office, but that seems to be the case. Because there's nothing else to do, I retrace my steps with a sense of pig-headedness, to rejoin the A1000. I fly my flag, refuse to be defeated.

At 7.30 p.m. I'm slogging along the Green towards Lemsford. I've been walking for eight hours and my feet throb with blisters. I think of Clare managing to reach Stevenage on his first night. His feet were hardened to it; but he was also driven by illness and hunger to get home. He could almost taste it.

If he felt like a prisoner on the run, the more streets and fields he put between himself and High Beach the greater his chance of freedom.

A blue tit sharpens its beak on a branch. I'm clapped out. I can't sustain Clare's punishing mileage. I need to pace myself, and think about the Hare and the Tortoise, although in my weary state I can't work out which of us should be the Hare, as Clare reached the finishing line a hundred and fifty years before me. I feel like the Tortoise this evening, repeating in my scaly brain *you must go on, I can't go on, I'll go on*, while Clare skips and skitters ahead, hare-coloured, leaping from his burdens, always a few tantalising miles out of sight. There's the faintest scent of him left in the air, and I'm England's slowest plodder, picking up his breadcrumbs, missing his paw-prints, his clues. He beats me hands down at this walking and poetry malarkey:

> *The timid hares throw daylight's fears away*
> *On the lane's road, to dust and dance and play.*

Five pigeons circle over open farmland, near elms and barley and spindly white sprigs. Sporadic traffic spurts alongside me and disappears. It's liberating to feel separated from the noise of the A1(M), unclogging my thoughts. As these pigeons flap in widening loops, I understand Dee and I are sweeping beyond each other's meadows, where the torment we caused might evaporate into clouds, like shreds of darkened paper torn and floating away. No marriage ends neatly; but I can salvage some self-respect by loosening my fist at last, where she's been beating her wings for months, and set her free, as

53

if her freedom's in my power. We might grant each other the grace of living apart. That means losing her laughter. I'm grasping grass and daisies, gulping air, while she does the same, miles away.

Verges spill over without pavements here, so as soon as I manage a reasonable walking rhythm another taxi speeds towards me, carrying passengers in their glad rags to a night out. I'm forced to pause and step off the road onto the verge again, doing my best to avoid landing ankle-deep in nettles.

With the pigeons gone, the evening sky trails dusky pink sprigs. That fire when the sun gives up fills the nearest puddle with flame. A map of light glimmers above a bank of grey-blue cloud. Three minutes later I realise it's the emerging moon, starting to make its presence known, smudged as someone's talcum-powder thumbprint.

By 8.45 p.m. I'm finished for the night and sitting in the Long Arm and Short Arm pub in Lemsford. My boots lie under the table; my toes twinkle inside sweaty socks. I need a decent toilet, so I hope this one has sparkling tiles and the scent of a perfumed garden. I plan to trek through the darkening village after my cider, find a secluded place to sleep outside. I'll set up my borrowed bivouac somewhere, if I can remember what my ex-Marine friend Simon taught me: secure the weather-proof sheeting, create a shelter for the night.

Men laugh with the barmaid, leaning on the dark-oak bar, and order another round. Two women eat a meal together: one a pensioner, the other thirty-something. They say so little while their cutlery clicks and scrapes across the plates, I assume they must be related. In the corner a quiet couple are absorbed by their child in a buggy, keeping them entertained. I scribble in my exercise book: 'Could've been us, but it isn't now, so live with it and get what happiness you can.' It reads like an order to myself. I wonder how I appear to the drinkers here: a man writing alone, rucksack lodged by the table, bag at my feet.

I've achieved nine hours' walking today: 15.6 miles according to the pedometer, although I'm no longer confident it's working properly. Checking the milometer in the car last Sunday, Ian wrote in the margin that this village was about 22 miles from Epping. I split the difference, allow for two miles an hour and estimate I've covered about eighteen miles. I hope I can manage the same rate tomorrow. Do eighty-five miles and be clean again.

My shoulders ache where the rucksack's pressed for hours into skin and bone. I'm edgy about finding a safe hideaway tonight, but it's my next challenge. I should be man enough to face it. I've never slept rough before, under the night with all its stars. My body insists I'm more than ready for sleep.

First Day 1841

Escape

July 18 1841. Felt very melancholly went a walk in the forest in the afternoon – fell in with some gipseys one of whom offered to assist in my escape from the madhouse

Am I coming or going?
When you dawdle under beech-leaves this evening
look both ways like mother said.

The red road or the white one?
Unhinge myself. Unhook this sack of stones,
walking out on a trail of breadcrumbs through the wood.

Am I coming or going? The red road or the white?
They're open as a woman's legs:
run after lines until your ink goes dry.

Nuts and berries patter on my plate.
Eat escape, eat it before the trap shuts.
Why do you wait?

I'm too blind for the journey.
Mother it's getting dark. Mister say which way.

A Length of Road

All Gone

On friday I went again but he did not seem so willing so I said little about it – On Sunday I went & they were all gone –

The Gypsy speaks:

I'll whistle for fifty quid easy as he can.
A fine promise! It's not worth the air it's written on.
Money up front or nothing. What's a fool to me?

We know the dangle of each leaf here,
the rabbits skinned, the pigeons roasted.

When I squat in a clearing long enough
to learn where the bullfinch sings
my bones niggle to get cracking.

Kill the fire. Creak our wheels again.
Let the three-legged flea dog itch and wag behind.

Crow Flies

July 19. Monday – Did nothing

> The crows did more than me today.
> It takes power
> to unlock a beak at early weather.
>
> I'm rooted, while their claws
> knot for the skinniest twig:
> make it seesaw, make it swing.
>
> Eighty feet higher than nothing
> that crux between two branches
> spills an inky feather on my boots.

Movement

July 20 Reconnitred the route the Gipsey pointed out & found it a legible one to make a movement & having only honest courage & myself in my army I led the way & my troops soon followed

I'm squint-eye flap-arm Nelson
puffing up sails as the wind blows,
squashing frogs like scummy jailers
quacks and whores and poxy printers.
If my head's whacked off by a cannonball
I can glue it back again.

Slow down lad. You're Random Jack,
simply aiming home. I've fallen on that word
and live to breathe under clouds I still remember,
to lift my children's waists between my hands –
raise them over my crown and carry them down again,
resting their butterfly's eyelash at the side of my smile.

Her arms will end my wilderness,
hedge me inside to graze her grass.
She'll turn when I knock the kissing-gate.
I'm barred from bee-tickled blades,
until a tongue slipped through her parted teeth
wets mine.

Clover

to my good luck I found some trusses of clover piled up about
six or more feet square which I gladly mounted & slept on

My luck's in, napping on four-leaf clover
when it could have been stones. I pluck one out,
doss down to count three leaves over and over,
count sheep till I'm dozy while they chew fat
from the land: each white or purple spider-flower
torn between teeth. Feed me meadow dreams tonight,
simple as that green scratch, fainter
than each clover-heart it arches through, slight
as this crescent at the base of my thumbnail
when I pinch its stem. Years ago as she lifted
her skirts – Mary or Patty, Betty or Nell –
I'd root through to what I wanted. She shifted
her shoulders to squash the clover flat,
while goose-grass and my bristles tickled her throat.

The Steering Point

I lay down with my head towards the north to show myself the steering point in the morning

My body's a compass. Toes dabble south,
back to the mad-house's hard edge of leaves
where they slammed my brain in a cattle-grid all season.

My open arms crucify east and west.
No thimbleful of blood dints either palm,
blessing four corners of the map's stained bedsheet.

Tattoo north across my forehead.
Winter vixens and arctic hares
circle their hunted hemispheres round my skull.

The chase dies when I lie straight as midnight,
to rise again like breath's miracle
on the second day.

Second Day

Saturday, 15 April 1995

6.25 a.m. Last night I slept near Sherrardspark Wood, with its slender birch trees and three-slatted wooden fence, alongside the B197 and the A1(M). Its wide fast road meant the sound of traffic kept me company. It reminded me of sleeping in my old bedroom in Collingwood House next to Cambridge Heath Road for all those years: a child, teenager and young unmarried man accustomed to cars being driven through his dreams. How can such a familiar noise become reassuring? Their thrum, swish and percussion reverberated like the music of continuity, as if that thread of cars last night linked me back to childhood sounds.

I made up a clumsy bivouac in the dark, tying the water-proof grey sheeting to the side of a fence for support and scrambling inside. I used my bags as prop and pillow. With the tightness of the sleeping bag wrapped round my limbs, it occasionally felt like lying inside a coffin. Although I snuggled into my sleeping bag at 10 p.m., I didn't drift to sleep until after midnight, often stirring to check my watch and feeling vulnerable outside in the night, imagining yobs or police might discover me, and I'd be beaten up or moved on. I managed to sleep with that uncertainty, but stayed aware of my foreignness under cold stars, where the dark belongs to other creatures and I was intruding.

An animal, perhaps a badger or fox, moved close and I flashed my light. It gave a grunt that sounded like a gasp, a rough intake of breath through its muzzle, and shuffled into undergrowth. When I lay down again, after half an hour or so, I heard what I assumed to be a hedgehog beside my ear: scrabbling in soil and leaves, its weird high-pitched snort answered by another further away. Clare said the hedgehog *whistles like a cricket as he goes*, as though he'd been as close to its sound as I was last night. I tried to scare it a few times by tapping the bivouac sheet and switching on my torch. It made no difference. Either I'd camped by its usual night spot, or it was drawn to my body for warmth. In the end we made a silent pact not to harm each other and I dozed off. I've heard on the radio that hedgehogs are as much at risk of disappearing as tigers, so my visitor was a rare blessing.

Apart from the hedgehog it was a relatively undisturbed night, though debates about the separation kept circling my head, breaking through black and echoing in and out of dreams. Become a hedgehog – roll up in a ball of thorns – breathe till it's over. It's been happening every night for months. I tell myself this too will pass, but want to cry and have her back, our differences dissolved like salt in water. I still love her and we can't live together. Both facts bear equal weight, and I'm twisting inside the paradox.

Clare wrote about his first night, when he slept on a

six-foot-high pile of clover in a shed: *I slept soundly but had a very uneasy dream I thought my first wife lay on my left arm & somebody took her away from my side which made me wake up rather unhappy I thought as I woke somebody said 'Mary' but nobody was near –*

Although they never married, in his head Clare's first love Mary became his first wife. Remaining constant to her seems bound up with his need to keep a sense of continuity about his transformation from childhood to adulthood, from country bumpkin to overnight success to forgotten poet: 'I'm the self-same John Clare. I live in Helpstone and I've always loved Mary. Whatever changes in my life, nothing changes that.' It's similar to his need for his childhood landscape to stay the same. Mary stands like an elm in his meadow, full of birdsong and never leaving him:

> *That form from boyhood loved and still loved on*
> *That voice – that look – that face of one delight*
> *Love's register for years, months, weeks – time past*
>   *and gone*
> *Her looks was ne'er forgot or out of sight*
> *– Mary the muse of every song I write*

Clare's instinct to keep his first love alive – burning a candle for her, the woman who'd already been killed in a fire – stayed mixed up with his childhood and identity, despite his real marriage, gnawing for years against his commitment to Patty. Why this urge to hold on? Why is the gap of Dee's absence beside my left arm (on my nights when I fall asleep and mornings when I wake) so appalling? We're walking back to women no longer there; yet walking back might make them come into our arms again, fulfil some grand reunion we barely believe. Walking home to prove our love might almost make it happen, if we want it hard enough.

When I kept waking last night with tormenting thoughts, the twenty-third Psalm came unexpectedly to me. I gave up on God years ago, but its words felt oddly soothing inside my sleeping bag, like a leftover comforter from childhood, when I believed such things:

> The Lord is my shepherd; I shall not want.
> He maketh me lie down in green pastures:
>   he leadeth me beside the still waters.
> He restoreth my soul . . .

I'm hungry for my soul to be restored, as if I've lost it these past six weeks, or longer since the marriage took a nosedive. Lying down in green pastures near Sherrardspark Wood might help to bring it back, even if I lay last night on chill soil, even if this morning I climbed over the wooden fence onto the roadside carrying all the awkward lumber for the walk, and broke the fence and scraped the back of my thigh where it niggles my skin with every step. I want someone to lead me, soothe me with a splash of still waters.

Here by the sign for the Ayots villages I come across another makeshift memorial to a young man: 'Vince' this time, with his red-and-white Labatt's Formula 1 cap pinned to the central reservation fence. Card messages from funeral bouquets are stapled to the fence of this hectic road, including one from his brother saying, 'Wishing you the best that anyone could wish for you.' This is two minutes' walk from where I slept.

The ghastly paleness of death rides his white stallion again, bringing me Clare's Thomas Drake falling from a load of hay, breaking his neck; Enfield Chase's John T. Cod from yesterday, aged twenty-nine; Vince, whose age I can't know, though I assume he was another young man, perhaps because of his cap; and Clifford dying at thirty-four from an AIDS-related illness. It's nearly four years since I heard his last three breaths in that white side-ward in the Infectious Diseases unit in Leicester. His partner Andrew stroked his arm and quietly said, 'He's gone.' I walked towards Clifford's pillow, bent my head between his head and bony shoulder and sobbed with the release of those five months watching him die, always wanting him to stay. Occasionally I sense his presence, but more often (like this minute) it's the exact, tough opposite. No voice in the air, giving an opinion, making me laugh; his hesitant 'Hel-*lo*' when he picked up the phone; the to-and-fro of jokes and conversations. Now there's only the certainty of life ahead without him, my ally in our aspirations; my best friend in the glory of that title.

Clare writes of one of his first friendships with Richard Turnill, who died of typhus at seventeen: *what happy discourses of planning pleasures did we talk over as we lay on the soft summer grass gazing into the blue sky shaping the passing clouds to things familiar with our memorys dreaming of the days to come when we shoud mix with the world & be men little thinking that we shoud chew the cud of sweet & bitter fancy when we met it but he never did.*

These young men swirl around me this morning, wishing their lives were longer. It's as if I touch my fingers to their names carved on Enfield Town's Glorious Dead memorial, as if I might read them like braille. I wish Clifford and Richard Turnill and Thomas Drake and John T. Cod and Vince the best that anyone could wish, but what help is that when their deaths didn't stop, and all the other young deaths keep coming, like the blanketed man in the road yesterday?

During his last illness Clifford's consultant started him on AZT to slow the disease, but his reaction was so nauseous he had to stop taking it after a few days. The possibility that we might have been close to saving him, if the right medication had been found in time, twists the knife deeper. From April till August in the year he died we had to watch the pounds fall from him inch by relentless inch: the scraping cough, the collapsed lung, the shingles, the breathlessness, the tuberculosis, the lung cancer grasping their savage opportunities to feed off his life, while he kept hoping he'd get better, despite the oxygen mask, the wheelchair, the weeks in and out of hospital, and all other evidence to the contrary. 'I've got the big A,' he told a friend, when he admitted his diagnosis, as it was like a shameful secret. Anti-gay feeling was high, on the back of Thatcher's government preventing the promotion of homosexuality as 'a pretended family relationship' with Section 28 of their Local Government Act. The *Sun* and the *Daily Mail* spat headlines, blaming gay men as outcasts who carried the plague. Across public toilet cubicle doors – alongside felt-tipped cocks and offers of sex – GOT AIDS YET? was often scrawled, as if that was the meaning of gay.

When he was allowed home from hospital, during a period of remission over those difficult months, I wrote a brief poem called 'Scared', using Clifford's words about how some people treated him:

'I bet that District Nurse'll douse herself in Dettol
when she gets back home.
I've seen people wash their hands
after talking to me.
Scared they'll catch something.
I'm the one who should be scared.
A cough or cold from them
could finish me off.'

In hospital, a few months before his death, Clifford asked
me, 'Am I on the road to dying?' I said, 'I bloody well hope
not,' though the doctor had already told us he only had four
months to live. We kept it from him. He was scared of dying
and we couldn't face putting him through months of anxiety.
He was a nervous man, with panic attacks that could leave
him shaking in claustrophobic situations. Since he was an only
child, I always saw it as my job to protect him, if I could, to
make things easier. Once at a party he said I was like a brother
to him. I wonder now if not telling him about his prognosis
was the right decision, but then I thought, what's a white lie
between friends?

One Saturday or Sunday morning years ago, when Clifford
was still with John, his first boyfriend, we gathered at the flat
of a drag queen, somewhere along the Mile End Road. I
remember a shy man, who was in love with the drag queen,
looking at him longingly across the room. I watched the plane
trees through glass shiver their leaves in the breeze below, and
traffic slowly trickle along the road. Clifford and John cracked
jokes with the drag queen, off-duty and without his wig and
make-up, while his devoted admirer looked on and a few other
warm spiky camp friends waited for the next double entendre.

What were their names? I thought 'I'll remember this,' though I can't remember why. All I can think now is we didn't know AIDS was around the corner, ready to stalk Clifford and those men less than a decade later. I wonder how many friends crowded into that sparse flat it infected or killed; but what good are such thoughts? They depress me and rescue no one I knew then. I lost track of them, followed only Clifford. They've vanished from my morning, along with their names.

Clifford eventually broke up messily with John and moved to a high-ceilinged flat in Stoke Newington with other students. He developed a crush on his flatmate, another Northern John with a neat moustache, pretty eyelashes and a winning smile. One night I sat with Clifford on the stone stairs at the foot of our flats when he admitted that John would always feel nothing but friendship for him. Several years later, on one of our last trips to London, when Clifford was already gaunt and coughing from his illness, we visited a pounding gay bar and Clifford recognised Northern John again through the crowd, laughing and flashing his smile at some fortunate man. I remember Clifford leaning against the dark wall, sweating and bowed by his illness, lost in coloured lights, while Northern John stood happily a few feet away performing his flirtations. I believed then that all those fit men in that bar wanted to avoid Clifford's cough and skinny limbs for what they might mean about him, or about them if their luck ran out one careless, passionate night. I wanted to defend him from the music, beat and lights, the flirtations, the crushes and healthy smiles.

After he graduated, Clifford moved to Brighton and a few years later fell in love with Andrew. They had met on the prom and started chatting. For their first damp basement flat together, Clifford painted a second-hand screen he'd bought

in some junk shop with bold Matisse-coloured blank-faced
women carrying parasols: lush pinks, citrus limes, yellows and
tangerines, based on a Chinese theme. I told him you needed
sunglasses to look at it.

One summer we took our mothers to one of his few exhib-
itions, in a small gallery along Brighton seafront. Mysterious
underwater landscapes were displayed alongside pictures full
of penises and men taking part in wanking contests. My
mother laughed and hooted at the rude ones until tears ran
down her face. Clifford's mother noted in the visitors' book
that she preferred the underwater landscapes.

There were years of self-doubt, when he had neither the
space, the money nor the confidence to paint. Then, the year
before he died, a waterfall of art poured from him again, as
if it might save him: a self-portrait with a feather; an autumn
cherry tree from his garden; portraits and simple charcoal
nudes of Andrew, a patient model; stand-up wooden cut-outs
of dogs and cats and abundant flowers in vases, which he
painted for money and never sold. Dozens of paintings,
sketches, pen-and-ink drawings with watercolour and chalk,
which he told me were all about energy, so a cluster of images
recurred in them. Cartoon-like pylons, chimney stacks,
cannons, telegraph poles, light bulbs, gasometers, power
stations and atomic mushroom clouds wrestled with river
shapes swathing through each picture. Nature played a part
in this energy. Suns and half-moons, seaweed, snail shells,
thistles, bulrushes, lily pads and fuchsias; a lightning bolt
withering an orchid, and throughout these images what I
assumed might be him confronting his impending death: a
phoenix again and again, triumphant or maimed, a blue bird
with outstretched wings. In one painting in my room in

Rothwell a phoenix transforms into a peacock, spraying the comet of its tail feathers over the paper, plugged into a snaking cable lead.

When we could afford it, Dee and I framed two of his oils for Holly House. After we separated we agreed we would keep one each, so these paintings glimmer on separate walls, miles apart, yellow suns and blue pylons still speaking to each other.

Cars, vans and lorries shoot an endless whiz and shudder either side of my shoulders. I can't stand here any longer. I must move on. I leave Vince's memorial and develop a marching pace, regain my purpose. No other pedestrians cross me. It's a fast road edged by woods, and cars zoom their appearing-disappearing act. Here and gone, here and gone rhythms through the tyres. Between their noises I notice a wood with its pool of bluebells glinting near the turn for the Ayots villages, like a glade where I can't afford to linger. Imagine stopping beside bluebells – swimming in their scent – if I allow myself five more minutes. I might lie there, like I hoped to lie in the birch-tree wood yesterday afternoon.

The day after Clifford died, I had emptiness instead of hospital visits, where those bedside hours felt worth it because they were full of him. I floated on my back in a swimming pool for as long as I could, and kidded myself I might cheat grief this way, held by water and wet cries. Echoey breathing in my ears proved I was still alive. Perhaps, like four years ago, I can lie between tracks while the grief train shackles over me, without even grazing my hair.

*

Thinking of Clifford has already slowed me down, so I keep going. The clouds are mountains above me, and the shadow of a rook flaps over.

As we drove our reconnoitre last week, Ian mentioned that George Bernard Shaw owned a house at Ayot St Lawrence. It's liberating to feel a stone's throw and miles away from that literary lifestyle I fantasised about as an adolescent writer, when I dreamt I was bound to make my big splash sometime, and Clifford and I would become the talk of the town. Adolescent plans swapped with each other through London's streets every half-term, its bookshops and galleries, where fame and fortune would kiss us one day. We pictured our lifelong dedication to art and literature, when we assumed we both had a future.

It's eight miles till I reach Stevenage.

The realisation that I won't achieve the recognition I dreamt about dawned gradually. Although the vaguest fantasy lingers, I admit that no such change will happen. I trudge along the muddy margin, while younger brighter names flash past in the fast lane.

Writing without recognition can feel like speaking in an empty room: no audience; no interest. When I started out, I believed I'd make a name for myself: that Faber or Cape or Bloodaxe would eventually snap me up. When – submission after submission, rejection after rejection – small triumphs failed to lead to bigger triumphs, I faced the possibility of writing without success. But how can you stop if it's written into your bones? This itch for words feels woven through how I see myself, how I understand the world. Was my adolescent dream of fame really the motivation to write, or does it reach further back? A boy stands on his bed at night, acting out stories he's making up to brothers who only want to roll over and sleep. Toying with words as a child plays with Lego: building a house, an aeroplane, a dragon from red and blue bricks. Fame and fortune's absence doesn't seem to have shut me up or stopped me playing. It didn't stop Clifford painting for all he was worth in the last year of his life. Over three-quarters of Clare's 3,500 poems that survive remained unpublished during his life. He wrote:

> *I felt that I'd a right to song*
> *And sung – . . .*

If he blazed his glorious trail, wasn't it partly to allow later working-class voices their own right to song? One word daisy chains the next, until a page is covered in handwriting – a page no one else could have written.

Clare's first collection, *Poems Descriptive of Rural Life and Scenery*, was published in 1820 when he was twenty-six and sold nearly four thousand copies in its first year. Its title page read 'By John Clare A Northamptonshire Peasant'; his lowly status became a calculated part of how Clare was packaged for the public, and probably a factor in the book's success. Before him, working-class poets Robert Burns and Robert Bloomfield had been successful, so – as his biographer Edward Storey says – 'A "peasant-poet" was a good item on any bookseller's list.' Six weeks after its publication in January, Clare took his first trip eighty-five miles down the Great North Road to London, to be introduced to his writer peers and celebrated there by his publishers, although his first biographer says he was 'unwilling to play the part of a newly-discovered monkey or hippopotamus.' Jolting in the early morning four-horse coach from Stamford, Clare noticed workmen *ploughing and ditching in the fields* alongside him, as he had toiled for years to keep bread on his parents' table. The contrast hit home: *while I was lolling in a coach the novelty created such strange feelings that I coud almost fancy that my identity as well as my occupations had changd that I was not the same John Clare but that some stranger soul had jumped into my skin –*

It was astute of Clare to recognise that early success might tempt him to change his identity, to become another John Clare for London or his public, allowing a stranger to occupy his skin. It's correct that he *was not the same John Clare* any more. Perhaps he could be both: John Clare the poet glowing inside the fur of John Clare the country mouse in London. He was disappointed by the Thames from Westminster Bridge: *it was less in my eye than Whittlesea Meer*, and he mistook prostitutes for fine ladies walking through the streets on his first night. He even swallowed a friend's tale that *pathways on the street (were) full of trapdoors which dropd down as soon as pressd on with the feet . . . after the unfortunate country-man had fallen into the deep hole . . . he woud be robd & murderd & thrown into boiling cauldrons kept continually boiling for that purpose & his bones sold to the doctors –* This was what London could do to a country man and, by implication, how success might boil John Clare's bones, if he didn't watch his step.

One pressure Clare had to contend with was that, although his poetry deepened and matured with each of the four collections published during his life, his reading public dwindled. This peasant poet turned out to be a nine-day wonder. The flavour of the month grew stale, and his readers moved on to the next new thing. Twenty-one years after his first success, largely forgotten again either in the asylum at High Beach or shortly after walking home to Northborough, he wrote wistfully:

> *Fame blazed upon me like a comets glare*
> *Fame waned and left me like a fallen star*

A milk float trundles past. The sun isn't up yet, and I'm still the only walker here. My legs ache already. Blisters on the right heel and ball of my foot are cushioned by blister-pads, but my shoulders no longer twinge so heavily from the rucksack's weight. Considering my night's sleep, they've recovered reasonably well.

At the Ford dealer blue and yellow pennants crinkle in the wind, like paper crumpled again and again. Cars and clouds accompany me every minute, bearing their contradictory messages: noise versus silence, speed versus stateliness; islands of cloud in blue sea – the sky a sea I drown under.

Passing allotments behind a fence at the edge of Welwyn by Dicket Mead I think about the work that goes into them: frames and plastic bottles balanced over the tops of delicate crops; netting and blue hoops; bamboo sticks; shrubs and sacks; digging and weeding. Weekends, afternoons and evenings ploughed into soil, nurturing the shoots. They're left to fend for themselves this morning. No one's bending here now. A magpie behind me emits its serrated note like rasping along a saw. Clare wrote *I kept one for years till it got drownd in a well it usd to see itself in the water I fancy it got down thinking to meet it.*

Seamus Heaney said, 'Clare refused to co-operate . . . Once upon a time John Clare was lured to the edge of his word-horizon and his tonal horizon, looked about him eagerly, tried out a few new words and accents, and then, wilfully and intelligently, withdrew and dug in his local heels.' While it was an intelligent decision when he faced the page, this wilfulness cost him his 'career' as a poet. It cost him success in the marketplace, even if that decision has brought him more readers today. After his first book triumphed, he began to be blanked critically and commercially, literally overlooked, as if he was no longer writing anything of note. How did an isolated poet, under financial and artistic pressures to conform, decide not to censor himself rather than knuckling down and behaving? That he produced such a self-affirming body of work remains virtually heroic. After wrangles with patrons and publisher about a poem that used a rhyme with 'shit' in his first edition, he was annoyed by the removal of two poems in the third edition without his permission, and wrote to his publisher's partner Hessey in July 1820: *I think to please all & offend all we shoud put out 215 pages of blank leaves & call it 'Clare in fashion' – . . . the gold is lickd off the gingerbread – . . . I have lost my tail by it, but never mind.* Despite these demands, he kept faith with his own estimation of his work. Towards the end of 'Don Juan' (mostly written at High Beach) he states:

> *Though laurel wreaths my brows did ne'er environ,*
> *I think myself as great a bard as Byron.*

The painful rhyme's a joke (mimicking Byron's 'Don Juan') but it remains a radical self-assertion from a working-class poet, by then virtually ignored by the public, living in an asylum, his recent poetry rarely published. He dares to think he's equal to Lord Byron and by writing those lines he retains his sense of worth, whether laurel leaves flicker against his forehead or not.

Years ago, when England was first discovering her, Sharon Olds said to me after a poetry reading at the City Gallery in Leicester, 'If I was writing wrong, it was the only way I knew.' Clare would understand that sentiment. In a letter to his friend and supporter Eliza Emmerson he wrote *all I wish now is to stand upon my own bottom as a poet without any apology as to want of education or any thing else.* By not doctoring his style to suit a fickle market, he reclaimed his right to add words to the page, despite periods of poverty, critical disinterest, literary isolation, mental illness and even during twenty-six years in two asylums. He understood the leaves of his poems could be weighed in the balance with fashion, and was prepared to risk it:

> *Thy green memorials these and they surpass*
> *The cobweb praise of fashion –*

My first collection sank like a stone, despite my high hopes. The waves closed over its red cover, with me as a warpaint angel flapping uselessly under the title. I suddenly feel sorry for Dee. How must it have felt to live with a man who kept half a mind on his writing and half a mind on his friend? What dregs did that leave her and the children? I sometimes saw my writing as a disloyalty to them, thought it made me a bad husband and father, because I wasn't focusing enough on them, my mind was elsewhere. I short-changed them. There were times I'd vow to give up writing to devote myself to my family, and I never succeeded. The pull towards my writing room upstairs – where three stone rabbits sat on a lidded chimney stack outside the window – felt irresistible, but my gaps in writing were often clumsy attempts to prove my love, make it better. Give up writing and family life will become easier: this bargain with myself, beating myself up for not being good enough at the daily work of love; always being too tired, a failing writer, husband, father. Self-pity for sure, but there must be fathers pushing elaborate buggies who succeed in spinning the plates, juggling the hoops, without plate or hoop crashing to the floorboards. There must be husbands making their wives happy, while mine's distracted and crying, and I fail to please her by my presence. I'm another burden, doing harm with my tensions and anger, the way I would discard her, walk out of the room when she was talking. It's no wonder she must have fallen out of love. In these past few years I think I wore away her love with every thoughtless act. I'm walking back to someone who's turned her face from me, so all I can see is her hair like a scarf unfurling in the breeze.

I'm standing on Hunstanton beach where she's dancing an improvised ballet before low waves: arabesques and pirouettes. She's turning towards me smiling, lifting her hand with an open gesture, as though offering a lily, but turning away again like Isadora towards the tide, whirling and leaping, absorbed in her dance. There's no one else near this curve of water. I'm overwhelmed by love, wherever those steps are taking her, towards the sea, across the sand where she dances barefoot far from me and her skirt twirls around her. She's a free spirit who wants to question, travel, explore. I admire that, not being one myself. I suppose I find her astonishing. My wife. The woman I love.

*

I pick up the route's most reassuring name again at a round-about signed the Great North Road. I'm walking on the B197 towards Stevenage.

A row of modest shops fringes Mardley Heath, where the North Star pub shows its empty early morning car park, as if last night's drinkers are still sleeping off Good Friday pints and shots. I slip between select red-bricked estates, with clipped gardens and shaped trees. Range Rovers, Jags and sports cars squat in driveways, ready to roar.

Estates eventually drift away to leave fields that feel in quiet competition with the road. The nearest field lifts towards another copse of thirty shaggy trees, and a big sign at head height says PRIVATE PROPERTY – KEEP OUT. I'm sure I was trespassing where I slept last night, and feel relieved again that no one found me. Shall I disobey that notice and stride to forbidden trees?

In his sonnet 'Trespass', written shortly before his move to High Beach, Clare catches the fear and dare of trespassing:

> *I dreaded walking where there was no path*
> *And pressed with cautious tread the meadow swath*
> *And always turned to look with wary eye*
> *And always feared the owner coming by;*
> *Yet everything about where I had gone*
> *Appeared so beautiful I ventured on*

Trespassing deeper into the beautiful country before him might have felt like a political act for Clare, an attempt to reclaim the common land he'd roamed across as a child and teenager, before the Enclosure Acts gave landowners rights to fence and divide, to take over the fields and heaths and woods where previously a labourer might have been able to keep his cow or pig. In 1809, when Clare was sixteen, the parish of Helpston was enclosed. Between 1809 and 1820 – from when he was sixteen until he was twenty-seven – more than half of Northamptonshire's acres were enclosed, during which some of Clare's favourite haunts and sights were either destroyed, damaged or fenced off. The land he wanted to stay as his Eden irrevocably changed. It's no wonder he wrote in his protest poem 'The Moors':

> *On paths to freedom and to childhood dear*
> *A board sticks up to notice 'no road here'*
> . . .
> *As though the very birds should learn to know*
> *When they go there they must no further go*

Clare probably felt free as a bird, before his sixteenth year, to wander for hours wherever his fancy took him. The policy of Enclosures was personal to him. It felt as unnatural as stopping birds from flying where they choose. To face what he saw as *lawless law's enclosure* gave him not only an abiding sense of injustice (there was no doubt where the poor stood in the pecking order) but a belief that the land he knew intimately had been stolen from his childhood, that growing up meant even the grass under his feet became a site for greed and loss. Given his poverty, he had no choice but to earn a temporary wage as a young man felling trees, digging ditches, planting hedges and hammering fences into earth where he once walked freely. Imagine that lesson banging home with every axe-blow, each hawthorn twig needling his knuckles as he worked. It's no surprise he followed his fellow-labourers and turned to drink for those months to help make it more bearable: *Poetry was for a season thrown by . . . I usd to work at setting down fencing & planting quicklines with partners whose whole study was continual striving how to get beer & the bottle was the general theme from week-end to week-end.*

Looking across the fields this morning, I see a landscape whose shape is supposed to show an idyll of England, a green and pleasant image of tranquillity. But the hedgerows tangled before me, the squares of fields where *Fence now meets fence in owners' little bounds* were laid over months of civil unrest, and now hedgerows are disappearing to provide more farmland. In 1816 Hunger Riots in Littleport (forty miles from Helpston) led to nineteen protestors being transported for life and five hanged. How can I accept today's landscape on face value, assume it's how things have always been, without balancing the costs for Clare, his family and neighbours, and now the costs for birds and voles, stoats and weasels? They're soaked into the soil, where grass spills its own green secrets.

I keep going, faithful to the tarmac path unspooling beneath my boots, and a continuous film of fields and milky sky. The B-road means there's fewer cars to disturb me. Apart from Vince's white stallion and the dead young men, it's been a kind morning so far.

Clare's other trespass is into the beautiful, forbidden country of literature, where he has to keep *walking where there was no path.* Adam Phillips calls him 'a trespasser in the poetic tradition', and a reviewer of his second collection *The Village Minstrel* complained about 'the evil of incompetent intruders into the walks of literature.' Clare said he and his fellow working-class poets *are looked upon as intruders and stray cattle in the fields of the Muses.* These fields were mainly owned and influenced by moneyed men, who had not only greater access to education and a fine way with words, but access to the politics of publishing, ensuring one vision gets accepted and promoted, while another's ignored.

At least Clare's early success took the edge off his poverty for a while. It led to a trust fund and annuity set up by titled patrons and rich fans. Some payments came with strings attached. Lord Radstock huffed and puffed and tried to censor Clare's 'radical slang', but the combined income gave him initially about forty pounds a year, 'a sum comfortably in excess of an average labouring wage.' He could labour over his pen at last, until interest rates fell, his family grew, and he took on field work and harvest work again to pay the bills. When some patrons wanted to clip his poetry's wings, he could vent to his sympathetic publisher Taylor: *damn that canting way of being forcd to please I say – I can't abide it & one day or other I will show my Independance more strongly then ever.*

Taylor did his best to respect Clare's dialect most of the time, and usually took what Clare called *the pruning hook* to his punctuation, grammar and spelling, and his nervous tic of repeating himself. Apart from Taylor's severe editing of *The Shepherd's Calendar*, on the whole they worked collaboratively. Editing Clare's cramped and messy manuscripts took its toll on Taylor, especially when months of effort only led to dwindling sales. A few months after its publication, *A Village Minstrel* had sold 800 copies of its 2,000 print run. *The Shepherd's Calendar* took six dragging years to see the light of print, with Taylor handing over editing to less competent colleagues, and Taylor's partnership with Hessey dissolving in the middle. Clare wondered if it would ever be published and dreamt *I had one of the proofs of the new poems from London & after looking at it awhile it shrank thro my hands like sand & crumbled into dust –*

The Shepherd's Calendar sold 425 copies in two years, and Clare wrote to Taylor in August 1827 (four months after its appearance): *I feel very dissapointed at the bad sale of the new Poems but I cannot help it if the public will not read rhymes.*

Taylor pulled out of publishing poetry. In the early 1830s Clare's lament that *the public will not read rhymes* proved painfully true. No publisher came sniffing around a poet in his early forties who was yesterday's man. He wrote to a poet friend: *when the cow grows too old in profits in milk she is fatted & sold to the butchers & when the horse has grown too old to work he is turned to the dogs – but an author is neither composed of the materials nessesary for the profit of butchers meat or dogs meat – he is turned up & forgotten –*

Clare pursued a plan to self-publish a fat, blossoming collection – *The Midsummer Cushion* – but it was a gamble and he had no money to throw a dice: he failed to find enough subscribers. So he grabbed the safer option of selling the first edition of his next collection for £40 to the publisher Whittaker in London. *The Rural Muse*, a far more conventionally titled book, took half of the poems from *The Midsummer Cushion* and laid them before a largely uninterested public in 1835. It was probably the finest collection to appear in his lifetime, but it was his last, in a publishing career covering fifteen years. Good reviews didn't help low sales, and his brief fractured letters from this period sound like a poet with the stuffing knocked out of him. A month after *The Rural Muse* appeared he wrote to Taylor: *I thank you kindly for the parcel & am very pleased with the review but I am scarcely able to do any thing I feel anxious to get up to London & think I should get better how would you advise me to come I dare not come up by myself do you think one of my childern would do to come with me . . . excuse a short letter for I am not able to say more.*

Yet this man who dared not travel alone to London was, around the same time, writing 'Trespass', a sonnet that opens with dread and caution, but pushes the poet and reader forward, because *everything . . . Appeared so beautiful*; so why not dare to keep writing, keep walking? He understands that the fields he doesn't own, the literature he can't quite claim, may not be his, but that won't stop him walking and thinking:

> *I've often thought, the day appeared so fine,*
> *How beautiful if such a place were mine;*
> *But, having naught, I never feel alone*
> *And cannot use another's as my own.*

It's an oddly ambivalent conclusion, with 'naught' and 'never' and 'cannot': three negatives. The poet who has nothing sounds proud about never feeling alone, presumably because he belongs to a class that is accustomed to having nothing. If he knows another's place can't be his own, he turns ownership on its head, by making something out of nothing: his own poem.

I should follow Clare's example: make myself less timid about trespassing. I've been a good boy, sticking to others' rules, the paths laid down, for too many years: observing notices telling me to Keep Out, abiding by the rule that told me boys from council estates in Whitechapel don't pick up a pen, don't develop ambitions to write and publish poetry collections. Now I'm straying into the field of Clare studies, where some academics have set up fences around his prim-roses, his nightingale nests.

A year before she died Virginia Woolf said to the Workers' Educational Association in Brighton,

> Let us trespass at once. Literature is no one's private ground; literature is common ground . . . Let us trespass freely and fearlessly and find our own way for ourselves. It is thus that English literature will survive . . . if commoners and outsiders like ourselves make that country our own country, if we teach ourselves how to read and how to write, how to preserve and how to create.

Clare wrote without a room of his own, yet she could have been speaking to us, flashing a message like a lighthouse over choppy waters, urging us both to be fearless, to set sail.

There's a prolonged gap of greenery edging occasional cars, with the pips of birdsong. Trees fringe the road and daisies sprinkle the verges, as if to reassure me nature holds my hand.

I ask myself what Dee's doing this minute, miles away. I'm aware of my isolation, while in Holly House the kids will have woken by now. Dressing gowns and breakfast; cartoons bouncing across the screen. I'm separate from it, and they've known six weeks of waking without me; my absence becoming more of a habit to them, the norm, the way their week is shaped. A cut-paper father and husband. Scissor carefully round him till he disappears.

*

A heron flies over me in the otherwise empty sky. At first I assume it might be a big seagull, but when I look closer I notice how long the grey wings are, their luxurious flap, see its hunched neck, spear beak and those twiggy legs trailing behind its tail. Clare describes how

> . . . *the old heron from the lonely lake*
> *Starts slow and flaps his melancholy wing*

About four and half years ago I watched a heron for fifteen minutes or so on a lake at Clapham Common. It was our last trip to London with Clifford. He was too ill to travel after that. At first, I thought it was a plastic decoy because it stood motionless in the water, as if it wanted the fish to think it had turned into a willow. I had half an hour to kill, before I was meeting up with Clifford and Andrew. I remember watching the heron silently, patiently, to work out whether or not it was real. After five minutes of absolute stillness, suddenly its beak jabbed the water. I don't think it caught a fish. I don't remember a guzzle or swallow, only that it took up its frozen pose again. After another five minutes of waiting and watching I became bored. I wanted it to fly, needed the drama of seeing it unwrap its grey wings. It didn't happen. Presumably if it hadn't caught a fish there was nothing to fly away for. It would stand for as long as it took for a fish to become careless again.

I ran out of time and hurried to meet Clifford, but from then on I associated him with herons, as if the phoenix in his final paintings had transformed itself into a heron for my sake. When I see one, I imagine it's his message from another kingdom. I want it to be a hopeful sign, that everything's all right.

Although we never told him he was dying, one afternoon by his hospital bed Clifford asked me to read Hopkins's sonnet 'My own heart let me more have pity on' at his funeral. During his last year, as his body thinned and art cascaded from his hand, he read Hopkins's poems over and over. He was amazed that this Victorian priest understood him more than a hundred years later, that he even talked in his sonnets about Clifford's life.

After I read the poem at his funeral Clifford's mother fretted that he might have seen himself as 'this tormented mind tormenting yet' because of all his anxieties. But the message from his hospital bed was one of hope, not torment. The poem's lesson to Clifford (and his gift through me to the crowd at his funeral) was for 'poor Jackself' to

> . . . let be; call off thoughts awhile
> Elsewhere; leave comfort root-room; . . .

He ordered me to read the poem in a hopeful way, and told me to emphasise the word 'lovely' in the last line:

> . . . – as skies
> Betweenpie mountains – lights a lovely mile.

This morning I can hear his voice, the way he said it, instructing me. He said he'd haunt me if I didn't read it hopefully. I promised I would, and allowed a tear to drop onto his sheet, its tiny blemish greying the white linen for an instant. We didn't talk about his funeral again. That afternoon we watched a *Carry On* film instead. He made his request and I kept my promise, though when I was introducing the poem at his funeral my voice cracked as I explained he wanted it to be hopeful. I had to breathe slowly for a minute to control myself, before I could read the words aloud. I'd give anything for him to haunt me now.

This grey and white creature crosses the sky. Once, when Clifford and I walked through Hyde Park on one of our London jaunts, a heron flew over us. When I looked up, marvelling at its flight, Clifford said it would crap on my face. Do I misremember that afternoon – was it a swan rather than a heron, maybe two swans, or surely it could have been a couple of Canada geese? Time's playing tricks. I remember its flight, and me marvelling and Clifford's joke; but it might have been any of three birds that afternoon in Hyde Park, echoing here twenty years later.

I noticed a heron last Sunday, when Ian, Joe and I were driving the route. I was worried we'd lost direction around Hatfield, until it flew alongside us down Green Lane, almost as if to show us we were finding the right way. I saw another a week ago, when my friend Brenda and I took a break from work and walked along the canal near Foxton at lunchtime. It kept alighting a dozen or so yards ahead of us, lifting and landing further along the path, with impressive wings, black quiff and awkward ironing-board legs.

My heron this morning stays away from the trees. I want Clifford to be safe from harm. I still want happiness for him, although he's dead, and death might be the ultimate harm or safety. As a younger man Clifford believed in the spiritual aspects of life, yet during his last illness, when his mother tried to comfort him with thoughts of heaven, he said, 'Sod the afterlife. When I'm dead I want to *be* dead.'

I expect this heron to be alone, but suddenly notice – with a wow spoken into my Dictaphone – another following it, a few feathers torn from its wing. They're both flying in the same direction as I walk, heading north.

Clifford and Dee may be two great losses I'm trying to understand on this road, but they're losses of different magnitudes, different natures. There's nothing I can do to change Clifford's life or death: all I can change is my understanding of them. Dee and I stand at the start of letting each other go. How we achieve this might alter with every statement we make when we meet, each action we choose to take. Our marriage may be finishing, but our relationship's still subject to change. How do you stay upright when your heart carries a crack across its centre? Tread carefully, so as not to spill from the lip. It's already filled to overflowing.

Beside a row of red-brick houses I pass a skinny pasty-looking boy pushing a trolley of newspapers, with an Easter egg balanced on top. Inside the houses, people are opening papers and weekend supplements over breakfast while I flicker past their windows: a jacketed, laden figure glimpsed and gone.

Just before eight o'clock it's two miles to Knebworth. I'll work on a hobbling average of two miles an hour. After walking eighteen miles yesterday I don't feel on top form, stepping gingerly to protect my blisters. I had a naive assumption I could carry on as chirpy as my first morning, but my pace is likely to reduce every day. I haven't yet checked the graze where I scraped the back of my thigh climbing the fence, but my skin nags against my jeans with every stride.

Overtaking another BP garage, I trudge past midriff-high railings and new developments of two-storey houses. Street lamps stand above six-foot-wide lawns, and a line of cars park their nearside tyres on the kerb. If possible, however slowly, painstakingly, I plan to soldier on until eight-thirty tonight. It'll mean about twelve hours walking, with stops to catch my breath.

At 8.15 a.m. the latest milestone reads STEVENAGE 4 MILES. It's as if I'm reaching a form of meditative state with this journey, whereby pain's no longer separated from walking, yet I'm unable to cease. I marvel again how my body stays vertical, my legs keep moving one after another – forward, forward – virtually of their own accord.

Although I thought Clare would have felt free from High Beach Asylum by now, his journal tells of his fear of capture after waking on his first morning: *Daylight was looking in on every side & fearing my garrison might be taken by storm & myself be made prisoner I left my lodging by the way I got in & thanked God for his kindness in procuring it.* He's the captain of an imaginary army, and war's still shooting in his head. I associate with his fear of being caught, as if daylight's spying on us both the moment our eyes open.

Why does a night outside spell danger? When I was searching for somewhere to sleep, I had an overpowering instinct to hide. Whether exhaustion made me feel like a limping fox, or whether there's always a dread of exposure, I knew I must find a secret place to feel halfway safe. I think of the desperation of sleeping rough every night. I knew I couldn't sleep around Lemsford, in case imaginary drunks stumbled across me. They'd be bound to smell my vulnerability, knock me sideways, nick my cash, kick in my teeth.

*

Along London Road in Knebworth, daylight's helping to unlock the first few shops. Clicks of keys, scrapes of bolts and shutters speak of Saturday business-as-usual, while I've stepped out of time's routines.

No café's open, so I can't sip the froth and grit of a cappuccino or see the waitress sprinkle a dusting of chocolate. I glug a mouthful of water instead, near the zebra crossing that links two rows of shops: the Nails and Beauty parlour; the barber; the bookmakers and pharmacy; the off-licence facing the tandoori; dry cleaners, fish & chips, the butchers, estate agents, funeral directors and a shut Barclays bank on the corner.

From the top of her stepladder a young Chinese woman with a ponytail washes the windows of the takeaway, swishing across the glass with her grey cloth. Over the road a fat young woman in a tight pink dress disappears into the Co-op.

I reach Stevenage at 9.30 a.m. and I'm knackered, having walked for three solid hours. I'm taking a new pedestrian pathway, and need to pick up the route again from Graveley on the other side of town. Stevenage would have changed beyond recognition since Clare's walk: he'd wonder where he was if he arrived today. Halfords, Currys and PC World edge the centre with their ambitious blocks, wide inviting windows and car parks filling up with Skodas beside Fords beside Nissans. The compass has just come in handy, because I could have been aiming south by mistake.

Clare's still half a day ahead. I remain impressed that he reached Stevenage on his first night. There's no way my legs could have carried me here from Epping Forest in a day, although his journal says, *being night I got over a gate (&)*

crossed over the corner to a green paddock where seeing a pond or hollow in the corner I (was) forced to stay off a respectable distance to keep from falling into it for my legs were nearly knocked up & began to stagger. Clare's Stevenage is bare essentials: a patch of ground before his restricted field of vision, whatever crosses his path in the dark. A gate he's managed to climb; a pond or hollow he avoids falling into and *higher pailings to clamber over to get into the shed or hovel* where he sleeps. It's his temporary resting place. So the Hare snoozes on clover, while the Tortoise snoozes several miles and a hundred and fifty years behind him, both of us wrestling with uneasy dreams.

By 9.50 a.m. I'm sitting in Burger King on the brink of Stevenage. Erasure fills the sound system with another cheerful song. This is the new England. I could be sitting anywhere, though the sign above the counter at the end tells me in silver capitals on a red background that I'm at the HOME OF THE WHOPPER. I make notes in the exercise book that carries Ian's directions. It's bare unfussy decor: white walls, red pillars and sharp edges, with circles of light in the grey tiled ceiling. A poster nearest to where I sip my tea proclaims 'Crispy French Fries – The Best Thing That Can Happen to a Potato', with a close-up of chips and a paper thimble of tomato ketchup as big as my head.

A man in blue overalls is ordering at the counter from a smart thirty-something Asian man in a grey cap and waistcoat. My feet in their socks are laid across the red chair opposite, while my boots breathe below me, cooling their empty leather. Five other customers sit at wood-effect Formica tables with

long beige padded seats and backrests. Three workmen from
the road, dressed in high-vis orange jackets, already tuck into
Big Kings on red plastic trays. A young couple ignore each
other a few tables from me, two iced Cokes chilled before
them.

Outside the large glass panels, flags on poles ruffle in the
wind. The names of stores flutter their bright letters, spelling
out Pizza Hut, Toys Я Us and Texas above our heads. My
pedometer has reset itself to nought but, according to a map
of the walk in the Clare book squashed in my rucksack,
Stevenage is about a quarter of the journey home. As my tea
steams in its cardboard cup, I open the pages again. The
simple drawing charts how far I've come. Am I going to
finish this? I'm slow and blisters make me flinch, but they're
no reason to stop. Consider the sense of failure if I didn't
fulfil the journey I planned a few months ago, when I
assumed my life's foundations would stay the same. Built on
a bedrock that included my wife, children, home, job. I was
intending to hold on to them, as if they'd become possessions,
as if I thought I had a right to expect I could. Now I'm cut
adrift, what will finishing this walk mean? That I can achieve
something, pull a scrawny rabbit out of the hat, like Clare
when he'd also hit rock bottom.

I play a fantasy that if I finish this walk Dee might say, 'I
see you can set your mind to something and achieve it. You're
a determined person. You have value.' As if finishing this might
make me more worthy in her eyes. Perhaps I'm trying to light
a meagre victory out of the ashes, simply by walking eighty-
five miles. What if I don't make it – will I feel more of a failure
than having had a marriage break up? I ask myself again: what
am I trying to prove and to whom?

I assume Dee may be similar to me at this moment: trying to get through the next hour, the next day and night, with as little damage as possible. Her thoughts aren't full of me. They're crammed with the minute-by-minute needs of our kids, with me a dot on her horizon. The stupidity of my fantasy is that sometimes Dee seems long gone herself: miles outside the marriage and heading for another horizon, where I figure as less than a tree whose leaves she studied months ago like the palm of her hand.

I freshen up in the bright Burger King toilet. My blisters aren't big enough to burst yet, though I manage to wash my feet and change the blister pads. I stick Savlon and a plaster on the graze at the back of my thigh. No one interrupts my work. I repair myself, make myself fit and ready for the next stretch. My mother would be proud of me.

As I leave, the Asian server is placing one cardboard crown with rubies and sapphires on each empty table.

Weaving my way through Stevenage is a frustrating nightmare, with numerous walkways and pedestrian underpasses where signs disappear. A toddler with blonde hair in bunches wheels past in a buggy steered by her mother. She cries, 'Oh not *another* tunnel!' Her mother ignores her and pushes grimly on.

There's a characterless feel about the place, with loads of show-off buildings jostling with seventies buildings past their prime. It's hardly the ideal that the Committee for New Towns foresaw in 1946 when Stevenage was chosen to be the first New Town. They were sure it would become 'an essay in civilisation . . . an opportunity to design, evolve and carry into execution for the benefit of coming generations the means for a happy and gracious way of life.'

I set my compass again and aim north.

Stevenage Arts and Leisure Centre looms like a warehouse with wide pale fawn tiles and a yellow and blue headband. I've obviously gone wrong. It's taken me far longer to trek through this town than I originally planned. Last autumn's brown leaves collect in a corner of the twentieth tunnel, alongside two abandoned shopping trolleys. Leaving this tunnel, I can't fail to notice a huge blue-glass Confederation Life Centre set back from the road. It looks very American, or very Stevenage.

Eventually I reach a quieter, more modest area called the Old Town. A red-and-black brick pub, the White Lion, has a sign that says it provided accommodation and fresh horse teams for coaches using the Great North Road. It sits beside Pizza Hut and the Old Town Fish Bar. Women carrying shopping bags look harassed and intent on bargains, while others in fleeces cluster round a couple of buggies, smoking and cracking a joke. An old woman in a khaki-coloured coat is coughing repeatedly. As I pass nearby she complains to a friend, 'I've got such a tickle!'

This area feels more life-sized compared to the centre of Stevenage, as if we've returned to a human scale again. I find the Graveley B197 road. A speckle-bellied thrush in the grass eyes me and decides not to fly. It watches me warily, cocking the side of its head, listening for worms. I lean my back against a tree on a patch of grass, pulling off these boots again to give my plastered feet a breeze. Two girls on white ponies trot by. It's 11.45 a.m. and I plan to stay here till noon.

Quiet minutes drag me back to our separation, that under-current troubling my thoughts. I think of us meeting at eighteen, how student love blossomed into young married love and young parent love; then it should have settled into a steadier love, but what happened? To be chucking the golden years away. Changing apart rather than together, as if our differences became as inevitable as growing up.

We drove to Cornwall for our honeymoon after a wedding night at the Red Lion in Salisbury, tendrils of red leaves against the brickwork outside and chicken sandwiches when we arrived late. The four-poster bed where we made love, with satin honeysuckle and branches above us. From an elderly artist named Lamorna we rented a one-room stone hut. It overlooked Lamorna Cove, with its jutting red cliff and a turquoise sea close to the toe of England. It was primitive, but we felt happy there and began our married life. Kidding ourselves we could be Lawrence and Frieda: learning each other's nakedness, sharing one room, strip-washing in front of each other on sunlit mornings within the sound of waves. We bought a woodcut edition of Lawrence's love poems *Look! We Have Come Through!* with its ecstatic nudes. We bought four hand-thrown blue dinner-plates with fish and hippyish designs in dulled gold. We thought we knew each other well by then, but found a difference living together, learning each other's daily ways. After a visit to Logan Rock, one rock balanced on the other at the edge of land, I wrote a love poem that ended:

> This far out there is feeling,
> Close as your move for my hollows
> Under sleep. Touch me
> Like the sun on that crashed colour.

97

Our love felt elemental then, as if her fingers on my skin sparked against the sea. Halfway through the honeymoon we bumped back to earth. One night I ate a dodgy burger and fell violently ill, with frequent trips to the outside toilet down stone steps under moonlight. In sickness and in health arrived sooner than expected. It was our first lesson of marriage: that closeness of another body could be too close; my farts and belches and foul breath; my sick bucket beside the bed. What an awakening! I'm not thinking day-to-dayness stifles love (even after food-poisoning on honeymoon) but it ruins romanticism. Maybe romanticism deserves to be ruined, if idealising the beloved does them a disservice, makes them more than they can possibly be.

What chance did Patty stand, competing in Clare's poetry with Mary Joyce? A muse you don't live with is easier to idealise; but I think one of Clare's uses of Mary was that she was bound up with his childhood, the part of his life he repeatedly returned to in his poetry and saw as his untainted years. If Mary stayed in his head (if not in his daily life, at least in his poetry) he could pretend the narrative continuity of his life story meant something. He could stay the same John Clare who fell in love with Mary when they were at school as the John Clare who declared his love to her throughout his married life, into his long asylum years.

I met Dee when we were eighteen. If that bond is breaking now what does it mean for my life? Snapped like a twig. Katherine Mansfield talks of 'our persistent yet mysterious belief in a self which is continuous and permanent.' If consistent figures disappear from my young years – Clifford; Dee – my life could shrink as easily, be fractured, extinguished, as though I represent the only continuous presence in my story. I suppose it's fear of mortality. If Clifford dies and I don't remember him the same extinction could happen to me. If Mary goes from his daily life and he doesn't honour her in poem after poem, Clare's sense of continuity vanishes with her. He was never quite able to admit to himself that she'd gone, even before she died. So she stays elusive but alive, the woman of his dreams, and his stanzas obsessively call her name.

In this break on the grass I open Clare's poems at 'The Enthusiast: A Daydream in Summer'. Its rhyming couplets follow a man into his daydream over seven pages, burnished by childhood's pleasures:

> *Heart bursting with unshackled joys*
> *The only heritage of boys*
> *That from the haunts of manhood flye*
> *Like songbirds from a winter sky*

Manhood sickens the poet, makes him turn with distaste from *life's realitys* to the compensation of reimagining childhood, culminating in a fantasy reunion with Mary:

> *And Mary, pride of pleasures gone,*
> *Was at his side to lead him on*

He delights in reliving her physical presence, their closeness:

> *The self-same voice as soft and dear,*

her blue eyes, her taking his hand to climb stiles, shielding her eyes to watch a skylark (*her favourite in the skies*). Mary's return blurs with the return of his youth, since when he calls her name again she answers

"Tis youth and Mary standing by'.

Yet it seems her return is not enough. He wants, and gets, a promise that they *would part no more*, and to seal that vow he makes the next move and tries to hold her, presumably to possess her sexually:

> *When her small waist he strove to clasp*
> *She shrunk like water from his grasp.*
> *He woke – all lonely as before*
> *He sat beside the rilling streams*
> *And felt that aching joy once more*
> *Akin to thought and pleasant dreams*

So the man sighs for security, represented by the woman; and though she promises never to leave, she literally disappears because he tries to grasp her. She becomes as impossible to catch as water. She won't be his audience, or even his muse, any longer and he's bereft, alone with his aching joy, facing himself rather than a fantasy. This long poem runs out of steam four lines after Mary vanishes. Even the rhyme-scheme changes in its final quatrain. Once she's no longer there he's lost for words. The woman's power to disappear at any moment she chooses haunts much of Clare's love poetry. That experience of aloneness, after the woman's disappearance, echoes into me sitting under this tree. Left for good. Left for dead. I deserve to be nurtured for ever by a mother or wife – my divine right. If they go, I dribble like water into mud.

I'm on my feet again, approaching Graveley. The landscape spreads out to fields after Stevenage. Graveley's a village with a couple of pubs, and two young sisters in pink and lilac on bicycles, wearing matching crash helmets. Blossoms scatter like sawdust in the kerb.

It's good to open the compass and read that it's bang on north. My map notes this section of the Great North Road was originally a Roman Road, and sure enough it does its job by lying straight as an arrow, giving a wide view over to the A1(M) on my left. This is a line carved into soil nineteen hundred years ago. Beside a growing number of cars, I add my steps to an ancient ritual where others have trod. I walk through time, where fields and hedgerows recover themselves, with overhanging trees and birdsong tinkering between branches. A willow stands halfway up the hill, like Ophelia tumbling her hair down on a green stage.

At 1.15 p.m. I skirt Jack's Hill Reservoir, calmly reflecting the clouds. I've walked for six hours, allowing for breaks and hobbling. According to the map, the milestone mentioned in Clare's account must be somewhere around here. A starling flies across the Great North Road with a strand of tissue paper in its beak, disappearing under guttering in a corner of the Highwayman pub. It's a wide road bordered by cow parsley and steep hedges, and cars keep coming. Tiny ticks of moisture tinge the air, as though weather's weighing the pros and cons of rain.

I pass a clump of dead nettles, with creamy globular flowers in a small steeple. Bending closer, each has three Elizabethan ruffs of furry pear-shaped petals rising to the top. Its leaves pretend to sting, while the flowers give the game away. I think again about all the lessons Dee taught me, including the difference between live and dead nettles. In our early trips to Northamptonshire she showed me how to stroke dead nettles and prove they'd do no harm, as if by magic. I copied her cautiously and my fingers didn't itch. I'd never have discovered this without her.

I suddenly find Clare's milestone:

34
MILES
from
LONDON

in chiselled and black-painted letters on a thigh-high pale stone pillar. Nettles and goosegrass surround its base, edging the tarmac walkway. I yank away the stems of an elderflower bush to uncover its face, like it could be an honoured monument. A line of ants is tracking across its foot. Its crown is spattered by a few mustard medallions of lichen, and a rod of iron must be staked through its centre, as I pick at a small black button that won't budge. I rest my back against it and reread Clare's account, to make sure it's the one he mentioned.

His journal carries a footnote: *On searching my pockets after the above was written I found part of a newspaper vide 'Morning Chronicle' on which the following fragments were pencilled . . . Wednesday – Jacks Hill is passed already consisting of a beer shop and some houses on the hill appearing newly built – the last Mile stone 35 Miles from London.* In fact 34 is carved, but what's a mile between friends? I feel certain Clare paused here to scribble that note. He couldn't stop writing, even through his exhaustion, and pencil on a scrap of newsprint would suffice.

I snap a photo like a tourist, lay my palm on stone for blessing. I imagine it, every midnight, spelling its message to foxes and whoever else may be passing. Whereas I'm usually hobbling behind Clare in the long shadow he's cast, for this minute stopped at a marker where I'm sure he stood in 1841, our shadows briefly cross. The Tortoise catches up with the Hare. If only for a moment, a halt in the race, we check each other eye to eye, as if this stone might now contain memories of us both. Although these dandelions, nettles and speedwell are the heirs of those that grew when Clare rested here, it feels like this place holds a resonance of him, a bell echoing fainter after the first scuff of his boots moved away.

Dozens of people are taking part in Easter Saturday golf at the Chesfield Downs Family Golf Centre, its little yellow flags flapping while they point and stride, whacking dimpled balls and trundling trolleys of clubs over the links. Three dead rabbits lie in the road opposite.

When I reach Baldock I'll have covered one Ordnance Survey map. I need to complete two more maps to finish the journey. My pace has probably slowed by half because of blisters. When I shuffle downhill, it's as though I'm walking barefoot with red-raw soles.

A chaffinch prinks on the branch ahead, a trill of the same notes over and over, punctuated by a tiny pause. It sings by a bare field, ploughed with nothing sown. A cluster of a dozen cowslips yellows the verge. Our old neighbour opposite Holly House mentioned that cowslips used to cover meadows in his childhood, and in a High Beach sonnet 'The Cowslips' Clare writes of their abundance:

> The dancing Cowslips come in pleasant hours;
> Though seldom sung, they're everybody's flowers:
> They hurry from the world, and leave the cold;
> And all the meadows turn from green to gold.

Cowslips *hurry from the world* and roads are added. Signs proclaim the construction of a new bypass between the A6141 south of Baldock and the A505 east of Baldock, to be known as the Baldock Bypass. A public enquiry is planned, so there's obviously local feeling around the issue. If it goes ahead this landscape will change again, fields and woods will be cut through, taking it further away from how Clare experienced it. Perhaps I've walked here just in time, because next year or in five or ten years, I'll find a host of changes. Walking's a brief form of ownership: seeing this place when I move through it imprints it on my thoughts. It carries me from one sight to the next, like a series of light bulbs strung above my path.

A young man sells expensive flowers by the wayside. Headphones are buzzing in his ears and he blinds his eyes with his hands when I'm alongside him, like he might be embarrassed or, for reasons I don't understand, wants to shield his face.

A smashed pigeon's a feathered catastrophe in the road, ribs and blood oozing onto tarmac. I'm glimpsed for a second by drivers, after which they carry on their journey while I'm pinned in mine. We brush against each other, get caught sometimes, and that entanglement can last for twenty years or more. Clifford and Dee were two great entanglements where I felt drawn to hear their next words. Whatever came out of their mouths intrigued me enough to stay around to hear more.

Four years ago, Clifford's last words to me were 'Thanks Rob,' which I hadn't heard properly because he said them softly, with a slurred groggy voice. Andrew had to repeat them for me. I took Clifford's hand and kissed his knuckles before I left his hospital room, as though he were a frail prince and I was pledging loyalty, bowing over his hand to say farewells. When I visited the next afternoon, he was in a heavy morphine sleep that lasted a day or two before he died. I remember the chalky blue of his fingertips, as I pressed a cold flannel against his burning red ear to cool him down, talking to him, telling him what I was doing, although he was sleeping. On his funeral wreath I wrote to thank him for twenty-three years of friendship. So we thanked each other. What else can we say but thank you to our friends? Perhaps friends shimmer off each other: their personalities melding and sparking like two virtually simultaneous waves.

One summer before he met Andrew, Dee and I spent an afternoon with Clifford on Brighton's nudist beach. They swam naked, Dee and Clifford, while I lay sunning myself on the pebbles. When they came back he marvelled in his painter's way about the shapes Dee's body made in the waves: her slinky pinks and octopus corals circling and swaying as she swam.

Pausing to drink water makes me realise how thirsty I've been. I've walked for eight hours. It's 2.30 p.m. and I deserve a break in Baldock: to slip out of these boots; change into trainers; shop for water, apples, Mars bars and blister pads. All the essentials. I can allow a good hour. I keep assuring myself there's no contest with Clare, since he's half a day ahead already, approaching Baldock on his second morning rather than my second afternoon.

Somewhere near here in the first light he came across two sleeping travellers. He wrote in his account: *on the left hand side the road under the bank like a cave I saw a Man and boy coiled up asleep which I hailed and they woke up to tell me the name of the next village.* I assume they were father and son – the wife and mother absent for reasons we'll never know – but I wonder what brought them to this road outside Baldock, sheltering under the bank like a cave where they might sleep safely, wrapped up together, half-protected from the elements. Broken from their dreams by a stranger asking the way. It reminds me of Clare's brief connection to another destitute outsider on his second visit to London in 1822: *I remember passing St Pauls one morning where stood a poor Affrican silently soliciting charity . . . I felt in my pockets but I had only fourpence in all and I felt almost ashamed to recieve the poor creatures thanks for so worthless a pittance and passed him but his looks spoke so feelingly that even a trifle would be acceptable that I ran back a long way and put the fourpence into his hand . . . I saw the poor creatures heart leap to thank*

*me and the tears steal down his cheeks . . . for his thanks and
suprise told me he had met with little of even such charity
as mine – and I determind the next day to get my pocket
recruited if possible and give him a shilling and my first walk
was to St Pauls but the poor affrican was gone and I never
saw him again –*

How did this African man end up in London? The slave
trade in Britain was abolished in 1807, though it continued in
the British Empire until 1834 and nine years longer in East
India Company territories. In 1832 Clare wrote to Thomas
Pringle, secretary to the Anti-Slavery Society: *I have a feeling
on the broad principle of common humanity that slavery is not
only unfeeling but disgraceful to a country professing religion.*
Perhaps this man was a freed slave cut adrift, unable to get
home; a servant out of work – an exotic novelty who'd outlived
his amusement value – dumped on London's pavements; a
soldier or seaman left to fend for himself after the end of the
Napoleonic Wars seven years before, Clare's sympathy the first
he'd seen in days from hard white faces closed as doors against
him. Where did he go after he left St Paul's, and how did he
survive into the next week, next month, if a peasant poet's
fourpence dropped like a miracle into his hand?

When I touch the outskirts of Baldock, blossoms from a horse-
chestnut confetti through the breeze. Someone's getting married
today. An empty cream wedding car smooths past: white
ribbons across its bonnet and white flowers on a shelf by the
rear window. Perhaps there's merely the ghost of a bride inside.

In the six years after our wedding, before we had children,
Dee and I used the opportunity to travel: the Greek Islands

one summer, followed by Venice and Rome another, and Northern India and Kashmir a couple of years before our first son Isaac was born. Our trip to the Greek island of Santorini coincided with another royal wedding: Charles and Diana. On the afternoon of their wedding we were miles from TV screens, walking along a dusty road towards some ruins or another beach, I can't remember which. I know we were determined to avoid the wedding. Although tensions surfaced on that holiday, there were happy times too: looking down on the bluest bay with people swimming naked in the waves below and thinking we'd found Eden; dancing to 'Psycho Killer' under the stars in some open air disco; coming across a café where a group of hippies were strumming guitars and singing 'Four Strong Winds'.

That afternoon I think we were getting on famously. It was a deserted road with no one else in sight, apart from a few bony goats nipping near olive groves on the hill, and cicadas shaking their tiny dice inside bushes. It was baking under the sun and we'd walked far too long. That may have made us tetchy or clumsy, but we suddenly collided on an otherwise empty road, bumping into each other's elbows and hips, tripping over each other's sandals. We landed on our arses in the dust, laughing like drains: a happy couple tripping each other up, giving each other belly laughs no one else would understand, while miles away in London a nervous bride and groom (or hundreds of brides and grooms) lifted veils and spoke their vows into air.

At 4 p.m., I'm sitting at a table in the Victoria pub, crisps and half a cider before me, jotting notes in my exercise book. Little pink and yellow lampshades are frilled either side of lattice windows near where I write. Blue, green and terracotta shields cover the flowery carpet under my boots, and terracotta scrolls run down the wallpaper to a green dado rail. Clumps of men in their forties drink, chat and smoke, staring over pints at horses on the screen above the gas fire and a plastic flower display. Golfing photos and portraits of horses clutter the wall behind the bar staff pulling pints. Three leprechaun mascots dangle by the racing calendar behind the bar, and a cabinet of silver trophies glints above me. A fruit machine twirls arrows, numbers and bonuses to itself in the corner.

The commentator says, 'Catch the Moonlight and Red Mystique race into the dip with Suburban Sky, Wind Fire, Little Better and Caledonia towards the outside. Southside Bay, Enchanted Garden and Lulu the Zulu are under a bit of pressure.' He speeds up as horses gallop towards the finish and the men start raising their voices at the screen. One shouts, 'Gara boy!' and Red Mystique is repeated by the commentator until Red Mystique is first past the post. Winners and losers check their betting slips, and something in the air relaxes, subsides.

As it does, an immaculately made-up young woman sits down at the far end of my table. Her boyfriend brings their drinks and sits beside her for a few minutes, occasionally passing a remark and sipping his lager, until he leaves. She waits for twenty minutes, tapping her magenta nails, trying hard not to look impatient, while I drink my cider, crunch my crisps and politely avoid her eyes in typical English fashion. Considering how scruffy I must look, I think about the effort she's made: the careful application of foundation, mascara and lipstick, the mirror telling her she's OK.

When the boyfriend returns, he doesn't speak, as though nothing has happened. I'm trying to work out what's going on between them, to decipher this silent code, when the penny drops that he's probably a gambler. Why else would he bring her to this betting pub and leave her for so long? Perhaps he popped out to place a bet or two and has lost again, and she knows he's lost, because he's saying nothing. He's caught in its talons, and I decide from a few feet away she's caught in the talons of loving him but wanting to move on to someone who pays her more attention, without half an eye on the horses, money falling through his fingers; sitting in a pub waiting for him to notice her.

Of course, I've no idea if this is true. We make up stories about what we see between two people: my mother and I used to do it all the time when we were out, clocking customers in cafés or couples on park benches, deciding their fates between us from a smattering of clues. My grandmother would have called us Nose-omels: her Yiddish term for nosey parkers. Did strangers do the same for me and Dee in the years of our marriage? Strolling past wedding photos snapped in a Bethnal Green park; smiling honeymooners sunbathing at Lamorna Cove, or, years later, a couple rowing in Boots in Kettering, where the woman says, 'If you walk away again I'll smash everything on this shelf,' so the man stands beside her but still doesn't answer. Glimpses of a couple's history over three points in England, as I'm glimpsing theirs now: captured at the same beer-ringed table or walking past and disappearing from each other's view.

I'm out on the Great North Road again, having passed a sign saying Icknield Way. Wires high across the road, from pylons over ploughed fields, are taut as thick black guitar strings.

Branches bend heavy with leaves. I needed that rest and should have taken it earlier, since I've been walking for over nine hours and I'm nearly a third of the way to Clare's home. I feel I can manage a few more hours, but I should treat myself more carefully.

My body's a vessel of water or wine, ready to smash if the path cracks. I'll smash everything on this shelf. Tied to her. Moods shut in a room. Why did I hit her with silence when all she wanted was communication? But when I'd say what I felt, she didn't want to hear that either. It only led to more words, more misunderstandings, so it felt safer to keep my mouth shut; both trapped in months of things not working between us; both gagged and bound. I feel sorry for the mess that couple ended up in, years after Lamorna Cove and Santorini.

Lines from Joni Mitchell's song 'Hejira' repeat in my head, about being glad to be on my own. I sing them to myself beside the cars. I'm liberated by solitude. It's a strange freedom not to have to adapt myself to someone, mould my likes and dislikes, attempt to please and fail again, getting more cack-handed with each attempt. I can begin to please myself. I want to come away from this walk with grand attitudes of forgiveness and compassion for Dee, cleansed by four days outside that torment. Eventually, I want to rise above these months without acrimony, blame or even regret. It might help to see whatever happens as the next event in my life, though it smacks of the temptation to make the heart a stone. Can I achieve a lump of marble in my chest, banging its cage?

Some people leave an indelible mark: run right through the skin to your bones. Driving to work last week I heard a woman on the radio talking about her husband: 'When I first met him the light shone through his hair.' I understood that pull to romanticise, until my eyes opened to see my wife as she stood before me: simply a woman as I'm a man, with no special powers, as flawed as anyone. I thought she might be more attuned to emotion because she found a vocabulary for what she was feeling. I was struck dumb by it, when she was only asking someone to say how they felt, and I couldn't find language for the mess inside. Saying any words I could find wouldn't give her the reassurance she needed. These past ten months we've been holding up flags to each other on separate hills – flags of truce, flags of semaphore – trying to signal *I love you – stay with me – work it out*, but the flags kept waving out of order and we couldn't even spell our names.

At ten past five the rabbits are out again. Wind is blowing the map-wallet looped around my neck until it feels like it'll throttle me. The first stretch is approaching where I'll be walking along the A1. I'm dreading it, like a trial of fire I'll have to endure to follow Clare's route. A sign ahead says WELCOME TO BEDFORDSHIRE – A PROGRESSIVE COUNTY. I wonder if any county would admit to not being progressive: WELCOME TO NORTHAMPTONSHIRE – A DYED-IN-THE-WOOL-COUNTY.

Somewhere around Baldock (he says in the account of his second day *Somewhere on the London side*), Clare was passed by a man in a slop-frock on horseback, near the Plough pub. If he was wearing a slop-frock he may have been a farmworker or drover, but he took pity on Clare, calling out – presumably to friends nearby – *'here's another of the broken-down haymakers.'* He threw Clare a penny *to get a half-pint of beer which I picked*

up & thanked him for & when I got to the Plough I called for
a half-pint & drank it & got a rest & escaped a very heavy
shower in the bargain by having a shelter till it was over – My
half-pint of cider at the Victoria has done me proud, and
though no horseback riders pass today, I might look broken-
down to any drivers.

Glancing over to the left as I join the A1, I make out the
honeyed tower of a distant church. The A1 brings me up hard
against an onslaught of two dual carriageways of speeding
traffic, fields following their own quiet business on either side.
Walking along the A1 is a mad, scary enterprise, leaving my
vulnerabilities more naked than before. I'm open to whatever
I see. The sky's bellied by clouds, where two buzzards sail
across air currents in an almost leisurely style, separate from
each other, scanning for prey.

Thistles and nettles prickle the verges, with occasional
narrow walkways and the wallop of tyres over four lanes of
tarmac, careering past me like a *thump thump thump* against
my ears. I imagine Clare hearing the hoof-beats and rattle of
mail coaches, carts and carriages clattering up and down.
Maybe a neigh or two. He'd have probably passed walkers
going about their trades, trekking from village to village,
whereas I'm the only walker here, beside the pelt of a badger.
The most disturbing element is not facing the traffic, so I can't
tell if disaster's hurtling towards me at eighty miles an hour,
ready to knock me and the next badger dead in our tracks.

When I bought a paperback anthology of *Six Centuries of*
Great Poetry for fifteen pence with Clifford on one of our
jaunts round Charing Cross bookshops, Clare's sonnet
sequence on badger baiting was harsh and clear-sighted, his
sympathy for the badger made tougher by an absence of

philosophising about his plight. In the first lines the badger's alone, with no *dogs and men* to trouble him:

> *The badger grunting on his woodland track*
> *With shaggy hide and sharp nose scrowed with black*
> *Roots in the bushes and the woods and makes*
> *A great huge burrow in the ferns and brakes.*

When *a host of dogs and men* arrive at midnight the hunt is on, and though the badger fights back *and everyone's a foe*, Clare makes clear through relentless rhyming couplets that the odds are piled against him. The crowd scents blood and Clare's focus is the victim:

> *He falls as dead and kicked by boys and men,*
> *Then starts and grins and drives the crowd again,*
> *Till kicked and torn and beaten out he lies*
> *And leaves his hold and cackles, groans and dies.*

Clare's badger dies before mine. The finality of those lines marches with my rhythm down this killing road.

I've moved on to my third map. The A1's red line is the straightest route from A to B. It looked so easy when I spread them over my front-room carpet, but maps lie silent as unfolded paper. Cars, motorbikes, vans, lorries and coaches overtake each other back and forth, with only a gun-metal barrier and a margin of thistle-heads between their opposite directions.

I'm a daft poet – bonkers as the other one. Why put yourself through it, test your nerve? Plod on, stupid workhorse. Get wherever you want to be that isn't here.

*

A green A1 sign ahead says 'PETERBOROUGH 40' in white letters, so perhaps I'm nearly halfway home. I pass a place to stop for a drink, but decide to plough on and finish this dangerous lap. I'm unsure if I'll manage six miles to Biggleswade before the light fails, and tell myself perseverance must be the watchword. When I sang that hymn in junior school with its line 'Give us grace to persevere' I wondered who 'Percy Vere' was, but kept the question to myself. I sing the Lord is my shepherd to cheer myself up, even though I don't know all the words.

The grass verge remains bumpy to walk over, and I'm too close to traffic for comfort. After an hour or more I cut through a field by the gap in a hedge, scaring rabbits. It feels imperceptibly calmer here, a tinge less frantic because of the green before me, as if the colour and curves soften the traffic's damage, though engine after engine a few feet away sounds like the same assault. It's low flat land, with a shallow crop I try to skirt round, and a copse of trees rising towards the horizon. Half-a-dozen rabbits at the edge of a fence near a water tower haven't realised I've arrived, and carry on munching. A kestrel hangs like a wishbone in the air, wings and claws lifted for a minute, until it dives. There'll be flurry and death in the undergrowth. This wildlife continues without reference to the cars brushing past it, the drivers oblivious, eager to be gone.

Suddenly a fox-coloured hare as big as a terrier races across the field, tail flashing like a smudge of grubby snow. Clare describes it perfectly:

> *Through well known beaten paths each nimbling hare*
> *Sturts quick as fear – and seeks its hidden lair.*

He becomes my hare again, leaving me gawping, tired as a tortoise, a cumbersome rucksack overloading my shoulders and spine. He shows off his speed, but perhaps he's fearful of me pursuing his paw-prints, pinning him down. There's plenty in Clare's writing about secrecy and hiding, as though his brief glare of publicity dazzled him in the headlights, made him run for cover. I want to join his escape, creep inside my shell, when this late afternoon tips its balance towards early evening: safe from harm, safe from shuddering cars and hovering kestrels.

By 7 p.m. I'm exhausted, sick of tramping over rough verges, having to watch where my boots place every step. The sky tells me I've got about an hour while it's still light enough, so Biggleswade remains my Mecca. If I can reach there, I should be able to find somewhere safe to sleep tonight.

An old pocked milestone standing little higher than my knee says 42 miles from London, which indicates I've covered quite a patch of ground today. I'm passing Bleak Hall, a low black sign in the grass with blurred white letters. It's like an apple orchard with a 1970s red-brick house nestling beside it. My feelings are bleak enough. At this stage I'm moving by instinct, slowing down. My bones make me more able to appreciate Clare's words at the end of his first day: *my legs were nearly knocked up & began to stagger.* It would be easy enough to stagger now, if I don't tighten every tendon in my effort to stick to the straightest line ahead.

At 8 p.m., coming into Biggleswade, I landed a lift from a young man and his mother and sister or girlfriend, though

my thumb wasn't hooked to hitch a ride. I told him I was
heading for Biggleswade and he offered to take me the few
extra miles. I was impressed, especially as he'd been driving
in the opposite direction and I was taking him out of his way.
I thought, 'Is this bloke for real?' Perhaps weariness made me
wary. He said he felt sorry for me looking so tired on Easter
Saturday night and he wanted to help me into town. The
women in the backseat said nothing. I couldn't tell if they
supported his decision, or if his detour would make them late
and their silence was sullen.

We drove past rows of houses and the Potton turn I needed
for retracing Clare's walk; but having told him I wanted
Biggleswade I felt too embarrassed to change my story, too
knackered to explain. Easier to keep mum and be driven, give
myself up to his good deed. Just over Biggleswade's mini roundabout, he found a pub that offers beds for the night. Ever
helpful, he told me about others if I was unlucky there, giving
me names and complicated directions that were simply words.
I couldn't take them in, became a nodding dog and thanked
him for all his help before he drove away.

I hobble over the paved market square, where a tall stone cross
bears a sword carved to the Glory of God, in grateful memory
of the men from the parish who gave their lives in the Great
War. Names are listed down each side of its base.

Above the door of the New Inn a sign says that it's seven-
teenth century. Inside I find a sandstone-tiled floor, white and
grey chrysanthemums on black wallpaper. Chaka Khan sings
about being every woman. I buy another cider and sink into
a brown leather settee, scribbling lines in my exercise book

about the driver and this pub, thinking how far I've managed today.

Two young women in stilettos and tight skirts chat on high stools at the bar. 'And I was like, is he gonna leave, just tell me. And she was like, I don't know. And I phoned her and said I love you but I was like I can't keep taking it.'

The barmaid with hoop earrings and a ponytail pouts a kiss towards a regular as she pulls a pint. Drinkers here are preparing for a night on the tiles. I'm gearing myself up to spend a second night outside counting stars.

Second Day 1841

On My Left Arm

I slept soundly but had a very uneasy dream I thought my first wife lay on my left arm & somebody took her away from my side which made me wake up rather unhappy

Be apple-wood for my fire again
splash to my tongue,
a woman at my left side again:
slotting against this shoulder
as if hugging's the warmest wish
you care to make.

You who could sleep
where blossom skitters on your waking eyes
decide to snooze through my hair,
to breathe my breath.

Don't rise. Let no hand rob you from this holding:
I'll daisy-chain your wedding finger to mine.
When we're lying, two bodies in bed,
joined at the wrist and the hip
our gap measures less than an earlobe,
loose as a tooth.

Man and Boy

on the left hand side the road under the bank like a cave I saw
a Man and boy coiled up asleep which I hailed and they woke
up to tell me the name of the next village

The boy speaks:

> We coil like day-old pups. No milk. No mother.
> I nuzzle his beard's thicket,
> hook thumbs through his greatcoat buttonholes,
> hanging on.

> Some stoop under slate or thatch all winter,
> so I beg them. Does wind clack teeth
> and prickle their napes like mine?

> I'll bite a farthing to clap those crows away.
> When I scraped this dug-out deeper
> he laughed me his little workhorse, roughed
> my hair.

> Your yell kept pecking at my eardrums.
> Father names a place to make you happy.
> Mother's voice fades again the second I wake.

Dead-Nettle

Dead because she hides no sting
I slink fingers through the stalks of this green sister,
leaving the live ones to better men. My tongue
can lick these furry teeth: no blister
cuts my kissing lips. A ruff of petals
pearl-drops round her neck. These are the leaves
I need now, easy to stroke. Dead-nettles
tickle my touch. I'm sick of old loves
burning if I hold too tight.
More fool me to think I had a right to keep her.
She'll seed where she wants, reach her full height
without my grab or sickle. I look closer
at her map of veins. Four jagged sun-shades
shield a ring of creamy buds.

Here's Another

*a Man passed me on horseback in a slop-frock & said 'here's
another of the broken-down haymakers' & threw me a penny
to get a half-pint of beer which I picked up & thanked him for*

He speaks:

Being a high man astride a bay-mare
my voice counts for something down this street,
when I'm luckier than loose change in a pocket
and the saddle's steady, the hooves slow.

I note cloud-smoke and attic windows,
ponder the poor below: how many,
how my horse could slap dung onto waiting hands.

Here's another, broken as a bulrush,
his whipped look kindling a penny's pity.
Perhaps. Compassion learns its limits.

Mark my fidget between embarrassment and pleasure
when he dips his neck like a wag-tail,
his tongue a weathered flail I barely hear.

Wishes for Breakfast

I sat down half an hour & made a good many wishes for break-
fast but wishes were no hearty meal so I got up as hungry as I
sat down–

I'm all mouth—
eating a wish to escape
till it groans round the belly's well
where bacon and eggs, black pudding and bread
could toss like pennies to my pit
with the plip of an echo,
hollow as a wedding-ring I fall through
calling her name.

This fat gap where a soul should be
feeds on her face at my window again,
promising stars and moon by the water's lip.

For what we are about to receive.
While my heart cools its coals for half an hour
my fingers form their nest without eggs,
cupped hands a begging-bowl.
I would tramp from door to door
for crumbs chucked to sparrows from her plate.

Lace

*I called in a house to light my pipe in which was a civil old
woman and a young country wench makeing lace on a cushion
as round as a globe*

She speaks:

Windmills, brides and butterflies
rise from my pillow.

Fingers twist our living until candlelight:
pennies a yard, shillings a week.

I'll weave a snow kiss when it's warranted,
squint at bobbins whatever questions come

from the journeyman who sucks his pipe on our
doorstep,
this maze under my knuckles a lover's knot.

North or South

*I then suddenly forgot which was North or South and though
I narrowly examined both ways I could see no tree or bush or
stone heap that I could reccolect I had passed so I went on mile
after mile almost convinced I was going the same way I came*

The old question: where's your life going?
Answer. My life's going home.
That drum's two boots on a puddled highway,
walking home, walking the drumbeat home.

It's only the heart's percussion,
cracking hip-joints knees and ankles
on this road where I'd run barefoot
if I trusted the route rang true.

Walk a circle without hitting the sea.
Home's a pebble to suck and choke on
spat out before it's swallowed,
rattling North or South, back the way I came.

Third Day

Sunday, 16 April 1995

At 6.30 on Easter Sunday morning I crawl out from one of the box-shaped construction blocks, like huge white cavity liners, which I slept inside last night. MILTON is stamped in black on the side of each empty concrete rectangle, a dozen of them stacked two-high by the hedges of sprouting crop fields, alongside a housing estate near the Biggleswade sign. I take a photo of them in early light under a pale-cloud sky, though I've no idea what they're meant to do, apart from giving me somewhere for sleep and shelter. Since they're about eight feet long and wide, and only about five feet high, I was able to crouch inside the first one nearest the field's corner last night, kneel down to stack all my belongings in the dry, and sleep on its concrete bed, with more white concrete as my low ceiling.

On his second night Clare slept in the porch of *an odd house all alone near a wood . . . there was a large porch over the door & being weary I crept in & glad enough I was to find*

*I could lye with my legs straight the inmates were all gone to
roost for I could hear them turn over in bed so I lay at full
length on the stones in the porch – I slept here till daylight &
felt very much refreshed as I got up.* The immediacy of his
writing! I could be lying there full length myself when I read
it, hearing those sleepers roosting and rustling in feather beds
a wall away from Clare.

I wriggled into my sleeping bag at about ten o'clock last
night. I slept until six, managing about six hours of fitful sleep,
with all my usual disturbed waking, debates and repetitive
tunes ricocheting between dreams. I shivered in the dim hours,
teeth chattering with cold, because a slice of wind cut through
where I lay. As I half-woke in the night, turning or stirring
on my stone mattress, I thought I heard light rain, like coins
flicking one by one – heads or tails – onto darkened leaves.
When I walk in the open this morning a few puddles glint on
the road ahead, so I probably heard right. I wasn't dreaming.

Rain at night carries me back to our holiday years ago in
Rome, before the kids were born. It began pouring without
warning one night as we walked to our hotel after a pasta.
Torrents soaked our clothes in minutes, plastering flimsy
cotton to our chests and legs, dabbling our sandals through
streams along the street, washing over my glasses so I couldn't
see an inch in front of my nose. Dee wore contact lenses then.
I held her hand and she, the seeing one, led me through wet
black streets where I would have been lost without her. I felt
absolute trust in her ability to lead, talking to me calmly as if
she knew the way and in five minutes we'd be home and dry.
I gave myself up to her completely, in safety and blindness.

*

Walking past houses on the edge of Biggleswade last night felt disorientating, seeing families through lit windows carrying on their Saturday night routines: living together, relaxed or bickering, with me excluded on the path outside. No chance of stepping indoors for me. Before he found the porch to sleep in, Clare described walking past houses on his second night: *It now began to grow dark apace & the odd houses on the road began to light up & show the inside tenants' lots very comfortable & my outside lot very uncomfortable & very wretched – still I hobbled forward as well as I could.*

That phrase *my outside lot* reverberates for Clare. It echoes into how writing made him seem an outsider to his class – a class understandably wary of, and often excluded from, the written word. Yet that same class made him an outsider to those who owned the written word, and the books that were full of them. The language of books was theirs, written, published and read by them, as though their conversation was the only one worth having. Clare's use of dialect wasn't simply radical because he was determined to write poetry how he spoke, but it also brought words familiar to him (and unfamiliar to most of his readers) into pride of place on the page. *Ariff*, *bumbarrel*, *clumpsing*, *drabbled*, *elting* and *flaze* lit a fire inside his lines. Their vowels tasted like warm bread in his mouth. But no one listened any more. The toast of London was far outside those lit homes now.

Last night I came across a phone box and phoned Dee on my way to find somewhere to sleep. It felt comforting to hear her voice. The kids were tucked in bed, a family scene I felt months away from. We talked about me sleeping rough, and vagrancy being something the police could pick me up for. She joked that if I showed them papers about Clare's walk as my credentials, I'd end up certified. Slip my arms into a straitjacket. Gag and bind me.

No hedgehogs, badgers or foxes sniffed around while I slept, though I worried again about drunks swaggering home from pubs. This morning I noticed names and cartoons of cocks and cunts sprayed in black inside two of the concrete squares where I lay, so teenagers obviously use them as dens. I had a lucky escape.

Last night I walked into my dream as a child, needing to be held. I cuddled that boy like his father, as if I fathered myself. I feel as rejected now as I did when my father left when I was six; as if I couldn't keep him. Being myself – trying hard to be a good boy – wasn't enough to tie him to my side. The difference today, last night, is I can hold the child I was and tell myself I'll stick around. Someone has to comfort that left-alone boy in the dark and it might as well be me. I can care for myself like a father, instead of expecting someone else to do it for me, looking to Dee to comfort me like a wife or replacement mother. During those first desolate days and hour-by-hour weeks after our separation death became a temptation. Hold up your hands and surrender. I no longer need to exist. This white flag can wrap me like a shroud.

I've been fighting its seduction, admitting I'm no good – annulled – negated. It's a dangerous whirlpool under my nights; but I should protect the child I was, not kill him. My dream's telling me that. A daft expedition like this walk becomes one clumsy attempt to rebuild a house of self-worth: somewhere I can live. I'm years away from machismo, yet I've set myself a physical challenge – carrying bricks on my

back for eighty-five miles – as though beating my own endur-
ance test might make me a man.

It's cold and overcast this morning. I'm three miles from
Potton on achy legs, approaching a line of poplars with flat
farmland. Pylons are stretching in four rows overhead, their
wires sizzling when I walk underneath. Leaves at the top of
the poplars quiver in the wind. I scare two pheasants. The
female's flying above the hedges, and her dim-witted mate
follows with his clatter of wings.

I wrap my arms round my ribs, promise myself I won't
disappear.

Goldfinches fly into a tree, beside cows and a brown horse
nipping grass. I pass a small campsite, with seven or eight caravans and a couple of tents near Turnpike Farm. My blister-pads
are working wonders.

The quiet of this early morning – with the occasional car
and only birdsong for company – may be as good a time as
any to consider my parents, if I'm going to understand love.
Perhaps parents are our first examples of male and female, so
they become emblems of men and women to a watching child.
Perhaps we assume, for a while, the way they act together is
how the sexes relate, as if their lives show us mythic patterns
we struggle to decode.

The pattern my father gave me was that men leave. Or, to
be more precise, men stay for a while, and their presence makes
you happy enough to nearly forget the shouting you hear in the
next room when you're supposed to be asleep. Men sit on the
edge of your bed one evening after school and quietly say they're
going, and you know you won't be able to stop them. All the

crying in the world won't stop him. He's going because of something you've done or not done, and he's going because of that shouting in the other room night after night. Shouting through the walls where you can't make out the words, only the anger, but you can't get out of bed and tell them to stop. It's the weather of your days. You may as well tell the breeze to stop making you cold.

My father's leaving became the first big breakage in my life. I keep going back to mend it, but the pieces stay in my hands. For a while he visited us, on Saturdays or Sundays, every few weeks maybe. As far as I remember, he wouldn't come to the door. He hooted his car-horn below our flat, or my elder brother Peter (who'd left with him) came to collect us. I remember the awkwardness and guilty pleasure of those visits. It felt like Peter and my father were already becoming outsiders in our family by not living with us. Our pleasure in seeing them felt disloyal to our mother. I imagined her sitting alone in our flat with all the empty furniture around her, waiting for our return, as if her hours were suspended by our absence. There was nothing she could do but mope through the lonely time without us, until we came back.

One of these visits must have coincided with my sixth or seventh birthday, because I remember unwrapping a present from my father in the backseat of his car, tearing paper from a big box on my lap, uncovering zoo animals stuck in clear plastic: polar bear above a tiger, zebra beside a lion, a row of diminishing penguins, a hippopotamus, elephant, giraffe. A dozen animals in jungle or arctic colours. Their silent roars. I made up games and stories with them for afternoons across our bedroom carpet. Was playing with them like a loyalty to my father, keeping him there and fingering his absence, knocking their heads together, making them eat or stay with each other? Tiger stripes barred against zebra stripes, my heart hoping to become rhinoceros hide.

A few weeks later my mother bought a zoo on a board where they could live. I loved its cages, green hillocks, twisty grey pathways and the kidney-shaped penguin lake painted the deepest blue.

Our loyalties were ripped in two. How could my younger brother Stephen and I mend this family? What was in our power? After maybe six months of these visits, that upset and made us happy in the same hours, we hatched a clumsy plan to tell our mother we didn't want to see our father any more. Stephen was sixteen months younger than me, so I suppose he followed my lead. I imagine we soaked up the unspoken atmosphere around these meetings: force fields of loss and recrimination and trying to do their best criss-crossing through our chests, as if we were its targets. The sad reminders, month after month, of seeing our father and brother but they never came home. Perhaps it was a declaration of love to our mother. We were kids, stumbling with mixed feelings, maybe hoping if we cut off one source of those feelings our confusion might disappear.

Through the wooden slats inside a broken green-painted roundabout, where I'm tense and crouching, I watch my father waiting at the entrance to the housing estate's playground. He's waiting for me to come to him for our visit. I don't know where Stephen is. I stay where I am, hidden inside the stopped roundabout. I can't tell him I don't want to see him. I can't face him. I'm scared. If I stay small as a rabbit he'll go away, take the feelings with him. He's twenty or so yards away, looking a little lost and disconsolate between black iron railings, staring at an empty playground. Maybe he hangs around for ten minutes, maybe longer; but I have to crouch quietly where I am – frozen and invisible – hearing my own breathing, until he finally leaves and I can come out from my hiding place, sniffing the air without him. Our parents accepted our decision. We didn't talk about it, and my brother Stephen and I never saw our father again.

My shins are pulling. The B1040 towards Potton shows me acres of low crop-leaves in an absence of sun. I notice a yellowhammer by the corner of a field before it flits away. In his sonnet 'The Yellowhammer', written in Northampton Asylum, Clare associates yellowhammers with homesickness, asking:

> When shall I see the whitethorn leaves again,
> And yellowhammers gath'ring the dry bents
> By the dyke-side on stilly moor or fen,
> Feathered wi'love and nature's good intents?

It ends with a poignant sense of watching that ritual of choosing and building a home, as the watcher and speaker can't:

> In early spring when winds blow chilly cold
> The yellowhammer trailing grass will come
> To fix a place and choose an early home
> With yellow breast and head of solid gold.

The place I fixed has fallen from me. My nest in my rented room's a temporary shelter – where the children sleep a few nights a week – while I arrange my feathers, gather strength, search for a head of solid gold.

The few cars that pass me drive too fast for these narrow roads. While I hear my boots tramping on tarmac, one or two cars shudder a swipe of windscreen, blue or red bonnets, and vanish round the next bend. I'm alone again for several minutes – a car – alone again – a car; engine revs followed by quiet. Between these interruptions it's calm among fields, and I think of the teenager I was becoming without a father. I was getting by. My father had disappeared from the horizon, my mother doing her best to be father and mother. Several years later my elder brother Peter came back home, after our father threw him out, and he stayed with us. I can't remember questioning his return. I accepted it, swallowed whatever story I was given.

In my early teens Peter told me my father wasn't my father. It becomes the rasp of a crow skimming an elm this morning: 'father not your father – father not your father'. Crack your gold head, shuffle black wings and fly. He told me my real father was Tommy's younger brother Alf: that my brother Stephen and I were the result of an affair between my mother and her brother-in-law.

This revelation made my father unreal, my memories lies. I was reeling from the news. I feel sorry now for the teenager I was then. Today, years later, I know I should have asked my mother straight out: 'Who's my father? Tell me the truth, the story of my birth.' I didn't face her, didn't ask. Stuck in the roundabout, I was still hiding, and tried to continue acting as though nothing had happened, sharing a home with her. I'd done it before. I don't even remember telling Clifford, though I could easily have confided in him, my ally, my best school-friend. I gagged myself and trapped the story inside. It became my dirty secret, hidden from my brother Stephen, too. What did I think would happen if I let it out? The world would change.

For seventeen years I never asked my mother. It was as if I inherited her secret, her taboo, painted the shame onto my own skin. I still aimed to be a good boy; still wanted to please her, so she wouldn't follow my father and disappear. If you hold a piece of news under your tongue it becomes a grenade, and I fiddled with the pin against my teeth.

In our student years I told Dee. Poor woman – what a tale to inherit! She couldn't understand why I didn't ask my mother, but once the secret became its own burden, I couldn't imagine my life without it, or how my life would change if the secret was out. It shut me outside myself, and I'm sure it hampered the man Dee married, shut me off from her, stowed other secrets under my tongue.

Two years after we married I heard that Tommy – the man I'd seen as my father – died; so there was no way back: the door to meeting him again was barred for good, the green-painted slats of my roundabout torn down and hammered one by one across the locks.

I hear birds whose calls I can't recognise, songs between branches, more powerful than the cars and this thud of slow boots on the road. Hundreds of trees line my walk like a beneficent presence, shield me against a thousand cars.

Our first son Isaac was born five years after Tommy died. Having a son, becoming a father, sent shockwaves through my identity. I'd put off becoming a father for years, tried to avoid it like a train trundling towards me. The life I'd worked hard not to change changed under me: its tidal wave knocked me off my feet. I fell in love with Isaac the moment he opened one steady slate-blue eye, lying exhausted and just born on his mother's belly, taking his first glance at this unfamiliar world. I thought he looked like me, as if I might have been born again, as if this was my chance.

Where do I go for a father? My lack of a father set off echoes through my body, as I held my son by the window that first morning in Kettering Hospital. It was like holding my son meant I understood again – for a second, more anguished time – the meaning of losing my father.

When our second son, Joe, was born twenty-one months later I was delighted and confused by what Tillie Olsen calls 'the profound experience of children'. Joe was born at home in Holly House, our red-brick Victorian former Calvinist chapel in Northamptonshire. It was January and snow was falling across the fields outside. I loved these boys in ways I'd never encountered before. Those first months and years of caring for them extended my sense of self beyond anything I'd previously imagined. They carried me to the limits of love and tenderness, exhaustion and anger, until I hardly recognised myself. There were sleep problems, balancing needs, all the chores, my social work training and repeated broken nights. With two children under two I was struggling to become a good-enough father and beating myself up for not being perfect, eternally giving and sympathetic, always on tap and on top. I wasn't managing. Dee and I were bickering between the strains. Neither of us could ignore the problems any more. In the middle of the chaos my lack of a father, as example and guide, became almost an obsession. I started weekly therapy sessions in Leicester, where I attempted to make sense of the gaps and repair my contradictions, spilling all my secrets and paying to be heard.

The rows between Dee and me grew more furious, as though we were attacking each other for not coming up to the mark, failing to make each other happy. Eight months after our second son was born, after a particularly vicious argument full of accusations and the anger I'd heard through walls as a child, I took an overdose in the kitchen after midnight, when it was dark outside and Dee and the kids lay asleep upstairs. It was a closed-in self-absorbed act with such young children in the rooms above, but I was banging my head and trying to make things better had proved hopeless. It felt easier to surrender, give way at last, admit I was rotten to the core and needed things to finish. Standing in the kitchen counting tablets after each gulp of water felt logical, inevitable, like an irresistible action I'd been trying to shy away from for ages. *This is what you want.* I wanted a deep black sleep, preferably without dreams. I wanted my wife to stop. I wanted to end myself. I wanted to be with the man I saw as my father, as if dying might prove my love to him.

Although I planned to swallow fifty tablets, instinct stopped me at twenty-five. That obsessive ritual of drinking down one pill after another ended as abruptly as it had begun, as though it emptied itself of meaning, or became as futile as everything else. Why not eat tablets – why not stop eating tablets? My hands fell to my sides. A few minutes later, in the early hours when it was still dark, I walked upstairs to our bedroom and told Dee what I'd done.

After her frantic phone call, our good friends Helen and

Ian drove over to Holly House. Ian stayed to support Dee – with the boys thankfully still asleep – and Helen drove me in the night to Accident and Emergency in Kettering, the hospital where Isaac had been born only two years before. They gave me medicine to make me sick. Behind hospital curtains the bucket I held filled with tiny white flakes in fluid over and over, as if the tablets might have turned me to snow inside, or I'd become a snowman and could spill ice for ever from my mouth. But my blood was warm, and I must have wanted to live, apologising again and again to Helen as she gripped my hand. I spent one bleak restless night in hospital, sleeping near another young man who'd overdosed. The following morning, I met with a Community Psychiatric Nurse who gently asked me why, and didn't seem surprised when I talked of wanting to run into my dead father's arms. They let me go, with a follow-up note for my doctor and the promise that I'd talk to my therapist.

I think of Clare's mental illness, how they kept him hospitalised for years, how he believed he was Byron and Jack Randall the boxer and that Mary was his wife and still alive. When I overdosed I came close to delusions I believed were real: that taking tablets could prove my love for a dead man; that I needed the seduction of death with its welcoming sleep, which I've felt again these past six weeks like a returning friend, a familiar echo – like Clifford or my father calling me towards death – You don't need to exist. I resist their call, fight hard against them. It frightens me now.

That was seven years ago and I'm alive in the breeze on this road. The birds are out in force while the morning deepens:

their separate melodies, a far-off crow-croak and bass thrumming of woodpigeons as accompaniment underneath. Seven years ago, when I left hospital the next morning dazed and tentative about facing my shocked wife, another wren was singing here like the one I'm approaching this minute. It's half-hidden in the thicket, notes sparkling from a body the size of a brown leaf.

In his sonnet 'The Wren', Clare votes for the wren's song in competition with the cuckoo and nightingale. He sees it as his companion, sharer of his shelter:

> *And little wren that many a time hath sought*
> *Shelter from showers in huts where I did dwell*
> *In early spring, the tenant of the plain*
> *Tenting my sheep, and still they come to tell*
> *The happy stories of the past again.*

This past hasn't been a happy story, although the wren's song becomes my footnote, as if it's glad I stayed alive to hear its notes pour from the hedge like water to quench me; like words I might spout about turmoil and survival, about suffering one in order to catch the other.

My history's unreeling with the road. A dozen or so white flowers of cow parsley jostle along the hedgerow. I pass the John O'Gaunt Golf Club, occasional houses, industrial units, a farm shop, ploughed and sown fields, a few crows picking.

After the overdose I took five months off work with stress. It was a fragile time, Dee and I being careful with each other, Clifford uneasy because he was the nervous one, I was supposed to be the steady friend. I felt far from steady. Standing once in a baker's, when I was asked by a shop assistant what bread I wanted and, seeing all those loaves like a horrible test I was failing, unable to choose, too stunned to say a word. At night I grasped the cuff of Dee's nightdress as she slept beside me, thinking that holding tight to her inch of cotton was the only way to keep me from falling off a precipice, as if our bed was the edge of a mountain.

Through those months of confusion and recovery my instincts told me I needed to sort out my birth and move forward with the life I'd chosen, if only for the sake of my children, who didn't need a wreck as a father. When Dee pointedly asked my mother what she thought had caused the overdose, she said she didn't know, but we had to find out. So I finally asked my mother about my father. It became as simple as saying those questions for her to answer, though (in my therapist's Zen-like phrase) 'You're not ready until you're ready.'

At first my mother tried to sound evasive and I insisted I needed to know. It felt like my life depended on it. She admitted that my father was her brother-in-law. She and Alf had carried on a seven-year affair and we were the result. Tommy was unable to have children because of a low sperm count. After he discovered their affair, she'd wanted to set up home with Alf, but Tommy threatened he would keep us from her, and her beloved father threatened that he would never see her again. When she was a girl her father had hit her hand with a knife if she rested elbows on the table at mealtimes. When he walked through that crowd of striking dockers years before, she knew he was a man who'd keep his word, whatever the cost; an upright man of principle. In the sixties, in that close-knit class and community, where the council estate bristled with tittle-tattle like a village, what choice did those ultimatums leave her? She'd already smashed a houseful of taboos. A wicked woman; a Jezebel; adulterous wife and shameless daughter. She knuckled down and stayed in the marriage for the sake of the kids. She and Tommy tried to make it work, until it failed a year or so later, as it was bound to, with them both having walked through that fire, too scorched to trust each other again.

Big fields are dotted by trees, ivory clouds suspended over them. My boot avoids stepping on a flattened squirrel, its head black and obliterated, tail a squashed grey duster, claws ready to clutch at life.

Six months or so after I asked my mother all those questions, I met Alf, my father, who still lived in Hackney, half a mile from that old soap opera. To hear him say, 'Hello son,' as he opened his door with a smile and shook my hand, gave me a flinch of odd pleasure, as though this was some grand reunion. He said he knew someday I'd come to find him, seek him out. He said he owed it to me to answer all my questions. He talked about their affair: how he'd moved in to live with his brother and sister-in-law after his Jewish fiancée died of cancer. He said, 'I was in a state and they took me in, and I abused it. We were young. We knew no better. I was selfish then.' Seven years after their affair started Tommy found them in bed together. Perhaps they'd got careless. Perhaps one or other of my parents wanted to throw the dice and see how they fell.

He and Tommy never spoke afterwards, though they both worked in Spitalfields Market. He said Tommy would look through him as if he was air. His older brother died without forgiving him. He said, 'I want his forgiveness and he never gave it. Now he's gone. Yes, I know, I know, I should forgive myself.' He told me, 'I thought you were an ugly baby, honest. When you came I thought you made me a man.' His honesty helped me put some ghosts to sleep.

Alf also gave me himself, in place of an impossible fantasy. A joker, a charmer and storyteller, a smart fallible East End man, who might become a grandad figure to my children. His arrival gave me back parts of myself that the story of my birth had chipped away: an ear or shoulder, an elbow, a finger. I could glue myself together with shaky hands.

When I think of my parents this morning it's as if I have three parents, two fathers – or perhaps two halves of a father – the man I experienced as my father and the 'real' one. In my childhood the real one's unreal. He's never there – he's invisible – whereas in my life today Tommy becomes shadowy, half a presence and absence, standing behind the here-and-now of his charming younger brother. I'm becoming easier about accepting my difference, instead of seeing my story as a birthmark of shame.

The landscape's flat as an outstretched palm that might tell my fortune, lines of my life branching before me. I pause and check the basic map of Clare's walk. It shows me that when I reach Potton I'll be a fingertip from touching halfway home. I'm lifted by that fabulous possibility, telling myself I might manage to finish this walk. What a dream! I wish I could spring a few inches into the air, but there's no wings on my heels, and the rucksack on my shoulders weighs me down.

In his journal Clare says of the 21 July, *I then went through*

Potton & happened with a kind talking country man who told me the parson lived a good way from where I was or overseer I don't know which so I went on hopping with a crippled foot for the gravel had got into my old shoes one of which had nearly lost the sole. Clare's plan had been to beg the parson or overseer *for a shilling to carry me home,* so there was method in his madness. I imagine him trudging this road with gravel niggling his heels, and the shoes – that hadn't been prepared for so many miles – protesting with every creak. My boots plod like sturdy companions.

According to his journal Clare arrived at these roads around Potton in the *late evening* of his second day, so he's still half a day ahead. I've refused to compete, but there's a repeated sensation that Clare's a slippery ghost flickering over the next horizon, while I hobble along behind, with neither the talent nor legs to catch up.

I fold my map away and keep walking, burrow into my thoughts. My childhood's central figure was my mother; the effect of her personality runs through me like a watermark, and I think I've only been cutting the apron strings in the past few years.

She wanted to be father and mother to us, saw my adult questions about my father as implying she hadn't done her job properly, but also admitted she'd been terrified for years that we wouldn't love her if my brother Stephen and I knew the truth. It was as though, by hard work and force of character, she hoped to smother our need for anyone other than her. After the divorce when we were children she juggled three jobs: a morning receptionist and secretary at a small solicitor's firm along Bethnal Green Road, where she lied to get the job, saying she had experience of operating switchboards; an afternoon job as a secretary doing invoices at a local garage; and her outwork in the evening hand-finishing trousers: snipping, sewing and biting loose threads at our round dining table in the front room, while *Coronation Street* played across our screen. She managed all the practical aspects of single parenthood brilliantly: ensuring we were well turned-out for school every morning: the washing, ironing, housework, shopping, cooking, washing-up, bill-paying, so we didn't give it a second thought, assumed it happened as a matter of course. But her determination to cope meant buttoning up her emotions, keeping 'shtum', keeping 'mum'. It left more tender moments, of knowing we could share our feelings and be listened to, held, accepted, out in the cold.

My memory of being held and comforted after the separation doesn't feature my mother. One afternoon in my infant class at Berger School in Hackney, I must have suddenly broken down, or flipped and got upset, perhaps by being expected to finish one task too many, to keep pretending nothing had changed when ten streets away my home was crumbling around my ears. Either my teacher already knew about the separation or I blurted that my dad and brother had gone. Whatever the reason, Miss Jones – a thin elderly teacher, usually formal and firm and not to be crossed – cuddled me behind her desk, at the front of the class. She murmured soothing words in my ear and gently rocked me. Although my classmates started sniggering among themselves – and I noticed – my misery felt important on her unfamiliar lap. I felt proud for my sadness to be on show, as though my sobs had been rewarded.

As far as I knew, I was the only child in my class whose parents had split up. I felt ashamed because of a failure that was mine alone, like a scar across my face that none of my classmates wore. On Miss Jones's lap my grief was special enough to be displayed to the class: not ignored or an embarrassment, hidden in bed at night, like a dark secret. She could stop her teaching – in the afternoon before everyone – to let me be held.

The sun begins to jemmy through a triangular skylight in a cloud. Bluebells scatter dusky puddles in a wood, and a distinctive bird with a reddish throat and bold feather-markings on the wing – like a redwing or redpoll or cock linnet – hesitates on a branch at eye level. Clare could have identified it without checking a book, spending hours outside where birds live, listening to others who knew better and gave every bird the boy noticed its name.

Unlike Miss Jones, I think my mother felt grief should be bottled up, shut away. She came from generations of a class of tough women, who would rarely talk openly about their feelings. That's how they dealt with things. I'm wondering if giving voice to how they felt might open a floodgate. Her attitude to a painful past was to ignore it, almost pretend by her silence that it hadn't happened, wipe the years clean, mop up the mess. After we stopped seeing Tommy, we never mentioned his name again. Missing him was never discussed between us, so even acknowledging any feelings would have felt like disobeying her: a shock and shame better left unsaid.

This attempt at amnesia is coming horribly true for her. Now, in her early sixties, she's been showing signs of Alzheimer's, insidiously taking over her head and sentences. At first we ignored those signs. Once, I played Louis Armstrong in the car to please her as she always loved jazz, and when his gravelly song began, she said, 'I know him,' but couldn't think of his name. When Dee and I were still together a year ago my mother came from her kitchen to tell us a funny story and five minutes later returned to the front room to repeat the same story, with no recollection she'd already told us. We played along with her, then stared at each other in disbelief when she went back to peeling potatoes.

My mother fights her illness with all the fierce strength she's used before, when she was left alone by two brothers to bring up her sons. The illness is eating her words. Now she calls Tuesday 'That thing with a T' and a slice of bread 'That square white thing'.

My Aunt Suzie (who still lives in Redmill House nearby, on the same Whitechapel estate) works hard to keep her sister going: helping her with shopping and meals, all the tiring battles of supporting someone whose memory is disappearing. For Suzie it's an echo of the years she spent caring for her mother, who had dementia; because Suzie was at home and her three sisters worked, and her two brothers lived and worked in Essex, the burden of caring fell on her. As my grandmother's health deteriorated, she started making cups of tea for the photos in her front room, because she thought they were her guests. This moved on months later to becoming aggressive with her daughter, until eventually it became unsafe for her to live alone. She was taken to a nursing home, where she cradled a doll like a baby for years and words left her for good.

My mother's refused all help so far, apart from her sister's. Accepting help would mean she's not managing and she's too proud to surrender. Six weeks ago, I told her on the phone I'd left Dee. She got the new address of where I'm lodging from my brother Peter, and sent a letter there. I saved it in the drawer beside my bed, and read it again before I left my lodgings for this walk. I knew it was the last letter I'd receive from her, with its two red roses in the bottom corner of the page, and its wide handwriting:

> Dear Robert
> I hope you will be o.k. as
> Peter was at my home and he
> gave me the address of the
> person.
> I hope that you will be in
> time and I will help you to
> be o.k.
> Love you, if you need
> come over.
> Love you
>   Mum xxx

It felt like I was holding a treasure map in my hand. I sensed she was wrestling inside a fog of language, struggling to pin enough words on paper to state her message. She couldn't hold me, but she could hold me with words. In those first few weeks after moving out, when I didn't know if I could survive a new way of living, reading her letter over and over helped one minute link to the next, with all the hours stacked in front of me.

When I pass another clump of dead nettles I see petals I thought were pear-shaped may be tooth-shaped instead, a little ring of teeth. Love's a live nettle plucked from my muddy heart.

Not far from Potton, I'm trying to work out why Clare took a detour here, when he could have continued along the Great North Road through Sandy. The journal of his walk gives no clue, though his first mention of *Potton in Bedfordshire* relates to calling late in the evening *in a house to light my pipe in which was a civil old woman and a young country wench makeing lace on a cushion as round as a globe and a young fellow all civil people – I asked them a few questions as to the way and where the clergyman and overseer lived but they scarcely heard me or gave me no answer.* So his motive was probably to find that elusive clergyman or overseer, or he slightly lost the route, or might have felt a stressed need to find somewhere safe from the hubbub of the Great North Road for his second night. If he couldn't find the clergyman or overseer he needed to search for a hideaway to sleep.

Why didn't the civil people answer him? Perhaps his wild look – which he would scarcely have been aware of – unsettled them, and they wanted him to light his pipe and go, the sooner the better. Perhaps they worried that engaging him in conversation may tempt this stranger to linger, so a quiet conspiracy developed between the three of them to keep him at arm's length, stay evasive, not respond. Clare leaves the polite young woman weaving lace. It's the only way we and Clare experience her, seeing how she worked every evening, a white web inching under her fingers.

At 7.40 a.m., as a cuckoo begins to practise its name in two low notes somewhere through the trees, I reach Potton's terraced houses. In his poem 'The Cuckoo' Clare shows how his presence makes the bird disappear:

> *It heard me and above the trees*
> *Soon did its flight pursue*
> *Still waking summers melodies*
> *And singing as it flew.*

In his final stanza he observes how seasons change the cuckoo's song:

> *It cannot sing for all it tries*
> *'Cuck cuck' it cries and mocking boys*
> *Crie 'Cuck' and then it stutters more*
> *Till quite forgot its own sweet voice*
> *It seems to know itself no more.*

Clare implies that if the cuckoo forgets *its own sweet voice* it'll lose its identity, as if singing became part of him also, woven into his nature, and if he stopped singing – if poems stopped pouring from his pen, his throat – he'd cease to know himself.

The clouds have become huge blooms of cauliflower above another goldfinch on a branch. Because it's early, Potton only shows me a couple pulling up in their car at a BP garage and a workman picking up rubbish along the street. A newspaper boy makes a dog bark inside a house when a paper flaps through the letterbox. A young couple passes, the girl in high clumpy shoes. She looks as if her feet hurt her as much as mine.

A fan of black wires from telegraph poles string into terraced houses. It's a long straggly village, almost a town. After Bonnie and Clyde hairdressers, with hairdryers like a row of drooped tulips, I pass Chapel Street, Blackbird Street and Sun Street. Potton then opens into a square of shops:

Potton Vets and Potton Flooring by the library, Indian Cuisine and the Coach House Bar and Restaurant.

Potton has been extensively developed since Clare's walk. A new housing estate has young gardens and spick-and-span driveways, many curtains and blinds still closed. Allotments fringe the village again, with corrugated iron and rickety sheds, glass frames and green netting pinned over sprouting seeds. This early they're deserted.

Sun spreads a shadow of hedges across the lane, with a tractor in a field on the left and a long rind of orange peel dangling from a bush. I'm aiming for Everton now, the next village. As I leave the last houses of Potton I realise this would have been a harrowing stretch for Clare at night, where he asked *a kind talking countryman . . . whether he could tell me of a farmyard anywhere on the road where I could find a shed & some dry straw.* Although the man tries to help with directions to the Ram, *suddenly recolecting that he had a hamper on his shoulder & a lock-up bag in his hand cramfull to meet the coach which he feared missing – he started hastily & was soon out of sight –* Clare's exhaustion leads him to *lay down by a shed side under some elms between the wall & the trees . . . but the wind came in between them so cold that I lay still I quaked like the ague & quitted the lodging for a better at the Ram which I could hardly hope to find.*

Loneliness sends Clare a dark message, walking as he was without light: *the road was very lonely & dark in places being over-shaded with trees.* Daylight uncovers telegraph poles and ploughed fields wherever I look, to the right a low crop smelling of cabbage. Two parallel strips are veiled by long sheets of white plastic, blue bags at their edges holding them down like stones. Those strips resemble two ice rivers running over the field, where I could choose which one I want on a frozen morning. I'll skate across its glaze towards telegraph poles and crop land, lifted by the promise of a whiskery wood in the distance. There must be a better life where two swallows whirl around each other, as though their loops and curves are playing with the idea of mating. In his poem 'Passerine Birds' Clare observes how swallows

> *Skim and dip their sutty wing*
> . . .
> *Twitter round to catch the flye*
> *But with more majestic rise*
> *Practicing their exersise*

I'll have earned my rest at Everton, as I thread between hedges and grasses, seeing sheds and fences in distant fields. It's a shame I won't find a café open yet, with cream scones and a pot of tea. I lick my lips at the thought, but a mouthful of water keeps me going. Sparrows cheep in Everton's guttering, while outside 1960s pebble-dashed houses blackbirds add their trills. The church on my right sprouts four small steeples, each with a weather vane on the corner of a squat tower. I'd love to sit outside among mottled gravestones to ease my legs, but as it's Easter Sunday they might hold an early service. The possibility scares me away. My chin's bristling with stubble. Last night I glanced in the New Inn mirror, my complexion a little reddened by the sun. I look far from respectable, and shun the prospect of being gawped at by churchgoers. Wave your tattered flag and soldier on.

My brother Stephen and I went to Sunday school at

St Bartholomew's Church, two minutes' walk from our flats. They played tape-recorded bells from the Victorian tower at ten o'clock to welcome us. Going there presumably gave our mother a rest alone in the flat, but she also wanted us to have some knowledge of the Bible. Because her father was a Christian the Jewish faith dwindled for my mother and her siblings, though she liked the food and Yiddish phrases, and often wore a gold mezuzah as a necklace. Years later she said that, even if we rejected religion as adults, at least we'd be familiar with whatever we were rejecting.

The priest at St Bartholomew's was Father Dowse, a red-faced booming-voiced smiler who played the plump jolly vicar to perfection, a regular figure on the estate in his black cassock. If we told him the right answers about Jesus in his quiz, he'd hand out the rainbow colours of Smarties one by one into our palms before they melted. He called them blessings. When churchgoers gradually stopped attending St Bartholomew's a few years ago, it was converted into flats, changed for ever from the inside out.

Clare felt suspicious of what he experienced as 'cant and humbug' inside churches, especially after condescending visits from neighbouring clergymen when he became a local celebrity with his first book. His *religion of the fields* was experienced under skies, in heaths and woods, where he found *truth & . . . the Mystery that envelopes it.* That helped him with a sustained belief in God, a comfort during periods of depression when *I awoke in dreadful irritation thinking that the Italian liberators were kicking my head about for a foot ball.* He wrote to his publisher's partner Hessey: *As to religion my mind is compleatly at rest in that matter my late deplorable situation proved to me that I had read the Bible successfully for it was*

*an antidote to my deepest distress & I had not the least doubt
on my conviction of its truth.* His love for the Bible didn't blind
him to tolerance of other religions. One of his prose fragments
from the 1830s says, *My creed may be different from other creeds
but the difference is nothing when the end is the same . . . as
every religion is a rule leading to good by its professor the religions of all nations & creeds where that end is the aim ought
rather to be respected than scoffed at.*

At the edge of Everton, they're putting the finishing touches
to Church Fields, a select development of three, four- and
five-bedroom houses. A beautiful white couple and their blonde
daughter grin down from a hoarding stretched above the
windows of a show home, like they're giants of the perfect family.

I suddenly wonder if Dee has arranged an Easter-egg hunt
for the kids this morning, as we used to when we lived together.
Writing rhyming clues in secret the night before, each last rhymed
word left blank as the answer to where their next clue lay hidden.
They scooped up a handful of small pastel-coloured chocolate
eggs each time they guessed right, and raced on to the next clue
with squeals and shouts. The clue for their big boxed eggs lay
folded inside an Easter bunny hidden in our garden, tucked in
the crook of the leaning apple tree where they could reach. I
hope the three of them may be laughing and racing from rhyme
to rhyme this minute, nearly sixty miles away. I feel my gap from
them now. My absence twists like a knife.

I think of completing this walk over Easter, a time for agony
and rebirth. It can happen from the flames. Perhaps I've simply
been going through the fire, and my feet might be singed, but
I'll step out the other side transformed.

One Easter before the children were born, Dee and I travelled to Paris for a romantic holiday. Blossoms collected by the kerb along the boulevards, like white and pink coins, browning at the edges. Sparrows bellied in the dust in the Luxembourg Gardens, where gendarmes told us off for moving a metal chair. It must have been Good Friday when we visited Sacré-Coeur. As we trailed around the aisles in that echoing space, all the statues stood covered in purple cloth, muffled and blank, to give a sense of desolation after Christ's death. It took us a while to work out, in lowered voices to each other, what was happening. They looked surreal, trussed up in body bags, having suffered the passion, waiting for the resurrection, for the vigil mass on Easter Saturday, when the new fire is blessed and the Paschal candle lit. 'On the third day he rose.' That Easter striptease, when holy statues are uncovered, and Christ's blue eyes can blink awake again, like a bearded Ken doll.

Before I started this walk, I partly viewed it as a form of penance for what I've done to the children, how I've let them down, been unable to fulfil my duty and give them a home where their parents stay together. Perhaps it's no coincidence I started on Good Friday, a day for churches to be stripped, for the liturgy of penance.

The giant family follow me with their eyes. Their smug smiles know I tried to make that perfect home but didn't succeed. I might kid myself there's no template for families any more, but their teeth and shiny eyes know better. They know I should have worked harder. They know I've put myself before my children, passed on that legacy of failure, fracture, difference my father handed down to me.

I understand that few children want their parents to part,

though I've spoken to friends whose parents stayed together 'for the sake of the children' and they describe homes bristling with recrimination, rows or resentment, with disappointment and regret oozing from their parents like pus. I don't want my children to think that's how to be an adult, but I've let the chance of a successful marriage dribble through my fingers. Could Dee and I work at a smoother separation instead, even make it better than the marriage; become good parents apart if we can't be partners together?

The example my father – both fathers – left me was disappearance. The male vanishing act. I need to give my children a different example. When I return after this walk I'll have changed as a father. Not coming back, as we told them in the car in Epping two days ago, but not disappearing either. I miss, in a gaping physical way, waking to their shouts or cuddles, sorting out their clothes, food, squabbles, helping them to bed every night. The daily-ness of love. What must I replace it with?

When we met, Alf told me he was able to cut us out of his life because he saw it as the best solution at the time. Cauterisation. A clean cut. To make callous. Can the skin become armour, the heart ice? Is this what it costs to be a man? I suppose it became Alf's means of survival when I was a child: to decide 'I'm building a new life, so the old life – and all the people in it – must wither from my side, fend for themselves.' I can't follow his footsteps, although I might work with scissors and glue to collage a family where the father lives elsewhere, but stays in their lives. An ear, an eye, a mouth can make a father from the shreds of a man.

*

A couple on benches outside the Thornton Arms look like walkers, socks rolled above their boots and weatherproof jackets. I try my imperfect smile as I pass. The man ignores me. The woman glowers, as if a smile's an insult. I wonder how their marriage ticks, what they feel about each other when they wake every morning.

Clare was forced to live apart from his seven children for years, including the last twenty-three years of his life, due to his time in two asylums. When he was taken to High Beach on 15 July 1837 his eldest child, Anna, was seventeen and his youngest, Charles, was four. Six weeks after Anna was born, he'd written an anxious love-poem for her, published in his second rather than first collection, to shift readers off the scent that Patty was pregnant when they married. Although 'To an Infant Daughter' starts by calling Anna *Sweet gem of infant fairy-flowers*, by the fourth line he admits that her smiles *wake my fears*, and his second stanza starts *God help thee*. His fears about her meeting *the frowns of fate* move on to what she may have inherited from him. He particularly doesn't want her to *itch at rhymes*, and his fifth stanza's more explicit about what Anna may inherit:

> Lord help thee in thy coming years
> If thy mad father's picture 'pears
> Predominant – his feeling fears
> And jingling starts;
> I'd freely now gi' vent to tears
> To ease my heart.

This stanza was cut when it was first published, but it shows Clare's concern that writing poetry may have become destabilising for him. This goes beyond his class; perhaps he somehow links writing to his own instability:

> *May thou, unknown to rhyming bother,*
> *Be ignorant as is thy mother,*

although his letters from Northampton Asylum to his sons encourage them to educate themselves – *I would advise you to study Mathematics Astronomy Languages & Botany as the best amusements for instruction* – his final stanza to Anna brims with tenderness and a wish to protect her from whatever he suffers:

> *Lord knows my heart, it loves thee much;*
> *And may my feelings, aches and such,*
> *The pains I meet in folly's clutch*
> >*Be never thine:*
> *Child, it's a tender string to touch,*
> >*That sounds 'Thou'rt mine.'*

The field ahead deepens when a cloud swipes the sun away. I try to write a benediction for Dee, but it keeps slowing me down as I stop to jot or change another phrase. I'll do my best to shut it out of my head.

Tempsford is three miles further, and there is no pavement, which means I need to tread carefully, with infrequent cars gusting down the hill a few inches from my shoulder. Two joggers thud past, red-faced and panting words to each other. In the sloping field on my right a man in yellow plastic overalls carries a yellow plastic box on his back. He's squirting insecticide, head down, absorbed in spraying.

Sloe blossom tingles the air. Tiny white buds load the hedgerows, like spread tablecloths, while a McDonald's bag lies scrunched by my boot. The view across pylons stretches to woods and hills in the distance. A line of trees is slightly bent to the wind, leaning the way the wind shapes them. My calf-muscles twinge and blisters hurt. I feel as if I'm ninety, with Tempsford a slow time arriving. My shadow hobbles down the road in sudden sun.

During Clifford's last illness, when we were walking through a wood, I remember looking back and seeing him tentatively, hesitantly inching down a slope between silver birches, as if he was afraid every step might make him fall, leaning on the trunks as he tottered. I laughed and told him he reminded me of his grandad. What was I thinking, saying that? I was a giggling man who takes his body for granted, who never has to be careful.

Three months before he died, when he was painfully thin, he told me, 'I look down and think this isn't my body. Someone's taken my body and put this in its place.'

Two months before he died, when he had tuberculosis and lung cancer, Clifford told me and his partner Andrew he was planning to run across the park again. He talked about it like a defiant ambition. It scared us both and it never happened; but I imagine he wanted to feel – even for a breathless minute – how good it would be to live inside that young man's body again, when he could run across a park without being frightened, or weave his steps between untroubled trees.

Scrape
Scrape
Scrape
say my boots on the road.

159

A yellow band of oil-seed rape faces me. I reach a level crossing where lights are flashing and the barrier eases down. When a train rattles through and leaves a gap of quiet in its wake, I realise that for all my thoughts of death I still tread gingerly across the rails, so there must be some instinct to survive.

After Tempsford another long haul up the A1 rumbles ahead. I'm steeling myself in anticipation. I start to hear the ground-swell of traffic, a repeated drum I can't escape, coming closer. A father and son park their car beyond me and swap places. The teenage son moves out of the driver's seat and takes off his L-plates, giving way to his father before the A1 drive. They glance at me with mild curiosity.

After fearing he'd lost his way around here, during the dark trudge of his second night, Clare was guided by *a lamp shining as bright as the moon which on nearing I found was suspended over a Toll-gate.* There must have been a turnpike gate at Tempsford, although now I can't even find a bench to ease my legs. I see only a mossy pond fringed by teasels, a narrow road that calls itself 'Private' and, a hundred yards away across a lawn through sheep and trees, what I assume to be the red-brick and grand windows of Tempsford Hall. A couple of men burn rubbish in the grounds, their fire crackling below grey feathers of smoke. A snake with green and black markings is squashed at my feet.

Before he got through the turnpike gate Clare noted that *the man came out with a candle & eyed me narrowly.* Perhaps he was suspicious of someone travelling so late on foot, or wanted to check if a toll was due. Pedestrians didn't pay tollgate fees, so this gave Clare some bravado: *having no fear I stopt to ask him whether I was going northward & he said 'when you get through the gate you are' so I thanked him kindly & went through on the other side & gathered my old strength.* The other side meant returning to the Great North Road, but Clare's gate vanished long ago – along with his hand that pushed the gate, his voice that disappeared into the sky – while the A1's a few minutes away. I'll need to gather my own old strength for an hour, before I face it.

At 10.30 a.m. I lodge my rucksack against barbed wire and pee in the woods, piss spattering onto bracken. It's bliss to tend my blisters, drink water, chomp on a Mars bar and read Clare. I lean back against a fence and sit with bare feet spread apart on the grass in the sun.

I take my time rereading the thirty pages of Clare's sequence 'Child Harold', written during his four years at High Beach, although some stanzas were completed after his walk home. It's a series of iambic pentameter poems, interspersed with twenty songs and four ballads, drenched by Mary's absence, calling her name on the road, through the forest and seasons.

Clare's first stanza teems with contrasts, as if he's trying to pin down where he might stand in relation to *flatterys page*, how best to use his pen, to stay *truly honest* in the poem he's starting to write:

> *Many are poets – though they use no pen*
> *To show their labours to the shuffling age*
> *Real poets must be truly honest men*
> *Tied to no mongrel laws on flatterys page*
> *No zeal have they for wrong or party rage*
> *– The life of labour is a rural song*
> *That hurts no cause – nor warfare tries to wage*
> *Toil like the brook in music wears along –*
> *Great little minds claim right to act the wrong*

In these lines, real poets can only be men. Perhaps Clare's trying to include himself among them, work out where he fits among 'many' poets. The title is an echo of Byron's 'Childe Harold's Pilgrimage', the poem that made Byron an overnight success. I read chunks of it with Clifford when we were teenagers, from a cheap *Byron: Selected Works* paperback he bought in Charing Cross Road.

After his first nine lines Clare throws away this initial approach before it's gained much traction and attempts another form, a different voice, when he introduces himself – uses I for the first time – in a ballad wanting readers (who he probably despaired of ever reaching again) to be in no doubt where he's writing from:

> *Summer morning is risen*
> *And to even it wends*
> *And still Im in prison*
> *Without any friends*

Clare's alternative title for this sequence was 'Prison Amusements'. He throws away that second approach and tries a third, in the first song that addresses Mary directly:

> *Mary thou ace of hearts thou muse of song*
> *The pole star of my being and decay*
> *Earths coward foes my shattered bark may wrong*
> *Still thourt the sunrise of my natal day*

This polyphonic sequence – with its restless approaches, spiralling changes of voice and form, sense of incompletion – proves that Mary's disappearance increases the poet's need for her.

He mimics what he calls a *chain of contradictions* in the apparent feelings of love from a man towards a woman. There can be no single, consistent stance. This is shown after another song to the vanished *angel Mary*, when he starts again but instantly wants to blot ink across the words he's written, the romantic declaration he's just made:

> *My life hath been one love – no blot it out*
> *My life hath been one chain of contradictions*

Four stanzas later the poet who claimed *one love* then thought better of it admits:

> *I sigh for one and two – and still I sigh*
> *For many are the whispers I have heard*
> *From beautys lips – loves soul in many an eye*
> *Hath pierced my heart . . .*

Two stanzas later he comes clean:

> *I have had many loves – and seek no more –*
> *These solitudes my last delights shall be*
> *The leaf hid forest – and the lonely shore*
> *Seem to my mind like beings that are free*

This section of 'Child Harold' frequently unsettles both his own and the reader's position. There's no calm resting place. The man who repeats Mary's name as his mantra even slips *Sweet Susan . . . And Bessey of the glen* into this stanza, as if he subverts each statement he makes about Mary soon after making it, so during his grand declarations of love he's whispering 'don't believe me' behind his hand. As 'Child Harold' develops, he attempts to turn towards the compensation of solitude, as though isolation is the only reliable state after love has deserted him or let him down:

> *Night finds me on this lengthening road alone*
> *Love is to me a thought that ever aches*
> *A frost bound thought that freezes life to stone*

Lines like this in 'Child Harold' reach the visionary heights of his later asylum poems:

> *England my country though my setting sun*
> *Sinks in the ocean gloom and dregs of life*
> *My muse can sing my Marys heart was won*
> *And joy was heaven when I called her wife*
> *The only harbour in my days of strife*
> *Was Mary when the sea roiled mountains high*

To prove how far desolation makes him travel from security and rural familiarity – and perhaps to mirror an aspect of Byron's 'pilgrimage' – Clare's imagery includes *Icelands snows, solitude in citys, Quicksands And Gulphs And Storms, Lapland Snows* and *fire and iceberg* as the sequence progresses. He's naked in his need for Mary, and often blends her identity with nature. Her name's a raft he crawls onto after *the giddy mast* has snapped and he's drowning in a chaos of thoughts. In the sequence's last two stanzas he returns, exhausted, to

Where solitude is queen and riegns in state
Hid in green trees . . .

. . .

Sweet is the song of Birds for that restores
The soul to harmony the mind to love
Tis natures song of freedom out of doors

What messages might I learn from Clare, about love or need or solitude, about the claims men make on the women they swear to love? Solitude can calm me out of doors, when a blackbird whistles through the trees. I can't find it yet, but it sings to me as its only listener, and I can set Dee free from all my tedious needs. Let our years in common fall from us both. I'll grant her peace, stop calling her name. I'll leave her be.

Tying my bootlaces again, I leave Tempsford at 11.50 a.m., having enjoyed a longer break than I intended, carried away into reading, losing track of time.

The A1's busy as ever when I cross. I have to find a gap to slip through, between a hundred cars. I discover a dead thrush, perfectly formed, with no apparent injury. There's no walkway here at first, so I tread carefully along the grass verge, minding my steps. Eventually I reach a tarmac strip, laid to link the villages for pedestrians. It makes this section safer, but it's demoralising to trek beside never-ending traffic whose river drowns me out, swallows me whole.

The A1 runs its spine up England's body, and mine's mangled, heavy with the rucksack's chains, shoulders twisted wires, boots clodhoppers on the road. I'm a packhorse, wearied by my burden. Speed follows speed, stinging my nerves – tyres beating my legs, come and gone, come and gone. Each roar bangs my eardrums, fist hammering my forehead's door. You're daft to tramp here, beggar and fool, plodding home to no home. Clare's my beacon, walker ahead, whose footsteps scorch the way.

Twenty swans rest near the river, moored galleons – yards from the in-my-face vans – rootling in grass or nestling heads in their wings. Rabbits scoot under hedges. Tempsford Bridge humps honey stones over the Great Ouse. Did Clare cross its back before me? Teams of ladybirds climb grass stalks by my boots, tiny red berries dropped on the ground or flying. I might become a ladybird in Clare's asylum poem 'Clock-a-Clay':

> My home it shakes in wind and showers,
> Pale green pillar topped wi' flowers,
> Bending at the wild wind's breath
> Till I touch the grass beneath;

Why fly away home? A grass column toppling in the breeze. My house is on fire, my children are gone: black spots on my back, no wings. I cross a burning bridge, while bridge-slats crumble to ash behind me.

A time-pocked milestone at Roxton reads '50 Miles from London' in barely decipherable letters. A Beetle car drives past with my initials RJH on its number plate: a good omen. I've walked for nearly five hours with an hour's break. A shiny green sign ahead says 'Peterborough 27 Miles' in white, closer than I expected. With the wind in my sails I may even reach Buckden tonight, though lorries and cars keep winning.

An advert for food tempts me outside the Wait for the Waggon pub, but I flog on in a bid to finish this stretch without stopping. I think with longing of a hot meal, cooked vegetables. A perky Jack Russell terrier starts to trot by my heels. As I'm faster than him and pay him no attention, apart from a wan 'Hello,' he thinks better of it and abandons me, pads back brightly to the pub.

Fag-ends of minutes spat out, extinguished. I cram another hour with walking: thoughts blunt and ragged, telling myself 'get there get there.' I swig water. Crows' nests in bare branches at the tops of trees blot like tar spots on a smoker's lung.

Near the turn for St Neots I reach a junkyard of dead cars: two pyramids of crushed and broken metal three times higher than me. Will they topple like grass stalks? Dust whirls across the empty forecourt, blowing grit into my face as though I'm some moody stranger passing through. I wait for another gap in traffic and cross the A1 again. It's 1.30 p.m. and I'm hungry. Dandelions sprout on both sides of my path.

By 2.30 p.m. I've eaten mushroom omelette and chips and drunk half a cider in The Bell towards St Neots. In the gents I washed my face and combed my hair, which stuck out in a wind-blown mess. I wondered why the barman was giving me funny looks.

While I ate, I reread Clare's account of his walk, noticing he didn't enter St Neots. He was *within a mile and a half or less* outside, so this area of Eaton Socon might have seen him around the end of his second day.

Loaded with rucksack and bags again, I pass an obelisk, fifteen feet high, surrounded by stubby pillars and a black chain circling rows of names, ranks and battalions – 'ERECTED WITH GRATITUDE TO THE GLORIOUS MEMORY OF THE MEN OF THIS PARISH WHO GAVE THEIR LIVES TO SECURE VICTORY IN THE GREAT WAR. THEIR NAME LIVETH FOR EVERMORE'. A mellow stone church stands behind a low wall, with a St George's flag dangling.

This village green's horse chestnut and war memorial should stir a sniff of patriotism in me for why those young men fought and died, though it all seems wasted now. I associate that red cross on white with shouts of 'Enger-lund! Enger-lund!' rising from football crowds or racists. I suddenly feel threatened by it, as if someone wrapped in a St George's flag wants to shut out my Portuguese-Jewish ancestors from this version of little England. I think of my family boarding a boat from the Netherlands in the 1830s, ending up in London as wives or boatmen on the Thames. I want that red cross to stand for more than a white island mind with dreams of Empire. I want it to become the signature of my ancestors who couldn't speak English when they moved here, or Patty's wobbly cross when she signed the register to marry Clare. I imagine Clare calling *England my country though my setting sun* from his asylum, as if an open version of England includes not only the glorious memory of soldiers under a setting sun, but Portuguese boatmen working on the Thames.

Half an hour's amble from the village green, I pass ten caravans. Jeans, dresses, vests and knickers loll along the washing lines, above a tethered horse and the inevitable dog barking outside a trailer.

I remember my childhood neighbours in Gascoyne House, who lived in a caravan before they moved to the flat next door, and how living in a caravan sounded dramatic then. Aunt Suzie told me that, because of her black hair and olive skin, she was suspected of being a Gypsy by Uncle Laurie's family, when they first began courting after the war. She laughed when she talked about it, the ridiculousness of it; but Uncle Laurie hadn't forgiven them. He still spoke in injured tones about how his parents judged Suzie; how they refused to attend their wedding, because they wrongly believed she was pregnant. Why else would a cockney of lily-white stock marry a Gypsy, this 'darky' who steals your milk and your son with her witchy ways?

A year or so before our marriage ended, when Dee and I were struggling again to repair the damage, I bought a lace tablecloth for my half-brother's wedding from a sallow middle-aged Gypsy who came to the door, selling pegs, tablecloths and handkerchiefs. As I handed over the money she said abruptly out of nowhere, with a sharp stare, 'You love her, but you won't be able to please her.' I flinched from her eyes, mumbled, 'Well, we'll see,' and closed the door, the tablecloth a dead weight in my hands. I never told Dee, because there was nothing she could do with the information. Did my air of weariness that afternoon give the game away? Did this woman find a frazzled man standing before her, and say whatever jumped into her head?

Clare's mother, Ann, was described as 'gypsy-like in her appearance'. Clare sided with Gypsies, users of the common land. He was fascinated by their customs and dialects, ending his High Beach sonnet 'The Gypsy Camp' by calling them

> . . .– *a picture to the place,*
> *A quiet, pilfering, unprotected race.*

He learned to play the fiddle from *the Smiths gang of gipseys* and from *the Boswell Crew as they were calld a popular tribe well known about here & famous for fiddlers & fortune tellers.* Before he married he immersed himself in their lives, when he wasn't working or writing: *I usd to spend my Sundays & summer evenings among them learning to play the fiddle in their manner by the ear & fancy in their pastimes of jumping dancing & other amusements I became so instructed in their ways & habits that I was often tempted to join them.* So this home-loving man, rooted for years in a few familiar miles, dared to think about uprooting himself, to leave Helpston and travel with Gypsies as *a young fellow that I workd with at the limekiln did join with them & married one of their gipseys his name was James Mills and he's with them still.* Clare was drawn to their difference. He, who could have seen their lives as an affront to his settled ways, was appalled by the clergyman Justice of the Peace who said, 'This atrosious tribe of wandering vagabonds ought to be made outlaws in every civilizd kingdom and exterminated from the face of the earth.' That attitude to otherness seems to distinguish us from each other: whether we blame them because they're not like us, or learn from them for the same reason.

Two reasons kept Clare from following Gypsies: *I usd to dislike their cooking which was done in a slovenly manner & the dread of winters cold was much against my inclinations.* Winter and bad cooking persuaded him to stay home, but in Epping Forest he was drawn again to Gypsies, since they still represented freedom, this time from High Beach rather than Helpston. The second entry in his journal shows a Gypsy siding with Clare's outsider status as a lunatic in an asylum. These two oppressed men discover in their common outsider-hood a conspiracy to effect escape, though the Gypsy's too poor to do something for nothing, and Clare couldn't afford to pay him: *fell in with some gipseys, one of whom offered to assist in my escape from the madhouse by hiding me in his camp to which I almost agreed but told him I had no money to start with . . . On friday I went again but he did not seem so willing so I said little about it – On Sunday I went & they were all gone -*

The Gypsy's offer had sown its seed, alongside the hunger for Mary expressed in 'Child Harold'. Nine days after their original conversation – only two days after the Gypsy camp's disappearance – Clare decides it's now or never and starts his walk.

When I was rereading the journal over lunch, I noticed on the basic map of the journey that the Ram Inn Clare mentioned on his second evening is highlighted past St Neots, just off the Great North Road. It would mean a walk out of my way, but I'm tempted to see if I can find the building about which Clare wrote: *the shutters were not closed & the lighted windows looked very cheering.*

My bootlace is coming undone, so I kneel to re-knot it. Suddenly, more than anything, I want to find the Ram Inn, see its windows as Clare saw them, in today's afternoon sun while he watched them in darkness. I find a phone box and use a couple of coins to phone Peter Moyse from the John Clare Society, to check if he's any idea of the Ram Inn's whereabouts. A few weeks before my walk, I'd visited Peter in Helpston to help me plan the route. Today he's happy to hear me, and impressed by how far I've travelled, but can't be certain where the Ram Inn stood without checking his books and papers. As I close the phone-box door and step onto the street again, I realise how bizarre it must have been for him to hear my voice out of the blue, expecting answers this minute to a finicky question. The Ram's not an inn any more, so directory enquiries can't help. I assure myself I might find it at Hail Weston. That hunch makes me think it's worth a shot, especially since it'll shield me from toiling beside the A1 for a little longer.

I check with a plump anoraked woman leading her Alsatian whether I'm going in the right direction. She confirms I'm on the road for Hail Weston, a mile or so away.

When I'm quiet again, moving forward, my head still rings with Dee's voice, telling her side of the story: statements, arguments, laughter, pressing on either temple like a thumb-print held too hard, a subtle bruise. It strikes me again how strange it is to copy this journey: two men *in extremis*, hunting their way home. Clare's trudging these roads with me now, mentally ill, wanting to recapture a woman who's gone. I see scores of Clares, hundreds of him, scattered across roads like this throughout England – walking with their bags this minute, chucked out of their last homes, needing to make another: build a house of sticks, a house of stones.

The sun's closed its eye behind a cloud. Wind stings my face, as if I'm battling against it. If this is where Clare tramped at night, searching for the Ram Inn, he was moving far from the easiest route, though this flat landscape might have helped him feel vaguely at home, miles from it as he still was. For a moment there's no one else on the horizon, although one crow skims the crown of distant elms. In Northampton Asylum Clare called crows *chimney sweeps* and *the sooty crew*, saying *I love I love I love* three times in seven lines in his sonnet about them:

> *How peaceable it seems for lonely men*
> *To see a crow fly in the thin blue line*
> *Over the woods and fields, o'er level fen:*
> *It speaks of villages or cottage nigh*
> *Behind the neighbouring woods . . .*

Does that crow make me peaceable or remind me I'm one of Clare's lonely men, craving the hope of a cottage behind the woods? I suddenly feel alone, with a crash that drags me down, as if I can't see any good in it. Futility knocks me sideways: searching for the Ram Inn at Hail Weston. What am I doing here? Half an hour ago I felt confident I'd find it. Now I know just as certainly it isn't there, as I know I can't walk back to Dee. She's not there either. I'm rocked by a sense of finality. Slog one foot after the other, or stand still and never move because you can't reach her. She's vanished from your side. My self-respect is decimated, a shrunk kernel cracked open by experience, ruined in front of my face.

A group of young walkers yell twenty minutes or so ahead, planted field on my right and scrubland on my left. Their shouts echo. A jogger pounding towards me after he's passed them asks, 'Can't you keep up?' I say, 'I'm not with them.' I'm years after them, or some of them might become me years later when they fall in love, raise kids and lose their wives, as if it's a fate waiting to trip any carefree hiker.

At Hail Weston I can't find the Ram Inn anywhere. I find St Nicholas, a squat brown church with a tiled spire and golden cockerel; slanting old and upright new gravestones; daffodils fading on a bank beside a magnolia; houses flaunting a mix of brickwork and gables, ages and styles. They look pleased with themselves, as though they've accomplished security, a tidy life with every shut door facing me, while Clare and I represent the excluded, the failures. Nothing says Ram Inn. Why should it? Clare never walked inside, and neither can I. He wrote, *I had no money & did not like to go in there was a sort of shed or gig-house at the end but I did not like to lie there as the people were up – so I still travelled on.*

We don't belong here. I'll move on to the next lap of my pilgrimage, work my slow way back towards the A1 down Ford End. I've lost heart, wearying myself on a fool's errand, hoping to lay my hand on a wall that isn't even here.

At ten to five on a road the width of a car with passing places, the shouting lads ahead keep disappearing into Little Paxton Wood, probably to set up camp for the night. It's three hours before dark. Where will I sleep? I want to be small as a pebble that can't smash.

The wood is fringed by a line of snowy blackthorn; thistles and ferns at my feet; brambles either side. A nursery rhyme drags its dogged rhythm with my boots, words I used to read to the children:

The north wind doth blow
and we shall have snow
and what will poor robin do then, poor thing?
He'll sit in a barn
and keep himself warm
and hide his head under his wing, poor thing.

I've sunk to my lowest ebb, feeling I entered marriage like a child expecting happiness. I've snapped a home in two: absented myself, fled the scene of the crime. Crap-father crap-husband becomes a litany.

I'm trapped by a sensation of endless slogging after this wrong direction, puddles and ruts either side and teasels in ditches. I want to rest and switch off my head, but if I stop my feet throb harder. They feel wrapped in a dozen bandages, still burning. Perhaps the secret, which Clare discovered, is one foot shadowing the other achieves more than standing still. Rumi said, 'Straying maps the path' and he didn't lie. Wasting an hour's become part of this journey, taught me facts I might not have faced if I'd stuck to the A1. My path's wherever I walk, and I catch a hint of triumph through my exhaustion. Not finding the Ram Inn, look what I found instead: worthless as I may be, I choose to grit my teeth and soldier on.

When I approach a ford before Little Paxton Wood it seems as if the river's flooded. There's a narrow wooden bridge for pedestrians, with metal mesh and handrails. A couple of slow cars manage to steer through wet inches below me, water fanning either side of their tyres. The river's a muddy current under the little bridge. Weeds hug its edge, slippery green, with a half-submerged old crate and the hull of a pram like a dumped coracle.

A year ago, I dragged our second-hand pram down from the loft and drove it to the local tip. We agreed in a business-like fashion it had to go; our tacit admission that Amy, our daughter, would be our last child.

The A1 splinters my thoughts again. Three motorbikes weave between each other/a flock of chaffinches enters a tree/traffic's a steady storm/pylons, skeletal giants, play tug of war/that crow jabs a crust from the hard shoulder/tyres like discarded black zeroes by the crash barrier/fat white arrows tall as me on the tarmac/pointing north.

Four lanes of traffic, where I toil through a volley of noise. The heavier boom of lorries and coaches, whine and buzz of motorbikes, whiz and swish of cars unsettles my breathing: a song of speed, even a song of death. I shouldn't be walking these unsafe stretches at 6.15. Keep your eyes down and keep marching. Buckden must be another three miles, about an hour and a half if my energy holds up; but since the sky's growing an edge of duskiness I fret about fading light.

Clare slept on his second night before reaching here, some-where around St Neots. When he woke he *could not help blessing the Queen*, and on this road before Buckden – forty-eight hours since he'd eaten – he scribbled his confusion in the morning, *The man whose daughter is the queen of England is now sitting on a stone heap on the high way to bugden without a farthing in his pocket and without tasting a bit of food ever since yesterday morning –* . . . *O Mary mary if you knew how anxious I am to see you and dear Patty with the childern I think you would come and meet me.*

Allowing for my two one-hour stops I've been walking for ten hours today. I'm hoping Buckden has a pub and a reasonable hideaway where I can curl up and sleep tonight, out of harm's way.

I notice another cross beside the road: 'Alex – Safe in God's arms – Our love to you.' This madness is the risk I run. Everything's mangled here: twists of rusty metal; smashed glass like glitters of ice; a sense of skidding off the road into a crash. Although I might feel safer facing the traffic, at least I can block it with my back again, fool myself it's not juddering towards me.

Somewhere near here on his third morning, when he was finishing his note about his daughter being the Queen of England, a tall Gypsy met Clare and they walked together for a while. Clare described her as *a young woman of an honest-looking countenance rather handsome.* She also made up her mind about his appearance and – like the Gypsy in Epping Forest – gave him advice: *she cautioned me on the way to put something in my hat to keep the crown up & said in a lower tone 'You'll be noticed' but not knowing what she hinted I took no notice & made no reply.* The tall Gypsy – standing out from the crowd with her olive skin, her height – had learnt the knack of blending in to get by. She'd already sussed Clare stood out, with his odd manner, his *old wide-awake hat* left by the Epping Forest Gypsy five days before. It's the advice of a fellow low-status outsider, warily spoken in a quieter voice, as though they're co-conspirators who might be overheard by anyone in power. Clare knew enough to remember it, jot it down later, but he missed her clues.

Her second piece of advice met the same fate: *she pointed to a tower-church which she called Shefford Church & advised me to go on a footway which... would take me direct to it & should shorten my journey fifteen miles by doing so.* Clare meant to write Offord Church, but didn't trust himself to *be able to find the north Road again*, so stuck to the road his feet were bound to, as are mine, slowing down at last towards Buckden in anticipation of rest, seeing on my map that Buckden's two-thirds of the way to Clare's home. Cars hurtle through evening light towards their destinations.

At 7.40 p.m. I nurse my cider in The Vine at Buckden. Clusters of faded flowers carpet the floor. A metal statue of an antlered stag rests on the windowsill between two brown leather chairs, in one of which a greyhound has folded his legs and is dozing.

A red-brick fireplace in the centre divides the bar from the dining area and the snooker table, where a cue waits across the baize. Five men in T-shirts lean by the bar or balance on high stools. While a middle-aged man in a tracksuit feeds coins into the fruit machine, a wizened man is saying to his mates, with the barmaid listening: 'If you turn left to Blenheim Way there's a pub that used to be owned by bikers. I only remember two pubs in Yaxley. Unless the one I'm thinking of is closed. When my sister moved there that pub was open. Queen's Head I think it was. Up the A1 to Yaxley, past the Little Chef.'

The barmaid says, 'That's not the way I'd go.'

'Am I thinking of Sawtry not Yaxley?' They all laugh. 'I was miles off the mark.'

Eric Clapton's 'Wonderful Tonight' smooches from the

sound system, with its gentle guitar. The tune reminds me of Dee, our best years, when love songs made sense: his voice crooning tender words to a silent woman. Sometimes this separation feels like an interruption, a temporary intrusion. We'll return to normal life again soon, licking our wounds: the park with the kids, our domesticity, watching television together, our squabbles, lists, meals and love songs. Normal service will be resumed.

Those months of Clifford's illness and death four years ago felt like a similar bubble, where we were gasping for air inside the ward, while everyone else played outside, oblivious, and we could hear them enjoying a pint, laughing about Yaxley or Sawtry. When Clifford was confined to bed in hospital – after reaching the sink to brush his teeth led to hours strapped to an oxygen-mask – he told me about a dream he'd had the night before. He was walking through a supermarket, guiding his trolley, ticking a list, as if mundane routines had become something to dream about.

The glass is chill against my fingers. Quenching my thirst on this sweet and bitter cider, I talk myself into searching for somewhere to sleep while there's still enough light, rising early again tomorrow. The prospect of more miles along the A1 is far from enticing. I feel bound on a wheel, although in three days I've covered fifty to sixty miles, with only twenty left to reach Peterborough. Maths was never my strong point, but for once the miles are adding up.

Third Day 1841

Two Wives

I blest my two wives & both their familys when I lay down &
when I got up

> Living without living with them.
> Kiss them all for me. Keep them safe
> until I wake to children's cries in the first light,
> their bad dreams breaking my sleep
> instead of my own.
>
> Halfway home to seven kids or seventeen
> I dive into one wife's net, I'm caught by two
> and spin to be caught
> as they dredge me from the wreck, this wreck
>   myself,
> I dabble their tongues with the same mouth.
> One woman lulls my hand, the other my hair.

Father and husband to all
I bless them
when I piggy-back them over high nettles again
rub dock-leaves down shin-hairs if they're stung
bless them
when we dib grass quills in cuckoo-spit's white ink
and when our children roost through my branches
bless their mothers
for each plucking a hailstone from this harebell
nestling it on their palms until it melts.

A Tall Gypsy

I saw a tall Gipsey come out of the Lodge gate & make down the road . . . I got up & went on to the next town with her – she cautioned me on the way to put something in my hat to keep the crown up & said in a lower tone 'You'll be noticed' but not knowing what she hinted I took no notice & made no reply

She speaks:

I live this skin, wanting no other:
not to be some milk-face supping indoors.
They quake politely when I read their smiles
as if I'll blab which husband bores, who dies
                                        tomorrow.

We side with each other
for ten furlongs into town,
talk of heading north and why swifts won't land
before I warn his gawky look.

Ape them or you'll be noticed.
Straighten your hat. Stiffen its crown
and you can skip their questions.
Take a short cut. Drop the road you're on.

A Length of Road

Candle Lights

*I then entered a town & some of the chamber windows had
candle lights shining in them*

If I could cradle a flame
from weather's whistle,
I'd cup my hand
round a flickery notion of being inside.
I'd be a good boy, keep my promises.
Let me in
and I'll not want outside again.

Open windows.
I could burgle their teacups,
breaking into candles behind glass
where a woman lifts her hands
to plait her hair,
while a man leans on their sill
and shuts the catch.

I want haloes from a hundred tapers,
warm wax between my fingers
to push holes for her eyes with my thumbprints,
pinch the rise of her nose,
her white cheek
still bewitching me.
Watch it burn.

The Coach

The Coach did pass me as I sat under some trees by a high wall
and the lumps lasshed in my face and wakened me up from a
doze when I knocked the gravel out of my shoes and started

For those dumped at the road-side
compensations:

1. Stop running. Doze under an elm's shadow,
pinch lavender in your fingers and sniff.

2. The coach wasn't early. You weren't late:
you were never meant to ride there.

3. The legs that took you this far
take you further.

A Length of Road

Eating the Grass

*on the third day I satisfied my hunger by eating the grass by
the roadside which seemed to taste something like bread*

Become horse. Mane and flanks. Teeth clenched on
                                              the bit
free now. Unbridled. I whinny in the sun
or roll through damp hay for the joy of it,
do you hear? No masters. So what if I stun
a hedgehog with my hoof, he's my brother. So what
if this grass was sluiced by fox-piss
in the night, it still tastes green. I eat
whatever's to hand, lick puddles when I'm lucky.
                                              This
is the earth's body. Swallow its bread,
suck its milk. I'm an animal like any other
until I speak. Given paper instead
I wipe myself, or
wipe words on it. Cover that white
with grass-stains, bird-droppings, names for things
                                              I write.

Went Sleep

one night I lay in a dyke bottom from the wind and went sleep
half an hour when I suddenly awoke and found one side wet
through from the sock in the dyke bottom, so I got out and
went on –

I saw monsters again tonight mother.
I'm wet to the skin again. Change me.
Where's the moon? Lying low,
so the wind won't knock it sideways.

Flat on my back I sing for spiders,
cross arms over my chest and point my feet
waking to that goose-pimpled man again:
myself vowing *I'll walk always beside you.*

Get me home
and I'll honour dandelions on my doorstep,
carry the moon in a bucket of water
without slopping a drop.

Fourth Day

Monday, 17 April 1995

6 a.m. Up with the lark – though there is no lark – I'm walking under a tunnel towards the A1. Blue-green walls have graffiti painted over in blocks of white either side. Strip lights line a riveted white metal ceiling a few feet above my forehead, where the tyres spin. Straight ahead is a square of daylight that's taking me to the next stretch of the A1.

When I reach a couple of yellow metal barriers before the slope up towards the road a sign says:

> HORSES – Any person who rides or leads
> a horse through this pedestrian subway
> is responsible for clearing away any
> manure that may be deposited in the
> subway by that animal. Failure to do so
> will result in prosecution.
> By Order of Buckden Parish Council

189

The sign appears to be successful. This is a manure-free subway.

As far as I could tell from the streets I saw last night after my drink at The Vine, Buckden seemed a pleasant, unassuming place. Another long straight road through the village, with Eloise Lingerie (swimwear and nightwear) leading to a cream-painted Lion Hotel, facing a long red-bricked George Hotel.

I phoned the kids at about eight, before they went to bed. I imagined them in their pyjamas, getting ready to brush their teeth, Amy already asleep. I spoke to Isaac, Joe and Dee. When I told Isaac there was about twenty miles to Peterborough he asked, 'Are you going to walk to Peterborough tonight then?' He's nine, so I told him it takes hours to walk twenty miles. Dee said she'd try to show them my whereabouts on the map, how far I've walked. I wanted them to be a little more impressed, but miles become Dee's fingertip travelling a few inches up the country. It takes a moment.

Last night I walked past Buckden Towers, with neat lawns, red-brick crenellated parapets and a sign saying 'Residence of Bishops of Lincoln 1186–1842'; although treading pavements for somewhere to sleep gives a particular slant on what amenities a village offers. Not that doorway, not that bench: too public. Once again, I felt the need to hide myself in the dark.

I found a recreation ground on the far side of the village, and bedded down behind a clump of straggly bushes across the grass. I managed to knot the grey sheeting of my bivouac between one handy branch and another. My exhaustion, and the cramped conditions where I crouched inside the undergrowth, meant that I didn't make the most comfortable shelter. I snuggled into my sleeping bag, but felt edgy through the night, because earlier that evening I'd noticed a police car cruising the streets, looking for trouble. I assume the police could see what I'm doing as vagrancy or trespass, adding to my dread of exposure.

Like others, last night was broken by worries circling my head, or by turning over for comfort on hard earth. Occasionally I thought I heard a patter of rain, but none arrived. I slept in a jumper, so although my teeth chattered with cold when I half-woke in the late and early hours, it wasn't as rough as the night before. I dreamt I came across a pond where Clare found water lilies in Epping Forest:

The pleasant leaves upon the water float;
The dragon-fly would come and stay for hours,
And when the water pushed the pleasure boat,
Would find a safer place among the flowers:

In my dream it felt as though Clare had been standing by the water only seconds before, and my approach startled him, made him hide behind trees. I hoped to find the water lilies Clare had called ... *'Ladies of the Lake'*, but though their leaves floated like small green tea-plates, the *white and yellow flowers* had gone. Perhaps I made Clare and his water lilies disappear, as if my arrival scares everything away.

My plan to leave early makes the start of today's walk easier, since there's not much traffic along the A1. Gaps of hush between a rumble and rush over tarmac, and occasional thumps of music vanish with the minutes. A lorry goes as quickly as it comes, leaves emptiness in its wake. The Fool's rhyme from *King Lear* sings through my head as I trudge beside cow parsley:

> He that has and a little tiny wit
> With hey, ho, the wind and the rain,
> Must make content with his fortunes fit,
> Though the rain it raineth every day.

Am I making content fit my fortunes, fool that I am? Another sign confirms this as the Great North Road. I scare a rabbit again. Later in my dream Margaret Thatcher was telling me she was prepared to consider she may have made a few mistakes. She was comparing her memoirs to some political analysis of her years in power. She sounded keen to explain herself, make sure I understood. I was relatively polite in the dream, considering she was Thatcher.

A spongy mattress has been discarded by the side of the road. The sky doesn't know it's morning, asks nothing of me, though it starts a conversation with the day. How much do I owe the sky?

A road sign's been knocked down, buckled at the knee. As another flurry of cars sweeps past in both directions it doesn't inspire me with confidence about the safety of this venture. Safety makes me think about what it must be like to be a woman, how that might change this journey. If I were a woman walking alone alongside the A1, my fear and courage would be of a different order. Would I be restricted by the threat, refuse to be defined by it? I've felt scared at night, but not usually in daylight. It's a basic infringement of freedom: who's allowed to walk where they please, who does the allowing. Even the fact that Dee's caring for our children feels like another curtailment, another allocation of roles we didn't talk about when I left her in Epping Forest: who's expected to walk, who's still expected to stay with the kids. I didn't consider my sense of entitlement until this morning, trekking here. I want my daughter to feel free to walk anywhere – to see everything – unimpeded, unafraid.

The exit coming up in half a mile is for the Midlands, with Kettering and Corby on a sign for the A14, white letters against green. Reading those familiar names feels like turning towards home, but I can't slip inside that life again. I don't belong there. We moved to Kettering as newlyweds after our honeymoon, to an area known as Poet's Corner. We lived in a bungalow that had belonged to Dee's grandparents, a few months after her grandad had died. We began that tricky process of trying to adjust to each other's ways. We tacked up one of Clifford's six-foot canvases from St Martin's onto Dee's grandparents' wallpaper. Abstract Expressionist blue and red swirls, yellow blotches and drips made a statement in the front room.

Our children didn't know that bungalow – we lived there before they were born, as if our pre-children marriage was sealed inside, ghostly schooner in a bottle. After I won a Northamptonshire poetry competition I was photographed for the local paper leaning awkwardly on the Byron Road street sign where we lived, apparently for inspiration, a coat slung over my shoulder in Byronic fashion, the local photographer's idea of how poets spent their days. For my birthday that year our artist friend Ian drew a pen-and-ink card of a tousled Lord Byron leaning on a Hamberger Road sign for inspiration.

What does Dee do with such memories, if she has them?

Apart from the children and our twenty years together, it feels like we've little left in common. Even those twenty years don't feel in common any more: we interpret and remember a different selection of scenes from such divergent perspectives we can't claim them as the same experience. They happened in the same house to two people. Maybe a loved one's ultimately unknowable: compelling enough to want to know more; outside each other's skin, even when we make love, beached in separate feelings, hoping our ecstasies meet. After years of intimacy our knowledge of each other led to disappointment rather than joy. We grew less, rather than more, familiar to each other, our marriage a finite series of events, so today we view every episode through the diminishing telescope of its end.

This flat country leans towards a hill of oil-seed rape, another slab of yellow brushing the horizon. On my right, car and no car. It's no wonder Clare reported little from this stretch of his journey. There's little to report apart from walking. He wrote: *I then got up & pushed onward seeing little to notice for the road very often looked as stupid as myself & I was very often half asleep as I went on the third day I satisfied my hunger by eating the grass by the roadside which seemed to taste something like bread I was hungry & eat heartily till I was satisfied & in fact the meal seemed to do me good.*

I remember my Welsh art teacher talked with bitterness about Churchill saying the striking miners could eat grass. For Clare grass becomes bread that nature offers, so he's grateful for its spiky gift, his third day's meal: sedge; cock's-foot; quaking grass;

Italian rye-grass; meadow fescue; Timothy; tor-grass. He's a sword-swallower, guzzling a hundred blades.

Bulrushes fringing a ditch stand bearded by fawn-colour fur. Under pylons near an artificial lake twenty or so swans lie dozing. I want them to be the same swans I saw yesterday afternoon beside the Ouse, accompanying me as snow-feathered guardians, keeping watch for my sake. This is quite a view: spacious fields at either shoulder, a blue-grey sky overhead and what Clare called *a length of road* straight in front of my boots, showing me how the next few hours are bound to be spent. I think of my Jewish ancestors in the 1800s on their own lengths of road, walking not towards home but away. The home you and your children love goes wrong, becomes dangerous enough for you to take your children in your arms, whatever you can carry on your back, and step away. It's courage born through desperation, which my ancestors needed to travel from Portugal to the Netherlands and then on to London, and Clare took in his hands on 20 July 1841 when he left High Beach.

On his second night Clare sang to keep himself company: *as my doubts vanished I soon cheered up & hummed the air of 'highland Mary' as I went on*, a traditional tune he picked up for his fiddle from the Gypsy Wisdom Smith sixteen years earlier, on the day he *caught a cold in the wet grass*. 'Highland Mary' is a Burns poem, lilting with love and farewells for another lost Mary who 'Death's untimely frost . . . nipt my Flower sae early.' I sing Joni Mitchell instead, to make me feel revived and blue in the same breath, showing my age to no one on this empty road. All those songs about pretty lies and still being on my feet dwindle from my lips into early weather.

A car's backing up and indicating on my side of the road: a square white glow from the reverse light and a winking orange. It appears to be waiting for me.

7.35 a.m. I've had a brilliant stroke of luck, so much so that I'll ignore the fact I've cheated. A man has driven me from the Alconbury to the Stilton turn. That must have been nearly ten miles, because we passed a sign that read '8 Miles to Peterborough', along with signs for the villages of Upton, Sawtry and Glatton. Those villages really are names on a map to me now: flashed through fields, clouds and roads, like flicking three pages.

When he stopped, indicating on the roadside for a few minutes while I struggled with rucksack and bags to reach his car, I felt again that initial suspicion about a stranger's motives. Before I reached him, I thought he might speed off without me for a joke. The moment I threw my rucksack onto his backseat I thought he could steal it and drive away. He did neither.

I caught his name as Tony. On the drive we swapped potted life stories as a bargain between two travellers passing the time, shooting past dandelions and cowslips, the hump of a wood on the horizon. He was in his thirties; London accent; T-shirt and jeans, a rough relaxed look about him with unbrushed hair and quick smile. I assumed he was single: there was no mention of a partner. He was self-employed, minicabbing and driving lorries. He said he'd be driving a lorry next week. His minicab mike was clipped near the dashboard, CDs scattered by the glove compartment. A little sandy-coloured pug squatted behind the driver's seat, looking up at me with soulful eyes.

Tony said he'd been driving his cab round Clapham all night. He'd had no sleep and looked weary. He said his radio, and struggling to keep his car steady in the wind, was helping him stay awake. I imagine he offered a lift partly for company and to help keep his eyes open. He'd driven minicabs for ten years and liked working mainly at night because there's less traffic. He bought his car from new. It had already gone round the clock. He said he'd abused it for years, but his tone sounded affectionate. He's travelling up to visit his parents for Bank Holiday Monday in Sleaford. I said, 'That's a hell of a trek,' and he replied, 'They're worth it.' They aren't expecting him till next week, so it's meant as a surprise. I chatted about where I was going, that I come from Whitechapel originally and I'm following the Great North Road. I didn't mention Clare. I kept it light.

I sometimes wonder why no one offered Clare a ride, especially as he came across more travellers than I have. I feel luckier than him. The nearest he got were neighbours in a cart from his home village of Helpston, on the last leg of his walk: *before I got to Peterborough a man & woman passed me in a cart & on hailing me as they passed I found they were neighbours from Helpstone where I used to live – I told them I was knocked up which they could easily see & that I had neither eat nor drunk anything since I left Essex.* Clare doesn't say he was angling for a lift, but presumably it could have been possible, especially if they were returning to Helpston, only four miles from his Northborough cottage. Whether the cart was already loaded, or whether he looked too mad or dishevelled (coupled with a wariness shown to Clare by many of his fellow villagers and probable gossip about him being 'locked away'), his neighbours rode on without him. Don't get involved.

But his story moved them enough to help: *they clubbed together & threw me fivepence out of the cart*, which paid for his first real meal in two days – *two half pints of ale & two pen'orth of bread & cheese.*

I must have looked a little mad to Tony as he drove towards me, traipsing along the A1 in the early morning. His ten-minute lift has saved me nearly five hours' walk and revived my spirits. So why should it make me feel guilty? As if I'm a fraud in the face of Clare's challenge. It would have been daft to refuse that gift-horse on a risky stretch. Peel off your hair shirt for ten minutes – skin tingles in a penance-free breeze.

Tony's lift has thrown my timetable. I'll easily reach Peterborough today, may even finish the walk in Clare's four days. It's helped me catch up half a day's slog, where I always lagged behind. The Tortoise creeps to level pegging with the Hare, even if he cheated to get here. Before Clare turns away in disgust I might look him squarely in the eyes – ask to shake his hand – if we meet as brother travellers; but he won't stop to talk. He's too restless, must keep on the move.

Stilton seems calm and quiet on this Bank Holiday morning. A tortoiseshell butterfly zigzags past. It's hard to believe the A1 is so near. Birdsong close at hand mingles with a low shush-and-thrum. All the hotels and pubs look closed in the spacious North Street and High Street carving through the village, cars parked either side of the Bell Inn's mullioned windows. Its red and gold painted sign is suspended above the door by black metal curls. An elderly man in an electric wheelchair trundles past, asking if I want a lift. Two clouds follow each other in the sky like albino camels.

To celebrate my good fortune I wriggle out of my rucksack and rest on a bench by the village pump, thick as a fat man's leg, with its onion-domed hat. It stands on a plinth surrounded by posts and a spiky black chain. I click open a can of drink, unwrap a chocolate bar near the phone box. A confident man in a pink shirt steps out of his Range Rover to buy a paper at the newsagents. He calls to me: 'You look very comfortable there, young man.'

'I am. Loving every minute.'

'Will y'be stopping all day?'

I laugh and say, 'I don't think so.' Another man asks if I'm doing the Great North walk. I tell him about Clare. He says they've done some filming in Stilton about it before, and wishes me luck.

Facing an eleven-windowed Georgian house, I open Clare again, with half an hour to kill. I dip into his pages at 'Don Juan', that strange misogynist poem written at High Beach (like 'Child Harold' and also modelled on Byron), though some of it was probably finished after his walk. Like 'Child Harold', its first line mentions poets, but he veers 'Don Juan' in a radically different direction inside that first line:

> *'Poets are born' – and so are whores – the trade is*
> *Grown universal – . . .*

No agonising, as in 'Child Harold', about where he stands as a poet: they're all whores anyway, selling their names like their bodies, ready to turn a trick to get on. Clare's alternative title for 'Don Juan' was 'The Sale of Old Wigs and Sundries', and in this poem everything's for sale, including the stanzas we're reading. It ends:

> *So reader now the money till unlock it*
> *And buy the book and help to fill my pocket*

In 'Don Juan' Clare becomes a ventriloquist. He tries on Byron's voice, a cynical swivel-eyed dummy who gives these verses a disturbing almost reckless energy, leapfrogging from one subject to the next with a jagged, improvisatory force. In his second stanza (probably added when he returned to Northborough) he chucks *Paradise Lost* into the performance, to discard it just as swiftly:

> *Milton sung Eden and the fall of man*
> *Not woman for the name implies a wh–e*
> . . .
> *Wherever mischief is tis womans brewing*
> *Created from manself – to be mans ruin*

It's as if Clare admits the history of misogyny (this voice he's trying on and gloating over) starts with Eve: the fall of man, and man's eternal excuse to hate women. I wondered before this walk how 'Child Harold' and 'Don Juan' could come from one man in the same manuscript, from the same asylum years and pen, until it dawns on me that misogyny's the underbelly of idealising women: the whore and madonna woven into men's inability to accept women as they are. Jacqueline Rose says, 'the idealisation of the woman . . . and the aggression are the fully interdependent and reverse sides of the same coin.'

Clare's hatred of women unleashes him into pouring scorn on the *driveling hoax* of marriage, politics, *that patched broken old state clock*, a young Queen Victoria, prostitutes, playhouses and madhouses as *state prisons for the queen*, mixed up in a whirl of punning rhymes about oral sex and his fondness for cunt, where he even admits to losing his train of thought:

> *I really cant tell what this poem will be*
> *About – nor yet what trade I am to follow*
> *I thought to buy old wigs – but that will kill me*
> *With cold starvation – as they're beaten hollow*

What does it mean for a poet to try on voices, lay various selves against his skin? To want to be different from the skin he's born into: Byron one minute and a Dickensian cockney mocking Byron the next:

> *Lord Byron poh – the man wot rites the werses*
> *And is just what he is and nothing more*
> *Who with his pen lies like the mist disperses*
> *And makes all nothing as it was before*

While Clare implies everything becomes nothing again, after the fog of lies clears, he dares to be more than *just what he is* – to say: 'There are more John Clares than the green voice you're used to. Hear another.'

A great example of Clare offering an alternative version arrives just over halfway through 'Don Juan' when he unexpectedly breaks a lyrical love song into the poem's stop-start panache, after he writes a stanza that (in typical Clare fashion) has four lines starting *I love*. It's as if his switch from urban

to rural imagery throws a romantic voice from 'Child Harold'
into the melting pot of 'Don Juan' to calm it down:

> *Eliza now the summer tells*
> *Of spots where love and beauty dwells*
> *Come and spend a day with me*
> *Underneath the forest tree*
> *. . .*
> *Come dear Eliza set me free*
> *And oer the forest roam with me*

Even inside a diatribe against women as *A hell incarnate*, he
can't resist smuggling through a message that simultaneously
sees women as a liberating force for a trapped man.

When an editor, Cyrus Redding, visited him at High Beach
two months before he left, Clare 'spoke of his loneliness away
from his wife, expressing a great desire to go home, and to
have the society of women'. It's as if in 'Child Harold' Clare's
banishment from 'the society of women' leads to mourning
the absence of a female principle he can barely find in himself;
whereas in 'Don Juan' it leads to despising and attacking
women for not being there. By the contrasts in both poems
Clare uncovers how heterosexual men need and desire the
sexual availability of women, yet are aware it might be withheld
from them. In 'Don Juan' men use physical or economic power
to gain 'the society of women', although the poem doesn't
always revel in the sexual availability of wives, prostitutes,
ladies, Queen Victoria and female asylum patients. He admits
he's witnessed the sexual assault of women patients in *Docter
Bottle imp*'s asylum and his tone is appalled:

Where men close prisoners are and women ravished
I've often seen such dirty sights as these

Clare's bravest attempt to try on another skin sneaks into the penultimate stanza of 'Don Juan', cutting across the poem by allowing an opposing thought:

I have two wives and I should like to see them
Both by my side before another hour
If both are honest I should like to be them
For both are fair and bonny as a flower

Clare seems to be hoping that he could become both his wives – take on their lives or identities – but only on condition that both of them are honest. He might be reinforcing the poem's misogyny by implying there's no chance for his wives to be honest, so it's equally impossible for him to 'be' them. Yet there might also be an elusive wish to identify with the women on whom he's poured such vitriol through the rest of the poem, wanting to be as *fair and bonny* as them. He writes *I wish I wish I wish* seventeen times in the poem's early stanzas, and risks the boldest wish of all towards its close: to become the opposite sex. This echoes Clare's intriguing assertions in his brief essay 'Self-Identity' written in the autumn after his walk, before his move to Northampton Asylum: *But I cannot forget that I'm a man & it would be dishonest & unmanly in me to do so . . . there are two impossibillitys that can never happen – I shall never be in three places at once nor ever change to a woman & that ought to be some comfort amid this moral or immoral 'changing' in life* – Clare's concept of 'self-identity' appears relatively fluid at times, but the immutability of his gender seems central to a consistent sense of himself. For him it is *some comfort* amid all the changes in his life that he can never *change to a woman*. Yet even writing it, both here and towards the end of 'Don Juan', his polyphonic vision flirts with that impossible possibility.

Clare's twin sister Bessey died within a month of their births, so the lost female part of himself, the woman inside, might have had greater resonance. In his early sonnet 'To an Infant Sister in Heaven' he says:

> *Bessey, when memory turns thy lot to see,*
> *A brother's bosom yearns thy bliss to prove*
> *And sighs o'er wishes that was not to be.*

Jonathan Bate writes of Clare living out the 'Platonic quest' of 'wandering the earth in pursuit of our lost other half: such is the origin of desire . . . Perhaps that was because he was in a more literal sense split at birth, due to the early death of his twin sister.' Given that in 'Don Juan' a young Queen Victoria seems to represent a fantasy figure, Clare's resistance and attraction towards merging his sense of self with the lost woman appears again when he sees Victoria on her royal progress through Northampton in 1844 and claims to his keeper in the asylum 'O she said "I'm John Clare."'

The slipperiness of identity: being Byron or Jack Randall the boxer, Nelson or Shakespeare, Queen Victoria or his two wives. They all become John Clare and he becomes them. The need to self-define maleness by not being a woman can be breached, if he dares to imagine it. In an 1830 letter apparently about grammar Clare wrote: *I am growing out of myself into many existences & wish to become more entertaining in other genders for that the little personal pronoun 'I' is such a presumption ambitious swaggering little fellow that he thinks himself qualified for all company all places & all employments   go where you will there he is swaggering & bouncing.* Clare's writing dares to think 'I' doesn't have to stay a swaggering little fellow. He could grow into other genders, since he knows a writer can be anything. The difference between Clare and the skin separating him from the rest of the world dissolves, not as evidence of his supposed madness but his ability to admit alternatives. He's repeatedly driven to confront the elusiveness of women, how they are literally other, something he can never 'be', yet *If both are honest I should like to be them.* He can admit *it would be dishonest & unmanly in me* to believe what his gender has always taught him, to accept the limits of masculinity, to simply stay a man. Even Clare – writing and speaking – can play with the freedom to be both.

Being male and female makes me consider gender in my childhood. As a boy without a father I felt more at home with women. When I didn't feel at home my father's absence brimmed with longing. Fantasies of being found and loved by him diminished in my day-to-day routines, as they had to. How else could I survive such longing, the howl of a child who can't be comforted? My mother and her three sisters peopled life. Any father became a mirage in their company. After school my mother met my aunts and cousins at my nan's first-floor flat in Bullen House, on our estate. My fierce nan, with her olive skin and flowery pinafore, made us sugar sandwiches – the granules tiny diamonds stuck in butter – and said, 'I'll crack ya' if we bickered. Playing on the carpet with my brothers and cousins, women's voices lilted a continual accompaniment, sharing jokes and stories with each other, another comment chucked into the mêlée of words, laughter suddenly blossoming over my head about a memory or someone they all knew: Beattie Orwell, Kitty Scaggs. Laughter I never fully understood, though I wanted to share it because it made me happy.

Men were more mysterious, unknown territory. My grandfather was dead, my father vanished. Most of my uncles were usually quieter, removed by long hours at work in the docks on the Thames or somewhere nameless and distant. Their occasional arrival at my nan's flat later in the day imperceptibly altered the atmosphere between the women. Did they become more subdued, less glowing, or was that change in my imagination? I couldn't quite tell. As a child I found men's mystery slightly troubling and attractive in the same breath. I couldn't conceive how I might grow up to become one.

When I was eight or nine, after a day trip to Southend with my mother and brother, my cousins, my Aunt Suzie and Uncle Laurie, our group of seven travelled home late on the train. Towels and trunks, flasks, spades and bags bulged in the netted racks above us. I dozed on my uncle's shoulder. When I half-woke in the jolting I pretended to stay asleep, since I liked the rough unfamiliar feel of his shoulder, his donkey jacket the colour of blue-black coal rubbing the side of my face. My father had left my life over two years before, because I'd pushed him away. Uncle Laurie's shoulder felt safe and solid, that sensation of being a child with a man again. For half an hour

I was comforted enough to pretend to dream between their tired voices, while the rails carried us home.

At 8.10 a.m. I buckle on my rucksack and check my compass through Stilton High Street. It points dead north. Here we go, hobbly man! When he reached Stilton on his last day Clare describes himself as *compleatly foot-foundered & broken down*, so exhausted he dozes on *a gravel causeway . . . half way through the town.* Two women leave their house along the High Street. The younger one calls him *'poor creature' &* *another more elderly said 'O he shams' But when I got up the latter said 'O no he don't' as I hobbled along very lame.* Clare's torment is reflected by those he meets on his journey, whether they show sympathy or scorn, or simply observe him as *another of the broken-down haymakers* when their paths collide.

Compared to Clare, my lift has helped me leave Stilton relatively refreshed, which makes my brief walk easier along the A1's final section. I feel untroubled by cars now, revving up in frequency as the morning progresses. I approach Norman Cross where I turn right towards Yaxley, past the low round block of an orange-bricked hotel. There's a tarred walkway where I part company with the A1, move away from its racket. It's the lightest of goodbyes. I don't even wave.

Two crows let themselves be raised by the wind, until they settle in the hedge straight ahead. Norman Cross shows me a wing-lifted bronze eagle peering down from a fifteen-foot stone column. A plaque covered in verdigris at the base of the column says IN MEMORIAM from 1914, although this time it's not the glorious dead of the Great War, but wars from a century before:

TO THE MEMORY OF ONE THOUSAND SEVEN
HUNDRED & SEVENTY SOLDIERS AND SAILORS
NATIVES OR ALLIES OF FRANCE TAKEN
PRISONERS OF WAR DURING THE REPUBLICAN
AND NAPOLEONIC WARS WITH GREAT BRITAIN
A· D 1793 – 1814 WHO DIED IN THE MILITARY
DEPOT AT NORMAN CROSS. WHICH FORMERLY
STOOD NEAR THIS SPOT. 1797 – 1814
DULCE ET DECORVM EST PRO PATRIA MORI

I look across placid fields on my left, where horses or cows
are too distant to tell which, and a wood pigeon flickers into
the nearest horse chestnut. Who would have known the world's
first purpose-built prisoner-of-war camp stood in these fields?
Clare wrote about it in one of his Northborough sonnets 'There
is a place', voicing sympathy for his supposed enemy, dying
far from home:

I looked & asked the coachman passing bye
Who laughed & said tis there (the) frenchmen lie
They fought for tyrants their reward was slaves
& england was their prison & their graves

The A15's two lanes replace the A1's four, so cars sound more
sporadic: occasional gaps where crow-croaks interrupt. Lorries
snooze in a few lay-bys and Friesian cows chew lazily in lush
grass. A couple of scarecrows stand in a ploughed field, one
like a black rooster with a scarlet crown, the other's arms
waving in the wind. It's liberating to leave the A1's noise. Last
night it was jolting my dreams.

Clare believed in a *Guardian spirit* who appeared to him in dreams across the years. He describes her as *a lovely creature in the shape of a young woman with dark & rather disordered hair & eyes that spoke more beauty than earth inherits.* Six months after he moved to Northborough in 1832 Clare wrote about how *my guardian genius* first came to him in a dream, years before, *when I had not written a line.* In that first dream she shows him *an immense crowd all around me,* with *soldiers on horseback* and *ladies in splendid dresses.* As if handing him a brilliant future she says *you are the only one of the crowd now,* and leads him to *a booksellers shop* where *on a shelf among a vast crowd of books were three vols lettered with my own name* – He published four volumes, but how was he to know that before he'd written a line? Years later she appears on Judgement Day in a dream when, despite his fear as his name is called, she *smiled in exstacy & uttered something as prophetic of happiness I knew all was right.*

Alongside mixed feelings for women portrayed so effectively in his poems, Clare imagines *a woman deity* related to his writing, and thereby to what he sees as his salvation. It's as if, despite his anger towards women in 'Don Juan', Clare was able to honour a benign feminine principle within or outside himself, *the lady divinity* guiding him towards happiness, even on the day of judgement: *I knew all was right.*

A submarine of grey cloud sails over me, with a lighter ridge along the horizon. The sky shifts as slowly as I walk, reminding my body how long it takes to cover a little distance, compared to a mile a minute in Tony's car. Now I'm upright again my thighs and calf muscles ache. Three crows battle in the sky. A

gun goes off and I flinch above banks of nettles. Four tall
chimneys smoke in the distance. A sign says 'Peterborough 5'
on the London Road. Here's a hedge alive with sparrows.

Quiet again at 9.20 a.m. Quiet unlatches a window I have
to peer through, as it pulls me back to my situation. Why do
I keep replaying a fantasy of Dee wanting me back after this
walk? My naivety – stupidity – innate resistance to change.
Despite all I thought earlier, there is a dogged unwillingness
to draw a line underneath us, acknowledge our marriage is
finished. To admit it's over means not only mourning, but
facing what comes after. I'll have the rest of my life to attend
to, even if I never intended the rest of my life to be spent
without her. Until six weeks ago I imagined that having a wife
and family defined me. A married man. What defines me
now? I might have used my marriage for safety, as a device
not to face myself. Everything feels fluid, changeable, uncertain. I admit to myself on the A15 that even my sexuality's
thrown in the air by this separation. Where will it land?

I unpeel another skin. Sylvia Plath called it 'The big strip tease'.
Where do I stand in relation to myself if I'm no longer married?

Four years or so into our marriage, when the feelings weren't
disappearing as I'd hoped, I admitted to myself and Dee that
I had attractions to men, attractions I had no intention of
acting on, but which needed acknowledging (by me at least).
After another of my many moods, I confessed this to Dee in
a hotel room on the south coast, before our children were
born. I thought our marriage was built on honesty, but it was
a high price for her to pay. I remember her anguish, her
suggestion we should end the marriage then, me saying I didn't

want to be with men, I wanted to be with her. That remained true throughout our years together. My attractions were an inconvenience, an unnecessary complication I fought against and would rather live without. At the same time, I foisted them on her, undid her self-esteem by having attractions outside our relationship. As though my fidelity might be a way of proving love, when it would have helped us better if my feelings hadn't existed in the first place, because having them was already a betrayal to her, to our love. How dare you look the woman you love in the face?

Birdsong between whitethorn, what Clare called *Loaded wi'mockery of snow*. Each branch tells the tyres to slow down as they swish past. What's more temporary, whitethorn or tyres?

I deliberately avoided looking at men when I was married. It became like a minor version of Gerard Manley Hopkins's 'discipline of the eyes', when 'The person undertaking this penance kept his eyes cast down, looking at neither persons nor objects around him', sometimes for months in Hopkins's case, as if beauty might lead to temptation and both could be blotted out by downcast eyes. Not to look men in the eye, to try to avoid glancing at their faces and bodies in the street, their bare chests and backs in summer, became a clumsy self-imposed attempt to blank out my attractions, pretend to myself the feelings and men weren't there. Not looking became a way of shutting the lid (literally) on desires I couldn't handle, didn't want. Lying heart. Mugging us both in the bargain. I can lie to myself out of shame, keep a side of my life in the shade: unacknowledged, unaddressed, left to wither.

Where did my desire start? How did that boy become me?

At Stewart Headlam Junior School most of my friends were girls: Rosie Patterson, Christine Connor, Susan Yassin, Jennifer Laurent, Susan Dempsey, Janice Spraggett, Georgina Mumford, while the boys stayed more apart, but I still spent time with them: Douglas Howe, John Uddin, Keith Worrow, Derek Arrowsmith. Their names come back like calling the register in Mr Muxworthy's class and they answer. Each name and voice saying Yes, like Clare's letter from Northampton Asylum to his son Charles, eight years after he'd lived at home, when the names of fifty-seven of his old friends and neighbours pour from his memory: *most of us Boys & Girls together.*

During playtimes I often felt like an honorary girl: the only boy playing with half-a-dozen girls. Talking mostly; some skipping games; knotting coloured elastic bands together in a long loop with a girl standing ankles apart at either end to hold them, and steps I never understood that tied bands around the main player's ankles, weaving complicated rainbow patterns.

In contrast most boys booted footballs around the strip of tarmac down the L-shaped playground, picking out teams during every break. I knew I'd never be good at that. I'd always be chosen last, as I was later at secondary school. It felt segregated along gender lines, with me as the single anomaly: noticeable, but happy to be different then. Rather that than trying and failing to fit in.

For a few years at Stewart Headlam my first friend who was a boy was Peter Stiller. I kept that friendship running parallel to all my friendships with girls. Peter was the bold one, who used to run naked into the girls' changing room after PE. He'd pretend he was playing a guitar, plucking his willy and wailing high-pitched electric-guitar noises. The girls couldn't keep their eyes away, pulling towels around themselves, hugging each other and squealing with a mix of embarrassment and delight.

We heard about becoming blood brothers from Steve, a self-assured thirty-something worker in our summer playscheme, who was a semi-professional wrestler and sported the glamour of a broken nose and cauliflower ear. Steve told us he had a blood brother who was a Native American wrestler. He showed us Laughing Eagle's black-and-white photo, in a wrestler's crouching pose and clawing hands, wearing trunks and an Indian chief's feather headdress. He said they mixed their blood together in a secret ceremony, which meant their blood would run through each other's veins for the rest of their lives. We were impressed. Steve asked me to sit on his lap sometimes when we were travelling in the play-scheme minibus. Now and then his fingers casually strayed up the lower hem of my shorts during these rides, where he gently stroked the skin of my thigh for a minute. I felt mesmerised by his soft strumming and the fact that neither of us said a word about it to each other, or showed we were aware it was happening. I told no one, not even Peter, though we'd become so close we decided we wanted to be blood brothers like Steve and Laughing Eagle. One afternoon break in the playground we nibbled tiny strips of skin alongside our thumbnails. We managed to squeeze a reluctant drop of blood from each little cut and held our thumbs together for a minute until we thought our blood had mixed. Or did I try that with Douglas Howe and not Peter? My memory's playing games. I can't be sure.

Once Peter lent me a pair of Levi jeans, while he stripped down to shorts to play football during a break. When I pulled them up my legs I realised that I'd never worn such a heavy pair of trousers in my life. I remember their thick blue creases, the strange feeling of being inside someone else's clothes, as if the denim had weathered itself to the shape of his legs, and my skin experienced its difference.

At eleven years old I was chosen for grammar school and Peter went to another school. I don't know where. We lost touch, moved off into divergent lives. Where has his life taken him? Is he happily married now; what children; what job – where is he this minute? Along with all my other school friends from those years, we crossed each other's history and disappeared afterwards, like snowflakes melting on the tongue.

Eagle Business Park shows blocks of faceless buildings on my left. Their industry's dead on Bank Holiday Monday, while I drudge through my life as its only star – trying to stitch one rag against another to sew a man.

Parmiter's was a boys' school, so my friendships with girls ended when I moved there. I met Clifford on our first morning, and we soon teamed up with Ian, who we nicknamed Len because his surname was Lenoir. We became known as the poofs, the butt of what's now recognised as homophobic bullying. It was hard to believe our natural behaviour, and all we represented, was despised in this male world. In our first year during breaks the three of us enjoyed mucking around behind the fire escape near the toilets, a secluded cul-de-sac in the playground where we felt relatively cut off and safe. We improvised little comedies and playlets. Clifford had read about Marie Antoinette, so our comedies often involved imperious heroines and rides to the guillotine.

Sometimes we acted out a Beverley Sisters dance routine: singing their theme song 'Sisters' and trying to perfect our pointing and finger-clicking in unison. Looking back, it was clearly camp behaviour (although we couldn't have named it as such at the time). It must have threatened the other boys struggling to perfect their East End machismo.

We wreaked an occasional revenge. One lunchtime Clifford had brought a flask of tea to school. A short boy called Priestley bullied Len repeatedly, and began taunting him with the usual poof insults. Clifford suddenly chucked a cup of tea over Priestley to shut him up. I watched Priestley's stunned expression, while fawn-coloured liquid dripped from his fringe and nose. That triumph was dubbed 'Tea Over Priestley' between us. The phrase set off conspiratorial giggles whenever he strode past us down the corridor.

Of course, we weren't sporty. The whole school was divided into four 'houses': Lee, Renvoize, Carter and Mayhew – Victorian philanthropists who'd played some part in founding the school and whose hard work and sacrifice we should aim to copy, to be model citizens, upstanding grammar schoolboys. Clifford was in Mayhew, so he couldn't be in our football team. Len and I were both in Carter (it meant a yellow stripe across our school tie). We were usually last in line to be chosen by captains to be part of their teams on games afternoons. Len and I were always placed together as defenders, where we could do the least damage. It gave us a good excuse to stand chatting outside our penalty box, ignoring the goalie and all the shouts, tackles, fouls and shots further up the field. As soon as the ball was lobbed towards us, or an attacker from the other team tore towards our goalmouth, Len would hurtle down the pitch as far from the ball as possible, leaving me as the helpless defender, while the goalie yelled furious advice, which I always failed to follow. A goal was scored every time. Such absence of team spirit hardly improved our popularity with the sporty types, who saw it as more proof that we were poofs. If our team was made of boys on the way to becoming competitive men, we couldn't pretend to be loyal, swallowing masculinity's message, one of the lads.

Masculinity's medicine – a spoonful of salt – pinch your nose and swallow. These stories unravel another of my selves inside the same body. He answers to my name; he changed under my skin to carry me here.

After squares of fields on either side a helicopter hovers above, like a noisy dragonfly. A big dog, the shape of a shaggy black footstool, noses down the edge of the street. An anxious young woman in gold trainers is dragged by its lead. I'll never see them again.

I pass a cemetery with mottled crosses and stone angels in the older section. A woman in the newer plot tilts a metal watering can. Loving memory rows of fathers, aunts, wives and devoted grandads who fell asleep in Yaxley, accompanied by a line of trees and pot after pot of bouquets. There's another parade of red-brick houses after the BP garage: front gardens behind low walls, trim hedges and cars stuck in driveways.

Whatever people seeing me today might think of this trudging man, I couldn't own the words 'poof' and 'queer' as relating to me in those first few years at Parmiter's. They sounded like words said with such loathing I didn't think they could explain me, describe what was happening to me. As puberty progressed I began developing attractions towards other boys at school: adolescent crushes on gorgeous profiles, bodies, glimpses in a pour of faces between classes after the bell. I wrote a line of teenage poetry, apparently describing a lascivious woman: 'Sheep eyes moon after streamlined boys', but I secretly admitted the sheep eyes were mine.

When I was thirteen or fourteen a classmate called me a *fucking queer* with such venom I heard it inside. His words hit home. I finally made the connection I'd been resisting between queer and my hidden crushes on boys. It felt as if that classmate had smelt something offensive simmering through my pores. Those passions and smothered thrills when I watched the beautiful face of a boy who ignored me on the stairs or in a corridor had a name. Queer.

As soon as I got home I locked myself in the bathroom and cried for an hour or so. I not only admitted that 'queer' could describe me, but wanted to disown myself, tear it out of my skin, because I saw that having those feelings led to staying on the outside. Even then I knew I wanted to meet a girl, settle, raise a family, live happily ever after like the stories and films insisted a man and woman would. The idea of two men being happy together in the same way was unthinkable, invisible. I believed then a man and man together meant temporary crushes, unfulfilled passions, desires that aroused and scared me. They could only lead to unhappiness and exclusion, and I wanted to be happy, break out of these miserable fears. I wanted to belong. Like the play-scheme secret of Steve stroking my thigh, I didn't admit these experiences to Clifford at the time, though I viewed him as my best friend. They were too shameful, too dark, unnameable. They stayed trapped in my skull, behind my teeth.

A couple of years later I kissed a girl for the first time, or rather, she kissed me. One Friday night, outside the aptly named Approach Tavern opposite the school, while we stood under the moon as her boyfriend disappeared inside for drinks, she suddenly said, 'D'you want me to show you how to kiss?' The tantalising slip of her tongue entered my mouth like the subtlest goldfish. Its wet flavour felt spectacular, despite the betrayal of her boyfriend. I wanted more, and nabbed a few furtive kisses from her in the next few weeks, but nothing else happened or was likely to happen. I felt attracted to girls, yet saw them as a race apart, after all my friendships with girls had ended so abruptly a few years before when I changed schools. I didn't know how to find a girl, or how to handle one if I managed to meet another for more of those kisses, but knew I'd like to try.

Clifford and I never went out to meet girls. We stayed locked in our intense friendship: long chatty walks through Victoria Park; reading *The Waves* or poetry to each other; visiting bookshops, galleries and museums; writing stories and poems on my part; painting and drawing on his. Arty pursuits for two East End boys, with high-flown ideas. Looking back, I imagine Clifford was privately acknowledging his gayness over those years, so going to pubs or clubs to chat up girls was the last thing he wanted.

Moving to Sussex University seemed my first chance to meet women properly – as more than another species. I met Dee on that first night. I was drawn to be around her, with her invitations to all and sundry to come for coffee, her questions and opinions, her glamorous look. After a couple of months I fell so wholeheartedly in love that my attractions to men receded. They drifted far out to sea: distant blots, tiny smudges. She took over my focus and desires. Once when we were picking potatoes in Northamptonshire as poor students, she raised herself from bending towards the turned earth. I looked up from kneeling in a furrow and she was standing in the field above me against the afternoon sun. She hinged the land to the sky, became my horizon.

If I knock on one of these doors I'll find another life. An unknown face curdles in the window, the owners too scared to let a stranger cross their threshold, allow difference inside. Keep it out. Shut it away, but what if the difference is yourself?

Early in my years at university, when we were in our late teens, Clifford came out as gay. He must have built himself up to our talk in Victoria Park, when he told me by the lake. His gayness didn't help me confront my latent feelings, because Dee was all I needed at that time. He wanted, understandably, to meet gay men but felt too insecure with his anxieties to visit clubs or discos alone, so he asked me to accompany him for moral support.

During university term breaks I went with him to Bang in Charing Cross Road, while Dee returned to her family in Kettering. It was at the height of disco: a flamboyant liberating period before AIDS was even heard of, so afterwards it took on a rosy almost innocent glow. The first time we visited Bang we got the day wrong and went on a straight night: both of us in our different ways feeling outside the confident hetero-sexuality on display, but dancing for the hell of it.

On our second visit we found the gay night, looking down from the balcony onto a crowded country we never knew existed: packed and sweaty with men enjoying themselves and each other in flashing lights through darkness, pulsing music – 'You Make

Me Feel (Mighty Real)' – 'Instant Replay' – 'Heart of Glass'. I saw a young man with Botticelli curls walking alongside the dance floor naked, apart from a leather harness and straps that covered his modesty and little else. I watched a handsome man in a suit kiss a younger man in a tight, white T-shirt with such slow-burning intensity it was fascinating. At the same time, I'd fallen in love with Dee. I hovered on the sidelines, observing from the edge, there to support Clifford as he began cruising dimly lit walkways, hanging around the bar, meeting men, flirting and dancing. Sometimes I would dance, absorbed in an irresistible song and my body and the short-haired moustached men in check shirts writhing two inches near me. They felt exciting and slightly threatening, and I convinced myself I didn't want them to speak to me or come any closer.

After a few visits Clifford occasionally started exchanging phone numbers with men he fancied, though he always decided in those early hours to take the night bus home with me. One man he seemed to be sparking with dropped Clifford the second he understood he wouldn't get the one-night stand he expected. On the night bus he'd tell me how each evening had gone – how they chatted, what was said – and I'd encourage him to follow his feelings and be careful in the same words. Wanting to protect my best friend: have a good time and stay safe.

During that period I didn't associate the men on the dance floor or Clifford's explorations with me. My buried desires resurfaced a few years into the marriage, before the children, when I found myself attracted – despite myself – to a married friend of ours. Wanting to be in his company. Lingering on how his mouth shaped the words, how he tilted his head and blew smoke from his cigarette, how his T-shirt lifted slightly to reveal the base of his spine when he crouched. It felt like the familiar echo of another adolescent crush. Being in my mid-twenties I realised with regret I couldn't dismiss it so smoothly. This was more threatening. It signified something about me I could no longer ignore, and led to that confession to Dee in the hotel room. It was twisting my feelings. I remained committed to Dee and never acted on my attractions to our friend or any other man. But I acknowledge in this street, moving forward between houses, that those unexpressed desires began corroding my moods – leading to silences and shutting Dee out – contributing to the thwarted unhappy man I was in danger of becoming.

Sky above and tarmac under my boots. Who poured and rollered this tarmac to make this street, build these houses? When did the fields disappear? I could have dropped a trail of breadcrumbs from Epping Forest to bring me this far – drifting into each green thought – a word-nest where I might hide.

Two young men stroll towards me, one wearing a butterflies T-shirt and rolled-up linen trousers. The other has small wings tattooed above each ankle and cobwebs lattice his elbows. He's saying, 'A dishwasher and a fridge' cheerfully to his friend. While he's talking about a dishwasher and fridge, I'm thinking I wasn't an easy man to live with in the children's early years. My sexuality stayed hidden, effaced by fatherhood, and I gave few distress signals to anyone. This was my closet. I became increasingly prone to mood swings, silences, sudden angers, shutting off. Although some of these traits may have been the effects of Dee and me being unsuited, they must have grown because of my repression.

Does this tale falsify my other stories – peck the crumbs along the trail that led me here – or do my stories weave between each other, alternative versions questioning and answering the version before? I'm my own unreliable narrator. My sexuality was an element I brought into the marriage to unstitch a few seams, add doubt and insecurity for Dee. It was the last thing she needed, shackled to a husband she didn't ask for. If I hadn't sorted out my sexuality, why drag her – an innocent party – into the mess of myself?

Street lamps line the road and more cars are lodged in driveways. A cabbage white butterfly flits beside the brambles. So what do I do now? If the marriage is as wrecked as it appears, there should be no need for fidelity towards anyone except myself. The rules I accepted and lived by have unravelled, as we both step outside the sacred circle of our marriage. I'm poised on the brink of changing my life. I need to decide if I address this shunned aspect of myself or keep it in shadow. Adrienne Rich calls it 'the audacity of claiming a stigmatized desire'. If I give that desire expression I don't know what person it would make me become. I'll be risking marginalisation, isolation, disgust and self-disgust, alongside the terrifying possibility of rejection by my children, the ultimate punishment. I can pass as heterosexual. I passed for twenty years, even (or almost) to myself, locked the lid on inconvenient attractions I didn't want to bring to light. Do I continue passing, feigning, shutting up and shutting off? I can choose instead to open windows, discover how it feels to touch a man.

Kim Taplin calls the phrase *solvitur ambulando* 'an old Latin tag (which) means something like "you can sort it out by walking"'. I haven't solved this by walking, but I've started to give it the attention it deserves, while a couple of miles have moved under my boots. Perhaps I've been trying *solvitur ambulando* these past four days. Finding a knot I can't unpick I've taken to the roads in the body I inhabit, the legs that steady me. All I own, beside my name and the gathering years. The least I can do is attempt to honour my desires. Perhaps I'm also trying a white bastardised version of the Aboriginal ritual of Walkabout: walking away as a rite of passage into adulthood, returning to the self to resolve whatever's been left, giving way – as Clare did – to an instinct to leave and thereby (eventually) return.

A lorry shakes past, gusting grit in my face. I keep my head down and momentarily shut my eyes. On his third day a coach threw dirt in Clare's face: *The Coach did pass me as I sat under some trees by a high wall and the lumps lasshed in my face and wakened me up from a doze.* I've dozed through half my life: sleepwalking, letting someone else lead because it was convenient to assume she was stronger, like my mother, connected to life in a way I wasn't, so I might be safer in her hands. As if falling in love and marrying gave me permission to fall asleep, do what was expected, con myself and my wife, get through the years with as little disruption as possible.

Yesterday morning I remembered Dee led me blind through the black streets of Rome in the rain. The rain's cleared and it's no longer night. I can let go of her hand now, open my eyes to see where I am, keep walking.

Feathery trees and hedgerows line this road.

I pass the grounds of the London Brick Company. Old clay pits lie on my right, one filled with water like a blue-grey lake. A clay smell clogs my nostrils, perhaps from smoke wavering from four tall chimneys at the brick works. Rubbish clutters this lay-by: an old car battery; a baby-wipe container; Kentucky Fried Chicken boxes and a blue plastic bag. Dusty nettles and dandelions by my boots. If I don't focus on my feet, I end up swaying over the pavement. Stepping down a kerb is a split second of agony because of my blisters.

A dead pheasant in the gutter looks beautifully unscathed, with fiery colours and lolled head. Even his tail feathers shine, undamaged. This decimated wildlife I pass each day at the side of the roads. In an early letter to a newspaper editor – where Clare says *It would be the top of my ambition* if his *humble effort* was published – he signed himself *John Clare A Northamptonshire Pheasant*. He's a bird, with fiery head and autumn wings they failed to clip, flapping above the wood before they could shoot him.

A sign says 'Peterborough 3 Miles'. I notice the iron-toned tic-tac shape of a woodlouse walking by my boots and manage not to tread on it. In Clare's poem 'Insects' his voice is one of wonder for the range of creatures he observes. Everything in nature's worthy of praise:

> *Thou tiney loiterer on the barleys beard*
> *And happy unit of a numerous herd*
> . . .
> *How merrily they creep and run and flye*
> *No kin they bear to labours drudgery*

Checking the map, I realise that as Tony was driving to Sleaford he could have dropped me off near Northborough, my destination. I might have saved myself the last hard slog. Quite a temptation, if I'd thought about it earlier, but I kid myself there's honour in perseverance. This part of the A15 is a long dull stretch, not as killing as the A1, but pretty characterless all the same.

Snippets of an old song we used to sing at my mother's Boxing Day parties float into my head. I hear my happy aunts and their husbands or boyfriends singing as the night wore on, when they'd had too much to drink. I sing into my Dictaphone, 'Strolling, just strolling,' about not envying the rich, and then I forget the words until the phrase about Shanks's pony. When I forget words like this I think about my grandmother's dementia, my mother's Alzheimer's, and reading in a paper recently that there may be as much as a 30 per cent chance of Alzheimer's being passed on. That figure went through me like a bullet with my name on it, as if the disease might already be hibernating inside me with teeth and claws. Let it sleep for twenty more years until I finish parenting my children, as if I could have any say in the matter. As if my mother could choose what's happening to her today, when she fights her Alzheimer's with whatever weapons come to hand. I shore up my defences with memories of her singing with sisters and friends. They give me a sense of self, and a sense of her self, the woman she was before her illness. Mythic stories I tell to convince me I own a past. Have I chosen which to remember, which to forget?

I catch my mother singing down the years – 'Call round any old time,' that lovely music-hall song about making yourself at home. Her funny, confident cousin Anna joins in with a rich singing voice after the first line. They sway together with drinks in their hands, my aunt flashy with

gold earrings, necklaces, bracelets and rings, balancing a fag
between her fingers.

We're in the crowded front room of our Whitechapel flat,
which we emptied of its three-piece suite late every Boxing Day
afternoon for about half-a-dozen years. My mother would grow
short-tempered after dinner, moaning that my brother Stephen
and I weren't pulling our weight shifting furniture, while she
buttered ham sandwiches, forked gherkins and pickled onions
into segmented stainless steel dishes. As soon as the guests start
arriving my mother's irritation flies out the window. Everything's
always ready on time, despite or because of her pre-party nags.
She can boogie with the best of them, and soon lets the party
spirit take over. Not a great drinker, her favourite's Martini
Rosso, after a few snowballs (each with its glacé cherry skewered
on a cocktail stick). It feels as if every local family member turns
up in glad rags, along with Clifford and his mother Peggy, who
both view Christmas as an ordeal to get through with as little
boredom and discomfort as possible.

My teenage cousins and I groan when the older generation
insists on Max Bygraves records late at night, once they've had
enough of dancing to the Beatles, Boney M. and Motown, 'My
Boy Lollipop' and 'I Will Survive'. At the start of punk I play
them the opening of Ian Dury's 'Plaistow Patricia' as loudly
as I can, with its five luscious swear words, for the satisfaction
of hearing my aunts tut and squeal to each other about his
language. It ain't called for. They feel more at home with
Singalongamax.

I need a break in the next few days, not only from walking
but from hearing and seeing another car. Their percussion

jangles my ears. I'm hooted by a young man in a van and think, *Do I know him?* At least he waved instead of waggling a wanker sign.

There's a repeated song from a bird I can't see or name, as if it's snipping the day neatly with one-two-one-two notes. A crisp packet like a yellow leaf is flipped over by gusts from passing cars. Traffic's building up: couples and families steering to Bank Holiday outings. White capitals painted on bricks under this bridge read SOCIAL WORKERS ARE SCUM. Another satisfied customer. I moved into social work around the start of my marriage because of a wish to 'help people', as I said in my interview. I think it was probably an instinct to repair, after such a broken childhood, to mend and make things better for the children I worked with, until it became too draining and I had to protect myself before my own children were born. After five years with children's services I shifted to working with adults with disabilities and older people with dementia, though my need to solve and mend was unchanged. It would help if I could solve myself.

I pass the parish boundary of Woodstone and Fletton on an old metal milestone. It was around this stretch, after he was told by two young women this road led to Peterborough, that Clare said, *as soon as ever I was on it I felt myself in homes way and went on rather more cheerfull though I forced to rest oftener then usual.* If Clare felt in home's way it's another street I've never walked down: here-and-gone stranger, trusting four days might bring me home. A young mum in orange with sunglasses wheels a fretful baby. On the right several piles of bricks mount like pyramids twice my height. A factory was probably pulled down, like the houses demolished a few weeks ago to make way for the M11 link road. I drove past the last remaining house in a street near Wanstead. A red flag swayed limply from a window above a painted wall saying HOMES NOT ROADS. The next time I drove there, on the way to visit my mother, the house had disappeared, as if it had never been built, as if the families who lived inside had evaporated like ghosts married to smoke. A long green fence topped with scrolls of barbed wire stood in its place.

A milestone says:

TO LONDON 80
PETERBOROUGH 1
STILTON 5

It looks like a football score. I stagger across the pavement again. Although the act of walking remains unconscious, automatic, I should respect each working bone in my legs, ankles and feet to conquer this exhaustion. There's no solution but walking to cover my days.

I phoned Dee. It was hard work even opening and closing the phone-box door, which proves how knackered I am. She agreed to pick me up about 7 p.m. from Northborough. As it's nearly noon I've got seven hours to reach there, allowing for breaks. She laughed and felt I'd cheated by accepting Tony's lift. I feel stupidly aggrieved afterwards, wanting to justify myself: 'If Clare had been offered a cart-ride by those neighbours he'd have grabbed it.' Another whiney squabble in my head.

In London Road, approaching Peterborough, Edwardian houses give way to bay-fronted houses. Magnolias in front gardens raise their petals like rosé wine. On the other side of the road a cool young man with headphones is followed by a pale young woman in glasses doing her best to disguise a limp. He ignores her while she walks meekly behind, as though she feels apologetic to share his pavement. Could it be another example of love, at least on her part, love in the face of his indifference?

Rap pumps its sluggish pulse from a window somewhere. Four black boys in baseball caps and trainers turn down Park Street, laughing. After a big sign that says ADVERTISE HERE I cross the railway bridge and pass a KFC opposite Kwik Fit. A smell of fried chicken wafts across me.

Under the scent of pink and white cherry blossom I enter the city with cars as accompaniment. Pavements are crowding with shoppers. Laddish lads and girly girls eye each other in segregated groups. I can hardly hobble over the zebra crossing fast enough for the traffic revving either side, ready to tear me apart for wasting a second. I hear Peterborough Cathedral's bells ahead, striking twelve. Women wearing the hijab mix with a baby wailing, while a soot-handed young man juggles flames. Shoppers with buggies stare at him, bored or curious in case he burns himself. I sense I'm walking in slow motion, compared with everyone else.

Willows line the river by a host of swans and a foamy pint-filled Easter Beer Festival hoarding. Crossing the bridge, I'd love to dip my feet in cool water, watch them hiss like red-hot horseshoes in a blacksmith's bucket. A shaven-headed man in a T-shirt has ENGLAND printed across his back, a sleeve of tattooed roses spiking his arm. A boy about three years old, dressed in combat trousers with 'Small But Dangerous' written across his T-shirt, shoots me with his toy Kalashnikov. To make him laugh I pretend to die standing up, expending as little energy as possible in the process. He scowls at me, not amused. He looks a few months older than my daughter Amy. I want to squeeze her tightly in my arms.

After four days of relatively empty roads, it's disorientating to be alone between couples and families, among the glass and rigid angles of plush new buildings. I poke a salty finger in the wound. Not living with my children will be the highest cost of leaving my marriage. Separation's a continuous ache, as if they've disappeared from my arms, being pressed against my ribs. In *Intimacy*, Hanif Kureishi asks: 'Where have all the fathers gone? . . . Do they think about their children? What better things do they have to do? . . . Where are the fathers hiding and what are they doing?' I won't hide from my children, yet removing myself from their daily lives could be experienced by them as hiding: separating myself, like the yolk from the white. I want to be with them, but don't want to crack open, as though the punishment for leaving might be letting go of their hands, when they cross a road or stroll under trees to school.

During Isaac and Joe's early years Dee and I had part-time jobs, tried to share their care as much as we could. My attempts were clumsy and faltering, often ending up as Dee's 'helper', a role that probably became a burden to her, leading to twice as much work. In sharing our roles, I took Isaac and Joe to various Mums and Toddlers groups around Market Harborough. It helped them mix with kids their age while I sat nearby; but if one of its aims was to reduce my isolation as a parent of toddlers, it failed. I was virtually always the only father in the group. Mothers politely avoided me, talking and laughing in their own clusters. I was an intruder into what must have felt like a safe space for many of them. Perhaps they were wary I'd chat them up or bore them with my knowledge of engine capacity and cricket scores. Some afternoons I left without having spoken to an adult, feeling more cut off than before. In Bowden Bouncers, a friendlier group in a nearby village, I came in handy to dress up as Father Christmas and give out presents, though Joe didn't realise it was me hiding behind the red hood and tickly white beard, putting on a fake fat 'Ho Ho Ho'. I eventually managed to meet a local father there. Anthony was another social worker who spent half his week at home with his kids. He helped me feel less like a freakish pioneer.

Having had two absent fathers, I believed in what Adrienne Rich called the 'work of love', believed her when she wrote: 'In learning to give care to children, men would have to cease being children; the privileges of fatherhood could not be toyed with, as they are now, without an equal share in the full experience of nurture.' Perhaps I'm toying with its privileges, assuming I can drop fatherhood because I've had enough. If leaving my wife stops me living with my kids, where's my attempt to take 'an equal share in the full experience of nurture'? Dee and I are choosing to change our lives, but the children are victims of our decisions, on the receiving end. Should I battle for an imaginary 'right' to have them half-time, part of each week, as if they're possessions whose days and nights can be divided like blocks of cheese? I might find a way to love them with the same gesture as letting go: give up an outmoded sense of rights or possession, the old paternal power.

A woman near my shoulder tells her child, 'We don't spit at people, do we?' Faces pass – a blur of colours, parade of expressions, ages, clothes and voices. I'm excluded, disconnected, hoping to love without needing – cat on a lap, flexing claws into skin, staking my claim. My desperate clingy fear that they'll disappear.

If I stand still my children fly from me like arrows. I might learn hard and early to rejoice in their flight. Moving my unhappiness outside their orbit helps them avoid its corrosion; but the prospect of not living with them feels like pieces of me torn up inside. Like the thought of never seeing Clifford again, it's unbearable and I must find a way to bear it, except there's no chance of another hour with him. Mine's a story of survival, not death. The children continue their three lives apart from me. I'll let go of their hands but whisper their names while they're piling sand in the orange sandpit, chalking circles on the patio, pushing their green wheelbarrow under the apple tree. They're busy, absorbed. I won't expect them to pause when I kiss their foreheads.

I feel sorry for Clare not wanting to make a fool of himself in front of the crowds here. After his meal from the five pence thrown by his neighbours *at a small public house near the bridge . . . I started quite refreshed only my feet was more crippled then ever and I could scarcely make a walk of it over the stones and being half ashamed to sit down in the street I forced to keep on the move and got through Peterborough better than I expected.* Through his exhaustion and mental illness he's aware that his appearance – or any unusual behaviour on his part – might mark him out. Everyone would gawp. He'd be embarrassed, want to hide. In Clare's dream his Guardian spirit showed him *an immense crowd all around me . . . – you are the only one of the crowd now she said*. It's a writer's ambition to stand above the crowd, *the only one*. He wanted, impossibly, to be both: the only one and to blend into a Peterborough crowd, belong if he could. Writing's a means of Clare acknowledging his difference: an observer making notes of other villagers, animals and birds, fields and woods he knew, his fascination with women; yet proving by his poems that the village and fields deserve to be recorded.

It's amazing to think I'll reach Northborough in a few hours: my aim, my bullseye. Another night sleeping rough would have been a strain. Near Cathedral Square a haggard young man sits cross-legged outside a NatWest bank, a patient dog curled beside him and a cap holding a few coins before him. He leans against his sleeping bag and a bulging bag of clothes, a blanket round his shoulders. He's reading a paperback with weary eyes. The wolf's come to his door, blown his house down. I want a roof for him, think again of homelessness as my life, night after night on pavements, the comfortless stones, hiding from rain. The battle of the days and how do I climb out of it? Hunger comes, but I step away easily from the young man, from New Look and Waterstones, into a loud empty bistro with dark panelled wood, where I order French onion soup because there's money in my pocket: the callousness of privilege, shutting off, pulling up my drawbridge again. I can forget the man with his sleeping bag and skinny dog, and smell my soup already: loops of onion curling above brown bubbles; tiny rafts of croutons bobbing in the steam. Like Clare in Peterborough, I worry how my feet will recover after this rest. I daren't pull off these boots, for fear they won't fit on again.

Where's the wolf at my door, blowing down my heart? I'm a man with an address, hungry for soup.

12.30 p.m. My bowl's clean and I'm ready to continue. The crowds are thinning further from the centre. As numbers on the pavement reduce, I might be able to count the people I meet. A line of taxis queues hopefully outside Tesco.

Through glass I see couples sitting in estate agents, talking about buying new homes. I'm walking towards Millfield, with Edwardian bay-fronted houses on my right facing terraced houses on my left. Across from a shop called Secondhand City, below a satellite dish, two shaven-headed men in tracksuits stand smoking and chatting. One taps on a window, asking to be let in. A neatly dressed black teenager with headphones, narrow jeans and gleaming white trainers passes me, staring purposefully ahead. He has somewhere to go. An elderly couple is entering Burghley Square Club before the roundabout, its Victorian red-brick gables and '1882' in stone above its door. He wears a smart blue blazer with a British Legion badge and gold buttons; she a salmon-pink jacket, with dyed hairdo and long sparkly earrings. He links his arm through hers as they leave the taxi.

I take my time through suburbs. A stubble-chinned man with a woollen hat pulled down over his ears steers an empty shopping trolley past me, shouting at the trolley, 'Do as I say! Do as I say!' People avoid meeting his eyes, like I do. Sparrows fuss in gutters, building their nests. Delicate trees are circled by cages. Bay-window terraces display dates and names: 'Hampstead House'; 'Oak Villa (1901)'.

Four Asian girls in front of me wear headscarves; two of them (presumably sisters) have matching lace flowers curling down their backs. One of the taller girls is obviously the leader. As they cross the road she says, 'Up two three four up two three four' while the others march obediently behind. She lines them up on the pavement and begins to stride ahead, playing a game of grandmother's footsteps. When she spins to face them they freeze.

A memory comes from nowhere. Does a glint of sunlight bring it? On a sunny afternoon a few weeks before Clifford died, I entered his hospital room for one of my visits, and found him and Andrew lying on the narrow hospital bed. I think Andrew was resting his head on Clifford's bony chest. I somehow see it happening in a calm, quiet light. It was the only time they could grab as a couple: a snatched opportunity in this place without privacy, and I interrupted it, blundered in. I apologised, but should have left the room, allowed them more time together. Andrew got up and their moment was broken. I can't re-enact that memory and get it right. I remember Andrew's unassuming heroism. He'd been diagnosed with HIV at the same time as Clifford, but devoted his energies to caring for him, sorting out his array of tablets, standing up for his rights, making things easier in those tough last months. I should have backed off, given them the hours they didn't have. I suddenly, stupidly, want them both to forgive me.

The roundabout sign doesn't correspond with the map. It says New England straight ahead, so I aim for that. I'm on the right track, since my compass points north.

An empty playground in a virtually empty park has stick figures chalked on tarmac. One pair looks like stick children fighting. A cyclist swerves near. Names are sprayed on the wall, one saying TOME, another MUNCH FRONTLINE RULES. A train shudders past. A flock of pigeons lilts on the air, a lifting falling motion, a few white under-wings catching this afternoon's light.

I ask a woman with a walking stick, to make sure of my direction. She doesn't know. This stage of the journey was familiar to Clare: he wouldn't need to ask. When he walked through this area towards Werrington, he presumably passed fields or a few scattered villages. It's now a spreading suburb of Peterborough, like a chain of old villages taken over by sprawl.

Walkways try to ensure I only walk through designated areas. Sprayed names under a subway tell me

RUSH
SPEED
ANTONY

live here in New England, staking their claim to stick children fighting, front lines ruling, pigeons circling and subways keeping me in my place. Daisies and dandelions sprinkle the A15's verges. I've almost forgotten the reason for doing this. The cumulative effect of my journey means I'm covering less ground now, but I continue to walk out of habit. Inch ahead – inch ahead. It's how I waste my days.

I'm near Walton, slogging along a pedestrian flyover to cross the busy roundabout beside a spate of parked Parcel Force lorries. It feels like a spaghetti junction walkway: an elaborate ring road for pedestrians suspended above the traffic. Fumes in my lungs, looking across the backsides of terraced houses, Tyre and Service Centre, Budget Rent-a-Car, Kwik Fit Motorist Centre with old exhausts piled in the corner, dual carriageways and hundreds of cars below. I think England's become a series of link roads, bypasses and motorways, places for drivers to live. There's no stopping this foggy river jostling bumper to bumper round the nation, Clare's warnings a voice of sanity rather than madness, as though roads have become our new enclosures. Clare becomes someone after whom a Peterborough car park's been named, his portrait by the ticket machine appropriately green, like the 'bright, grass-coloured coat' he wore for trips to London.

Clare was aware that his belief about respecting nature was likely to be dismissed as a fool's vision. In 1821 he wrote to his publisher Taylor: *my two favourite Elm trees at the back of the hut are condemned to dye . . . the savage who owns them thinks they have done their best & now wants to make use of the benefits he can get from selling them – O was this country Egypt & was I but a caliph the owner should loose his ears for his arragant presumption & the first wretch that buried his axe in their roots shoud hang on their branches as a terror to the rest – I have been several mornings to bid them farewell – had I £100 to spare I woud buy their reprieves – but they must dye – yet this mourning over trees is all foolishness they feel no pains they are but wood cut up or not – a second thought tells me I am a fool   was People all to feel & think as I do the world coud not be a carried on – a green woud not be ploughd a tree or bush woud not be cut for firing or furniture & every thing they found when boys would remain in that state till they dyd – this is my indisposition & you will laugh at it* – It's a measure of the man how, in this letter, his passion to honour and preserve is deflated by his jibe about the nostalgic element of such instincts.

Six stanzas into his early poem 'The Lamentations of Round-Oak Waters' Clare takes the radical step of letting the stream's words take over the remainder of the poem's twenty stanzas, as though the poet is left speechless, or stands respectfully aside to let the stream take centre stage, being more important than he is:

> *The bawks and Eddings are no more*
> > *The pastures too are gone*
> *The greens the Meadows and the moors*
> > *Are all cut up and done*
> *There's scarce a greensward spot remains*
> > *And scarce a single tree*
> *All naked are thy native plains*
> > *And yet they're dear to thee*
>
> *But O! my brook my injur'd brook*
> > *'Tis that I most deplore*
> *To think how once it us'd to look*
> > *How it must look no more*

Several years later Clare went further with his innovation by allowing a local stone quarry to speak for itself throughout the poem, as if we're hearing the quarry's voice, in 'The Lament of Swordy Well':

The bees fly round in feeble rings
And find no blossom by,
Then thrum their almost-weary wings
Upon the moss and die.
Rabbits that find my hills turned o'er
Forsake my poor abode –
They dread a workhouse like the poor
And nibble on the road

. . .

On pity's back I needn't jump,
My looks speak loud alone –
My only tree they've left a stump
And nought remains my own.

We're only just catching up with Clare's vision. The numbers of butterflies, bees and crickets, otters, hedgehogs and water voles, nightingales, lapwings, yellowhammers, cuckoos and skylarks are dropping by the year. I think of Reclaim the Streets marches and festivals where dancing along a road, sitting on tarmac, can stop cars being king for an afternoon. Compared with Clare I've spoken to fewer people on my journey, and even those few walkers have been reluctant to talk. The only people I've really talked to in four days are the two men who opened their doors, welcomed me into their space, let me sit beside them in cars.

Under a tunnel I read MELVYN LOVES ANGELA, though I don't read what Angela thinks of Melvyn. As usual Currys and Do It All edge the city in wide grey warehouses. If Clare walked back a hundred and fifty years later and stared across this landscape he'd feel any reverence for nature had been ignored. He'd feel *homeless at home* again, lost among grey warehouses, a green man out of place.

The road hives off pedestrians into a select estate of bungalows. There's no choice in the matter, as if here's where we all end up. The effect is chilling. Detached bungalow follows detached bungalow, as if pensioners disappear inside to age discreetly when they retire. No one's out when I plod down the street beside a few cars parked outside deserted bungalows. Nature's maintained within tidy limits. Each garden sprouts identical tulips, primulas and clipped rosebushes where thorns freeze.

Before I reach Werrington village two teenage girls whistle at a young man ahead, his long dark hair like a shawl stroking the back of his leather jacket. He glances over his shoulder, more offended than flattered. They giggle together.

There's a stream or brook, recent housing here, a second-hand car dealer and a Jet garage. I look along Church Street and discover the older part of the village, its pretty church and green accompanied by a horse chestnut, whiskery pine and dwindling daffodils. The lawn's enclosed by low wooden posts and looping chains. Birdsong reasserts itself. Telegraph wires like spokes of a wheel cross to the street's roofs. I rest on one of three black-metal benches, this one dedicated to a man who 'loved Werrington'. The Blue Bell pub sign squeaks in the wind, a long white-painted building that would have welcomed customers in 1841. Its blackboard by the front door states

MONTHLY MADNESS –
3 COURSE MEAL
£5

It's 2.30 p.m. Another two hours should see me safely into Northborough.

Here at Werrington Clare was met in a cart by his wife, Patty, and a villager and (presumably) one of his youngest sons. It's likely his Helpston neighbours got word to Patty that her husband was walking home, so she set out to find him. Clare wrote: *a cart met me with a man and woman and a boy in it   when nearing me the woman jumped out and caught fast hold of my hands and wished me to get into the cart but I refused and thought her either drunk or mad but when I was told it was my second wife Patty I got in.*

This captures his disassociation from the familiar. His wife and son have become merely a *woman and a boy*, without identity or any significance. He needed to be home and they were distractions, blocks in his path. The boy was probably Clare's youngest son, Charles, who was eight at the time Clare was found. Charles was four when his father disappeared into High Beach, so he may have been more of a stranger to Charles by then. This dishevelled frightening man causing his mother to jump from the cart and plead, probably calling John again and again to bring him back. How was Patty feeling? Her fight of emotions: relief to find him safe; clasping his familiar hands after four years' separation; anxiety at his condition; even hurt that he fails to recognise her. Their neighbour was possibly still a little wary of John: you don't know what madness does to a man; but he wants to carry him home safe to his family, help Patty out, a good loyal wife with seven mouths to feed and a harvest of trouble.

I imagine this scene from a villager's viewpoint, through the eyes of a man who loved Werrington, lived here all his life, and happened to be strolling past four strangers and a horse and cart one July afternoon. Shouts and drama for a few minutes disturbing the uneventful street. The woman pleading; a bewildered boy; the state of that man – repeated coaxing, like he's a beast to prod to market, until the shaggy oaf calms down enough to climb into the cart. Hoof-clops take them God knows where, for whatever reason, never to be seen again.

At Werrington one car has smashed into another near the mini-roundabout. No one's injured, but two glum drivers stand beside dented cars. A man offers to photograph it for them. A young man steps out of his parked car with his pregnant partner. A rough-looking man, he holds out his hand and she places hers immediately into his. It's a gesture of tenderness.

Passing the church I read a nearby lichen-dotted gravestone:

In Loving Memory of Susannah
Beloved Daughter of Samuel and Charlotte Green
Who died at Belgravia, London
January 10th 1897 aged 32 years

It wasn't only Clare who managed to reach London from these parts. Her parents were sufficiently impressed by the move to inscribe it on her gravestone, returning her home to rest, the flare of Belgravia like an exotic country mixing with her name. What happened in Susannah Green's life? How did she reach Belgravia and die so young?

Clifford's death at thirty-four – a hundred miles from his birthplace – hits me again. When he was talking in hospital about the changes in his body made by illness he got upset and said, 'I can't cry.' I said it was OK to cry if he needed to, and he explained, 'No I really can't. Some medication they've put me on dries up my tear ducts, so even if I want to cry I can't.' Wanting him to stay, but not wanting him to suffer. A few days before he died his doctor friend said to me, 'You know he's dying, don't you?' a little incredulously, as if he'd sussed what a slow learner I was. I thought his death was impossible, believing this was another bad phase we'd help him through. His illness was an awful trial his body had to endure for over a year, with no eventual outcome but his death. Death was all his suffering led to, as if it had no purpose but to hurt him.

One evening last week, as part of my rehearsal for this journey, I walked in my new boots through oil-seed rape fields, over a rickety bridge, to a corner of the wood near Houghton on the Hill. Pausing to stare across hills among birdsong, I admitted I'll die one day. I'm finite, temporary. Although it came too early for Clifford and Susannah, it's the way of things: my surprised recognition that death includes even me. Did you think you'd come through this fire unscathed? At that moment I noticed the burnt-red body and snow-tipped tail of a fox, slipping into the woods thirty yards away. I felt as much part of the fields as that fox and the arriving moon.

Now Clare has left me to it, carried away to Northborough, this last leg of the journey's my late gift to him, for a walk he never finished.

Apart from brief rests, I've been walking for virtually seven hours since I was dropped off by Tony, plus a couple of hours before then. A total of nine hours walking. I feel dazed, punch-drunk, pressing my palm gently against any wall I pass sometimes, in an effort to keep steady.

Light rain looks like it might set in for an hour or so this afternoon, though the clouds know better than me. I'm buttoned against it. Head down, trying to dodge the pattering, I stare at the path under my feet, an endless track. The rain contributes to my sense of slog. Thoughts flat and dead now – the air's gone out of them. I'm persevering, reliant on a will to persist. If I don't keep my skin together I might stumble over this path again, sit down and never stand up.

A diamond of spit marks the pavement, to be washed by the finest rain.

If Patty hadn't rescued Clare a few miles back, would he have stopped at Glinton to begin searching for Mary? He might have found her old house occupied by someone else, or expected to see her turning a corner to meet him again on one of their lovers' walks; as though the intervening years – and even her death – could be wished away if he wanted their reunion badly enough.

We don't know what Mary thought of him. In contrast to Clare's river of words about his feelings for her, Mary remains silent on the subject. Not even a puddle. No letters. No memoir. No reported speech. We can read whatever we choose into her silence: reciprocated love – embarrassment – admiration – boredom – indifference. We have no idea if she read any of his love poems, or what she might have thought of them. No idea if she envied Patty, or felt relieved to have this unstable man taken off her hands. Traditional male love poetry usually assumes silence on behalf of the beloved. Their role is to be beautiful, often unattainable, without words to contradict the poet's view of the relationship. On the manuscript of his poem 'The Flitting' Clare doodled the head and shoulders of a woman on a pedestal. Sometimes the love-object's placed so high the poet can't hear if she answers back.

Rain's crackling on my hood. I reach a slight incline extending to low fields, with dark cubes of intermittent farm buildings, a few spindly poplars and miles of sky. This is my side of the story.

Did Clare assume (in Carolyn G. Heilbrun's terms) 'he had a right to the life of (Mary) as an artistic property'? Had he 'usurped her narrative' for his own ends, describing her solely as his first and lost love? As though her autonomous life outside the enclosure of his poetry is of no consequence, as though that's all she could be, her only worthwhile identity. What was her life without him? She never married, a relatively unusual choice for 'the daughter of a prosperous farmer', but that may have nothing to do with Clare. The important aspects of her life remain an enigma, as unknown as her thoughts about him. Unlike Susannah Green in Werrington churchyard, Mary stayed put in her village, until her accidental death in 1838 aged forty-one. The summary of the inquest describes Mary as 'infirm of body' at the time of her accident, when she was alone in the brewhouse standing by the fire, so that she 'accidentally, casually and by misfortune' caught fire at noon, 'languishing' for six hours before she died. Her agony can only be imagined, and her infirmity or disability isn't known. Did it affect her decision not to marry or move from

Glinton? For how many years was her life hampered or restricted by her health condition? What limits did it place on her days?

Mary won't answer from Clare's margins. She's moved into her own inviolable sphere. She remains unresolved as a figure in his life. Like Dee, my own first love, she won't answer the questions I never thought to ask. How did she view the directions her life took? What choices did she feel entitled or constrained to make?

The rain's more intermittent, gradually easing off, leaving me this solitary speck drying out under an enormous sky. When the traffic pauses for a moment my boots reclaim their stubborn song. I'm not a tortoise any more. I'm a snail with a three-storey house on my back, tired in body and soul. This level of exhaustion blends the two together, battling the junk in my head. My feet feel bandaged and aching, as though mummified. My right heel twinges. I imagine sliding into a bath tonight. Soap and water's glory for my toes, to soak four days' dirt from my skin.

A milestone says '1929 – CITY OF PETERBOROUGH PRDC': fat lot of use for a milestone! I approach Glinton roundabout, ignore the driver's left sign for Northborough because these ring roads meant nothing to Clare. It tingles with a gleam of relief that I've nearly finished: closer to my target, love's destination. If I can whistle like the dreariest arrow over a couple of slow-motion miles I'll never have to touch this trek again.

St Benedict's spire towers before me, with two shuttered windows and a golden cockerel at the dizzying top. It comforted

Clare when he saw it and thought of Mary, because they attended school here together. Somewhere in the stone door frame 'JC 1808 MARY' is chiselled by his adolescent hand, his first stab at immortality, adding Mary to his name, hoping to entwine them in stone. I'm too weary to find it, but it comforts me to know I'm almost there. I want something to hug, so hug my bag. I must look pathetic to people passing in warm dry cars, talking to myself. When a red Fiesta swishes past I imagine it's Dee with the kids to meet me.

Ivy-draped walls surround the church, leaning gravestones stuck like large grey playing cards in the grass among yews and holly. A blackbird flits from branch to branch. The church strikes four bells. Mary's buried in the churchyard, but I won't pursue her. Let her sleep untroubled, her name obscured, hugging every secret to herself, elusive from me and Clare, hidden in long grass.

A sign near the footpath says

> Cycling Motorcycling and the Riding
> of Horses is Prohibited on this Public
> Footpath
> By Order of the Glinton Parish Council

Underneath someone has written 'BALLS'.

I nearly topple over, grab an elderberry bush to regain my balance. This last lap is drudgery, nagging my knees to drag one foot after the other. My nag's a workhorse fit for the knacker's yard, heart a braying donkey wanting home.

According to the map, Northborough's just over a mile away, a yellow relatively straight heart-line on a palm. Although Clare's still called a Northamptonshire poet, this landscape's nothing like the Northamptonshire I know, from the three parts of the county where I've lived over sixteen years. It's more like fenland, unfamiliar and slightly alien. I'm pinned between level ploughed fields. Sky's the abiding presence, shifting various moods of pewter and blue, continuous as a sea above me, entertaining my forehead with another sprinkle of rain.

I'm a frazzled machine. Sky's as indifferent as sea.

I pass the Bluebell pub, a fifties version in renovated stone, and turn left down the North Fen Road by the old village pump. A sign warns that the water's unfit for human consumption.

After houses behind hedges and low walls, and fawn-bricked bungalows with tulips, lilacs and grape hyacinths, the scene spreads into conifers and oil-seed rape fields. This lane's as lovely as I imagined it might be. Banked grasses. A dunnock signs the air with its song. A pheasant rasp lifts once from the hedge and a kestrel alights into the top of a tree, where it waits. If Patty hadn't found him, this is the path Clare would have taken to end his journey from Essex, because it's the direct route to Northborough – if Clare decided to return there, rather than linger in Glinton for a glimpse of Mary, or veer off to Helpston's magnet. When the family moved to Northborough, six years before his removal to High Beach, it brought Clare closer to Glinton. Mary's proximity becomes erotic and haunting, living proof of her closeness and elusiveness. As one of his 'Child Harold' ballads says:

The cloud that passes where she dwells
In less than half an hour
Darkens around these orchard dells
Or melts a sudden shower

The wind that leaves the sunny south
And fans the orchard tree
Might steal the kisses from her mouth
And waft her voice to me

Whether or not Clare met Mary again between Northborough and Glinton, it's clear from his Northborough and High Beach poems that he walked these lanes hoping to meet her, reminiscing. The love object lives on inside the lover. Whether the woman who lit such feelings is alive or dead, her use as adored one continues, an excuse – or inspiration – for poetry.

I've lost any sense of what Dee's thinking, but why did I assume I had the first idea when we were married? Perhaps everyone's a potential teacher. My three parents and three children, Dee and Clifford brush or bruise against me. Beckett called them 'all my little company': these people I've carried on my back over four days, telling their tales or mine. I choose one, Dee another and we move away, become more distant. Has the dialogue ended – is there silence from either party as our paths diverge?

Beside a tree blasted by lightning (greyed trunk, ungainly branches, singed to the root) a straight path unspools itself. I'll follow it. There's no lark ascending this early in the season, but despite horse dung spattered in front of my boots it's the quiet finale I need: a vacant sky, and on my left – my wedding ring hand with the ring gone – red and white DANGER DEEP WATER KEEP OUT signs.

Traffic hums in the distance. Far away on the left, like toy cars skating over a yellow band, must be the A15. I inhale a stink of oil-seed rape. Driving to work a week ago I heard a woman on the radio speaking Julian of Norwich's words out of the blue, and they helped: 'then our Lord opened my spiritual eyes and showed me my soul in the middle of my heart . . . it seemed to me to be a glorious city . . . And these words "You shall not be overcome" were said very loudly and clearly . . . He did not say, "You shall not be tormented, you shall not be troubled, you shall not be grieved", but he said, "You shall not be overcome."'

I haven't met God on this walk, but might have met my soul in the middle of my heart, like coming back to someone who's always been there, recognising him at last as myself. My glorious city's patched from a ragbag of experience. I might as well be proud of this promise to keep walking.

A far crow lets itself sail and dip, black feathers appearing to flirt with breezes, as though it enjoys its wings, gradually becoming a tick of ash, diminishing into cloud.

This hour's peaceful at the end of frantic activity. There's no need to hurry any more. No one's frowning over my shoulder to judge or tap their watch. Sprigs of whitethorn poke between blackberry hedges. Rain patters, while wind shuffles a line of poplars and the bushes nearby. This landscape's crossed by straight dykes. A sludgy ditch surrounds the oil-seed rape. A mallard flies hectically yards away. Clare describes it as: *The wild duck startles like a sudden thought.*

I reach the lichen-spotted bridge where Clare walked sometimes, two lines of stones across a muscling stream, which Edward Storey says of Clare and Mary 'could well have been their trysting place', if they'd been reunited after his Northborough move. We'll never know, so I throw the thought away. Four brown horses, one with a blue coat, crop grass by the dyke, opposite another field of ploughed soil, seeds and stones, with sticks and little white pennants. The possibility of green England recovers itself in my eyes and ears, as though it's been effaced by towns and traffic but is always waiting to be noticed again. An unobtrusive backbone linking Epping Forest to here. Is there a swan in that far field, a little blaze of snow?

A man and woman saunter past, easy in each other's company. They're followed by an overweight dachshund. The man glances behind him and says, 'Come on, Elvis.' It's not a swan – I'm too romantic – it's a stunted white post.

I notice the start of Northborough roofs ahead. Clare's move from his birthplace to Northborough – only four miles away – when he was thirty-nine, seemed to lead to dislocation from his past. Leaving his cottage for a larger three-bedroomed house and 'an Acre of Orchard and Garden' saw Clare put his family's interests first, but it carried a threat of displacement for him. A few months before his move he wrote in a letter about his birthplace: *there is no spot in the world that I shall like better only my affections now are fixed on other deeper interests & where my family are there will my home & my comfort be & they would make me a home every where & anywhere.*

251

His move might have felt like an echo of his childhood exploration across fields to find the end of the world: *I had imagind that the worlds end was at the edge of the orison and that a days journey was able to find it   so I went on with my heart full of hopes pleasures and discoverys expecting when I got to the brink of the world that I coud look down like looking into a large pit and see into its secrets the same as I believd I coud see heaven by looking into the water.* He discovers such a difference in nature that unfamiliarity makes the boy a stranger to himself and his world: *I got out of my knowledge when the very wild flowers and birds seemd to forget me and I imagind they were the inhabitants of new countrys   the very sun seemd to be a new one and shining in a different quarter of the sky.*

Clare's 1832 poem 'The Flitting' describes his house move, that loss of familiar space, with four stark moans in its opening line: *Ive left my own old home of homes.* The poem walks us over the woods, molehills, stone-pits, stiles, pastures, streams and springs that he loves and are inevitably becoming the past, with a clear echo of the sun's disorientation from his childhood sky:

> *The sun e'en seems to loose its way*
> *Nor knows the quarter it is in*

The break with his history's landscape threatens to shatter his relationship with nature:

> *Strange scenes mere shadows are to me*
> *Vague unpersonifying things*
> . . .

252

Here every tree is strange to me
All foreign things where ere I go
Theres none where boyhood made a swee
Or clambered up to rob a crow

I moved a hundred miles from my childhood home into marriage, and I'm leaving it for a sun that doesn't recognise which quarter of the sky it's in.

A sprig of four icy lemon daffodils flicker by my ankle. I turn left for the public footpath, so accustomed to moving I could walk in my sleep.

A man and his young son exercise two black dogs. The man clambers down the grassy slope near the dyke. The boy wants to copy him. He's hesitant and careful, but manages to reach his father without falling.

I creak like an old man, climbing nettled stairs towards the green-painted iron footbridge. Every muscle aches in the manoeuvre and my knees crack. Water pleats and ripples underneath. I see the bottom with gathered moss, one brown bottle resting. Is this the River Welland? I dare myself to touch dead nettles – love's itch or balm, needle or silk.

A distant gun pops the quiet. I broke a twig. It snapped in my hand. Beside catkins, a swarm of birds I can't name – sounding like skylarks, too small for starlings – twitter as they fly. They bob and waver like midges, disappearing over my head. Could they be goldcrests, sparks of energy, or maybe skylarks have already arrived? I feel my city ignorance again, twittering into the Dictaphone as I stumble along.

When the wind lessens, I have an inconsequential memory

of me and Clifford as teenagers sitting in an old train carriage. We were on a day trip with his mother Peggy, probably to Hever Castle or Petworth: all our visits to stately homes were during school holidays. We were steeped in the romance of history, imagining we could spy on it for the price of a ticket. The train stopped between stations for several minutes. It fell silent in our carriage, when a cheerful bespectacled old woman (I can see her face now) suddenly said, 'The wind's dropped.' Later we giggled like schoolgirls that she was talking about her flatulence.

I feel an urge to see him again, as if he could advise me about the end of my marriage, tell me how to mend myself. Clare wanted Mary to live – dreamed of it, sang to it – wearing down the dust on this footpath in search of the people they were. It's not too much to ask: the most natural wish in the world, which could easily be accomplished. To bump into Clifford at the next corner, meet my best friend again and pick up where we left off four years ago, as though our conversation has merely been interrupted by a petty obstacle like death.

A sheep balances her front legs on a fence, while she chews at one of the blossom trees. I'm dog-tired between elms and beeches, blue tits flitting and a robin's whistle, Glinton's needle-point steeple behind my back. Ivy-swaddled telegraph poles. Elderflower and hawthorn, brambles and the pink spear heads of a budded dog rose. This gently curving footpath with gravel and filled potholes. A bee hovers its low drone. Three white-bellied swallows rest forked tails on a telegraph wire. Nine repeated notes from a chaffinch on a branch are answered by another further off.

All the things I'm seeing on my walk feel like the *and then this and then this* chain of observations in Clare's Northborough sonnets. He's a man doing his best to record, to celebrate the apparently mundane. There's honour in that:

> *The weary rooks to distant woods are gone*
> *With length of tail the magpie winnows on*
> *To neighbouring tree & leaves the distant crow*
> *While small birds nestle in the hedge below*

In his marvellous untitled sonnet where he writes

> *I wandered out to take a pleasant walk*
> *& saw a strange formed nest on stoven tree*

it takes him until three lines before the poem's end to discover what creature made the nest:

> *When somthing bolted out I turned to see*
> *& a brown squirrel pattered up the tree*

For most of the poem Clare doesn't know what he's seeing, only that he's seeing it and *my heart jumpt at every thing that stirred.* He's been shown (and shows us) something amazing – a prize, *lined with moss & leaves compact & strong.* The last line leaves Clare and us like this: *I sluthered down & wondering went along.* His *highest glee* lies in sluthering and wondering. It's all he needs to say and his sonnet ends.

I'm sluthering through a slow sense of timelessness, cars an undercurrent, much less dominant now than birdsong below clouds.

255

Paradise Cottage displays a flare of red tulips and a 'Beware of the Dog' sign on its gate. An unseen dog barks on cue to warn me off. The arrow-points of a six-inch crop beside another dyke. A woodpigeon's wings flap open, like pages of a book from leafy shelves. A horse behind a fence stares at me, gets bored, dips its head again to nip at grass. Beside a yellow flurry of forsythia, I read that I've been walking down Paradise Lane, appropriately enough. I want a sumptuous Delius soundtrack for this final hour – his 'Walk to the Paradise Garden' – swirling strings, soaked in summer, as though I've been trudging towards Clare's Paradise Lane without even realising. I round the left corner to Northborough. This bend in the road might be anywhere: anonymous, without associations. I could be anyone.

This is the silence I hoped for. No one's here. A telegraph pole spreads taut wires, like spokes from an invisible umbrella, into nine 1950s bungalows on my right. I notice a gap under bushes, where I might have slept tonight. It'll be heaven to dream between covers again, my head on a pillow and sheets to myself.

Old thatched cottages on my left show gardens behind hedges, cars in driveways and a four-foot-high white windmill facing a wishing well full of daffodils. There's honesty in the hedgerow, like the honesty along the side of Holly House. My feet might give out at any second, though they've carried me this far. It must be thirty more steps, compared to the thousands I've taken. Rain has stopped before puddles start, and the edge of the village feels freshened. Broken snail shells crunch under my boots.

A long thatched cottage through a hedge and iron railings has 'JOHN CLARE'S COTTAGE' on a sign stuck in a clump by the lawn. A white cat with a smudge of grey near her nose eyes me narrowly. No one's in Clare's garden. A green watering can squats by the water butt. The walls are honey-coloured stone, with two black metal crosses like kisses above three small windows, another window indented in the heavy brown thatch, all four looking warily onto the road. Clare had been consulted about the cottage's design and 'asked that the house stood with its back to the road with no front door, the only door being the one that led straight into his garden.' I feel like a spy again (as I've nosed through Clare's secrets, while he's done his best to evade me), glimpsing the new owner's private life through bushes and railings. I snap a sly photo, don't linger.

The end of this journey brings a surge of relief and pride that I got myself here, attained my goal. I've achieved something of value, found a resilience I didn't know I had. Clare's house sits in my sights. I allow myself a moment to savour and swallow my little victory.

Monday Night, 17 April

11.15 p.m. The flowery curtains I didn't choose are drawn. I'll be sleeping under a ceiling tonight instead of sky. In the lamplit night inside my rented room I relax after my bath and remember two sentences from Eavan Boland: 'Only slowly did a story begin to emerge. Only gradually did I come to believe I could tell it.'

When they found me with bare feet and legs stretched lengthwise on a bench in the early evening outside Northborough's St Andrew's Church, the kids were excited, jumping round me, firing questions. Clare called it *my Childern all noising round me in bustling happiness.* Joe admitted he'd been worried I'd be eaten by a bear at night, so he looked relieved to see me back in one piece. It felt good to hold them again, after four days without their Isaac and Joe and Amy-ness, their voices, laughs and mannerisms our marriage's greatest gifts.

When Clare got back to Northborough his journal says he felt *homeless at home.* When I returned briefly to Holly House

– to get my car for the drive back alone to this room in Rothwell – I knew I didn't belong there any more. It's ceased to be my home, as if leaving it cut out the shape I inhabited and I'm gone in a blink, as if no husband or father with my name ever lived there. Dee sounded polite and interested about the walk, but it was no grand reconciliation, no hero's welcome. How could it be? The marriage is finished. I either repeat Clare's mistake of trying to keep this fantasy and woman alive in my life, or admit such an enterprise has no future. It's already been transformed into the past tense. I bow to it like an irrevocable fact.

I'd like to understand the mystery of two people falling in love and living together, having children, and what happens to them afterwards. It can branch in a thousand different ways, though perhaps there's only two conclusions for each couple: staying or parting. Already I find myself starting to think of Dee and me, the couple we were, as *them* rather than *us*, as if the marriage's end after a long illness helps us slough off our old useless skins. It was my life. It's not my life now. I could pity the two children who imagined they were adults because marriage is what grown-ups do. Two children, discovering a need in each other, married that need, believing love could make it better. Perhaps marriage helped them learn: one step that started with misguided love for each other ended with a clumsy half-understood love for themselves. It's as though the institution of marriage, or heterosexuality, kept guiding us back onto traditional tramlines that we were too compliant or overwhelmed to resist.

Tonight's unfinished, drawing breath, rather than a conclusion; although I could tie the four days of this walk with a lavender ribbon and offer them to Dee, like a bundle of love letters (even if they're no longer wanted) saying, 'This is how it was for me. How was it for you?'

I turn instead to what I hope might be the endless resourcefulness of parenthood: my determination for the children and me not to drift to the edge of each other's lives. My friend Bill said leaving his daughter felt like leaving his life at someone else's house. Driving away from Holly House I remembered how often I took the children to the hidden stream a field away from our garden: opening or climbing the shaky metal gate; finding whether the water under the hedge was bubbling at full throttle or had narrowed to a trickle. Taking them to the bluebell wood at Dingley every May since Isaac was born nine years ago, where they swung on a low bending branch. I'll take them again in a couple of weeks when the bluebells are at their best.

From now on will our relationship be constructed on a routine of me leaving and coming back? If they feel confident I'll return that won't stop the little losses of my leaving. When we next meet on Wednesday it'll be like a conversation barely interrupted, but interrupted all the same.

After his journey out of Essex, Clare stayed at home for five months until December 1841. Within three days of his return he completed his account of the walk, accompanied by an unposted letter to Mary, calling her Mary Clare and addressing her as *My dear wife   I have written an account of my journey or rather escape from Essex for your amusement and hope it may divert your leisure hours* – . . . He offers this harrowing account to amuse and divert her, as though reading his torment might entertain a spare hour or two.

Those months at home saw Clare adding angry stanzas to 'Don Juan' and continuing to work on 'Child Harold'. He wrote what he called 'Biblical Paraphrases', with lines that bled into his own life:

> *Who am I my God & my Lord*
> *& what is my house in thy eye*
> . . .
> *I was in prison ye came to me there*
> *& your talk made my bonds unconfined as the air*

He composed the brief essay on 'Self-Identity', writing *surely every man has the liberty to know himself*, and beautiful prose observations of nature following his autumn walks: *fish leaping up in the sunshine & leaving rings widening & quavering on the water with the plunge of a Pike in the weeds driving a host of roach into the clear water slanting now & then towards the top their bellies of silver light in the sunshine –*

Those months saw him finding the strains of married and family life hard to manage, combined with deepening depression as he fought the fact that *the people in the neighbourhood tells me that the one called 'Mary' has been dead these 8 years.* In the same letter to Dr Allen at High Beach around September he writes *having neither friends or home left but as it is called the 'Poet's cottage' I claimed a lodging in it where I now am –* . . . *I want to be independant & pay for board & lodging while I remain here – I look upon myself as a widow or bachellor I dont know which – I care nothing about the women now for they are faithless & decietfull* . . . *a man who possesses a woman possesses losses without gain – the worst is the road to ruin &*

the best is nothing like a good Cow – man I never did like and woman has long sickened me.

The misogyny in 'Don Juan' seems to have returned, and aberrant behaviour or possibly even violence came with it. Parson Mossop, who was visiting Clare and his family, said, 'the want of restraint soon generated conduct which became so alarming to his wife and family as to induce them to ask the aid of Earl Fitzwilliam.' Patty – who, after his return home 'thought him so much better that she wished to try him for a while' – had to protect their children and admit defeat. Clare's patron arranged for two doctors to assess him three days after Christmas. Their certificate of application for admission to Northampton General Lunatic Asylum notes the 'nature and causes of Insanity' as 'years addicted to poetical prosing'. They seem to assume not only was Clare's writing an unhelpful addiction, but that it contributed to his mental illness, instead of (perhaps) relieving him, giving him words to make sense of experience. Maybe Dr Skrimshire, who wrote the asylum admission papers, saw poetry as dangerous: much safer to stay placid, unexcitable – know your place – steer clear of words' explosions in your head.

Clare spent his last twenty-three years in Northampton Asylum, fifty miles from Northborough. Patty never saw him again, and even became known as 'Widow Clare' in the village, while Clare still lived in the asylum. So, as Clare continued to insist that Mary was alive, he was written off as dead before his time. Perhaps madness and asylums were seen as a living death.

Why didn't Clare escape from Northampton Asylum, slip his captors, return home for a second time? He assumed the role of patient, let it stick. Resistance was exhausted. He couldn't fight any more. It became enough to walk a mile into the centre of Northampton, and sit in the stone alcove of All Saints' Church, watching the world unwind, writing occasional love poems for acquaintances' wives or girlfriends, in exchange for tobacco or a pint: a poet for hire. This isn't a story of defeat. Clare's example is one of heroism in the face of circumstances that were meant to silence him and didn't. He wrote over eight hundred asylum poems. For Clare in the asylum writing remained a means of protest and observation, of saying in 'I Am', his most famous poem 'I am here and this is how it feels.' That stunning first line

I am – yet what I am, none cares or knows

hooks the reader with its first two words, which could start a declaration of joy in selfhood; although, like an angler drawing out his line, he immediately qualifies the statement, almost undercuts it. It's the voice of survival from a man who knows his worth, even his existence, is ignored by others. The third line – *I am the self-consumer of my woes* – could have come from Hopkins, unhappiness swallowing him whole, woes rising and thrashing uselessly, like a shadow of orgasm *in love-frenzied stifled throes*, which topple the poem into its next stanza. Waves of *nothingness* nearly overwhelm him, where his life's sea has become *waking dreams* that crash into a central image:

Where there is neither sense of life or joys
But the vast shipwreck of my life's esteems

His ambitions have broken on the rocks, where

> *Even the dearest that I love the best*
> *Are strange – nay, rather stranger than the rest.*

Dislocation from those he loves has returned, as when his wife and son in Werrington were a *woman and a boy*. With this pitch of despair at the end of its second stanza, where can Clare's poem take him? The final stanza journeys where death and childhood are curiously blended to comfort him, and the tone changes accordingly after the breath of the stanza break:

> *I long for scenes where man hath never trod,*
> *A place where woman never smiled or wept,*
> *There to abide with my Creator, God,*
> *And sleep as I in childhood sweetly slept,*
> *Untroubling and untroubled where I lie,*
> *The grass below – above, the vaulted sky.*

Humanity has disappeared, so he can no longer be hurt or disillusioned by the fact in his first line that no-one cares or knows him. His only relationship is with God. Refuge transforms death into a childhood memory of sleeping under the white space of sky that ends the poem, leaving the faintest impression on the grass.

Clare wrote this poem about seven years into his second captivity, in what he described to Patty in an 1848 letter as *the Land of Sodom where all the peoples brains are turned the wrong way . . . – You might come and fetch me away for I think I have been here long enough.*

Twelve years later he wrote one of his last known letters to a stranger who enquired after his health:

Dear Sir
I am in a Madhouse & quite forget your Name or who
you are   you must excuse me for I have nothing to commu-
nicate or tell of & why I am shut up I dont know   I have
nothing to say so I conclude
                    yours respectfully   John Clare

He stays polite and minds his manners, but the words have run out, though saying he has nothing to say speaks volumes. That summer he told a genteel lady-writer visiting the asylum: 'Why they have cut off my head and picked out all the letters in the alphabet – all the vowels and all the consonants and brought them out through my ears – and then they want me to write poetry! I can't do it.' Words have broken apart like alphabet soup in his brain – a paper chain of w's and o's and e's pulled from his ears. He's still a poet speaking in images, but words are instruments of torture, and he can't be their performing monkey any more.

Two years before he died, there's a photo of him staring into the camera under bushy white eyebrows and a high balding forehead, his snowy side-whiskers mutton-chops above a tight white collar, smart dark cravat, suit and waistcoat. He watches us, keeps his own counsel, and we can read whatever we like into his wary tight-lipped expression, the shut line of his mouth.

I've used Clare on this walk as a working-class poet who kept his voice whatever pressures ganged against him, a proud outsider who celebrated the woman he loved, walked home and found her gone. He's served my purpose. In Northampton he said to an editor of the local paper who challenged him after he claimed to have written the words of Byron and Shakespeare: 'It's all the same . . . I'm John Clare now. I was Byron and Shakespeare formerly. At different times you know I'm different people – that is the same person with different names . . . sometimes they called me Shakespeare and sometimes Byron and sometimes Clare.' Was it his mental illness talking, or was he playing a mad poet for a journalist? Maybe there's method in his madness: the idea that the identities of poets can morph into each other, ownership of names and poems can slide into the sea, because we're all shape-shifters writing one enormous unfinished poem – from Shakespeare to Byron to Clare – handing lines on to each other across the years, speaking to each other, signing, swapping and rubbing out our names.

Have I been changed by this walk? I could as easily ask if I'm changed by every day, moving – like Clare on his return to Northborough – from husband to single man again (as if it could be that simple), the difference being the children in my life. The wedding ring's slipped from my finger, leaving a pale dent around the skin, a constriction released for both of us.

What can I trust in this new loneliness? Family and friends of course, but apparently I can trust the persistence of self, this story my flimsy inheritance. A room rented six weeks ago can serve as home: magnolia walls with Clifford's pictures tacked onto them; my necessary books salvaged from Holly House; a lightshade and mirror; this writing table, lamp and bed. The essentials. Until I can afford a place of my own, be at home with myself. Looking at his paintings and sketches, I think of Clifford again – this bright nervous funny honest man.

Thinking of him dead and me alive feels like a form of disloyalty, but I carry him like a red ribbon on my lapel, pinned to my narrative. He can live as long as I live. There's an *Angels in America* line: 'Still. Bless me anyway. I want more life.' My useless wanting him here might be part of why Clare kept Mary alive in his head. Clifford would have wanted more bridges and afternoons, more Mozart and wet pavements, but what good's a wish for things to be different? Temporary life's built into every arum lily, wagtail and dragonfly. I can't be Clare and keep Mary alive because that road's the madhouse. Clifford's death and the end of my marriage are the fabric of my skin tonight.

I'm moving towards midnight, time for sleep. If I dream of a garden near the sea let there be goldfinches. Starting tomorrow there's the task of writing this journey and continuing the experiment of myself. I remember Beckett's phrases on the first afternoon of this walk: *you must go on, I can't go on, I'll go on.* If my feet are burning each step takes me forward.

Fourth Day 1841

The Name of Any Place

I don't reccolect the name of any place until I came to Stilton
where I was compleatly foot-foundered & broken down

Let me stop. End here.
I'd as soon call this place home
as anywhere:
gather stones, build a fire tonight,
plait willow-twigs for a roof perhaps –
snore to the sky
till it rains and my throat's a gutter.

I'll count grass-stalks
numbering the hairs on my head.
What happens if one follows two?
One step
two step
one for sorrow two for joy –
can you catch them? Here in my hand?

What happens when knees are smashed,
spokes of the great wheel broken?
Broken down haymaker. Me,
who dared to win the battle of the Nile
fought ten tigers bareknuckle and boxed their ears
wrote Child Harold on an oak-leaf baked in nutmeg
a broken down haycart

                        me
         a broken

           name
              who knows it?

           what happens after one?

        what glories of the Nile
        what battles lost and shipwrecked

        what
              battles   wrecked

          my name

Poor Creature

a young woman (so I guessed by the voice) came out of a house
& said 'poor creature' & another more elderly said 'O he shams'
But when I got up the latter said 'O no he don't' as I hobbled
along very lame

Young woman:

There but for the grace of God
I stumble, lie exhausted
as this scarcely man who shuts his eyes
for sleep and peace won't come.

Less than a fly fussing on a leaf
and still alive.

Should I comfort,
offer him a woman's outstretched hand?
He lifts his bag of bones again,
walks past us both as if he limps through flame.

Herb Robert

What flavour of man is this, whose tips
unpeel into flowers? His arrows blossom.
Five petals top each blood-line that dips
and lifts through the breeze. I've seen him
hide by the creaky bridge where lattice-water
dabbles a trout's tail while bubbles rise.
His leaves mimic ferns, his colour
campion. How can he be less than he is?
He lives his name. Two bulbs branch from every stem,
until I catch him taking over
the wood-side. A hundred buds swarm
their messages on the air.
If I eat his breath will it heal me?
Stroke him across my temples quietly, quietly.

Neighbours from Helpstone

a man & woman passed me in a cart & on hailing me as they passed I found they were neighbours from Helpstone where I used to live – I told them I was knocked up which they could easily see & that I had neither eat nor drunk anything since I left Essex when I told my story they clubbed together & threw me fivepence out of the cart

The man speaks:

> We sprouted in the same back garden:
> him a dog rose, me a bramble,
> but I've always fed my children.
> Can he say as much?
>
> Poetry's a wet harvest.
> Look at him. I knew he'd end up useless,
> his way with words
> enough to skin a pebble, nothing more.
>
> Do we cart him home?
> Now he's daft there's no knowing.
> He could eat us in our sleep.
> Click the reins. Best leave him where he is.
>
> His story shakes our pennies.
> We throw five and watch him grub the dust.
> When he's miles behind
> I keep hearing his children call us back.

Over the Stones

*I could scarcely make a walk of it over the stones and being half
ashamed to sit down in the street I forced to keep on the move*

When the body breaks its knees
the spirit whips its snorting horse
and drives him harder.

I'm walking to God
saying *can I have*
not happiness exactly, but calm –
sleeping on the breast of the woman I love,
with nowhere to go.

The Woman

when nearing me the woman jumped out and caught fast hold
of my hands and wished me to get into the cart but I refused
and thought her either drunk or mad but when I was told it
was my second wife Patty I got in and was soon at Northborough

Patty speaks:

> He blathers Mary like a love-whipped boy.
> He's blind to me. My scorched man,
> too long in the sun. If it rained
> who licked drops off his lashes,
> promised him tomorrow would be dry?
>
> Four years waiting and still no cure
> but I can mend him: patch his elbows,
> rest the shade of fingers over his eyes.
>
> I sang him asleep after the children,
> drunk from his wooing and glad to be so.
> Even now, squeezing his hands again,
> saying my name until he remembers
> I wake foot to finger at his side.

At Home

Mary was not there neither could I get any information about
her further than the old story of her being dead six years ago
. . . but I took no notice of the blarney having seen her myself
about a twelvemonth ago alive & well & as young as ever – so
here I am homeless at home

The woman who died is alive.
I watched her hem catch thistledown
when she walked through grass last summer
and blew a kiss.

Press an ear on the warmest wall
to hear it promise *you're home.*
You asked for this. You may sleep now.

I remember that fire, those flagstones,
the wife I lie beside,
but the children have changed their faces
and books here scratch another language.

One says *steal out tonight if you're hungry.*
There are miles more streets to walk.
Knock hard on a different door. It could be home.

Nothing

*July 24 1841. Returned home out of Essex & found no Mary her
& her family are nothing to me now – though she herself was
once the dearest of all – & how can I forget*

> Cut my brain in half and pluck her out:
> this woman where thought should be,
> stooping to touch the cowslips.
>
> I carry myself like spilt wine,
> my cup cracked
> with the memory of whoever I was.
>
> You can live on so little.
> Live on this breath leaving my mouth again,
> the song of a robin before it flies.

Afterword

Sunday, 9 April 2017

I'm sitting in the car by Helpston churchyard, making my final notes this afternoon, with my husband, Keith, beside me.

Over the past three years we've chosen a mid-April weekend and re-driven the route I walked, with me taking notes and photos as we kept parking the car along the way. Keith helps with the maps, and waits patiently in the car while I wander, make my observations, take my time to remember. I met him on 16 May 1995, a month after I finished my walk. My life is transformed. It's been strange revisiting the route of such anguish, as if I'm tracking two ghosts this time: Clare and the man I was when I was lost. Despite it not being the most rational decision, I think the walk arrived at the right time to save me, gave me a focus, a purpose inside the mess of separation, though sleeping rough and slogging along the A1 proved how desperate I was.

Yesterday saw us drive the final miles of the roads from

Stilton to Peterborough. Several stops, nine pages of scribbled notes and a dozen or so photos.

Today we drove to Glinton and I strolled again among birdsong down the North Fen Road, along Paradise Lane into Northborough, jotting notes of whatever I saw; clicking photos; noticing that the fence before Clare's lawn has changed from iron railings to white slats since I first saw it; sitting on the same bench by the church's two-bell turret where Dee and the children found me. Today's our last trip from our home in Brighton, because I've gathered the extra material I need. I've pored over the four Ordnance Survey maps and replayed the four old tapes I recorded with the Dictaphone, hearing my weary voice describing the things I saw, above traffic noise, bird calls and an occasional buffeting wind. I'm reaching the end stages of this book, before I think about the hunt for a publisher.

How much has changed over the twenty-two years since my journey, drafting and redrafting my story, laying it aside, picking it up again?

Once the walk was over, I realised that, as well as keeping up my evenings and alternate weekends with the kids, I needed to face my sexuality, jump one way or the other and sort myself out. I phoned Leicester Gay Switchboard for advice about any local social groups for bisexuals. There were none, but they offered Leicester Gay Group, which met weekly at the LGBT centre. What did I have to lose? I met Keith on my first night there, and afterwards in the Dover Castle at the end of the evening he asked for my number. I thought it was worth a shot, and a few nights later he phoned to suggest meeting up for a drink. We met at the New Inn in Kettering – my first date in twenty years – where I turned up deliberately late, so as not to appear too eager.

Love happened swiftly, much sooner than I expected at such an emotionally risky time, when I was porous to everything. Once I understood I might be falling in love with him I prepared myself for something to go wrong. Early on I remember saying, 'OK – spill the beans: you've got HIV or you're moving to Belgium.' There were no plans for Belgium and he didn't have HIV, as far as he knew. We went for an HIV test: little button plasters in the crooks of our arms like pink badges. We weren't HIV positive, but it felt like a challenge we had to face together, a bridge to cross towards commitment. He told me I could be myself, a crucial message to hear for someone who'd been hiding aspects of himself for years. I'm lucky to have fallen in love twice in my life: once with a woman, once with a man, and I've been fortunate enough to marry both.

Today I'm amazed how much HIV/AIDS medication has improved. I remember Andrew stitching Clifford's name onto his AIDS quilt, cutting and sewing two of Clifford's favourite shirts to make each letter, and how he asked friends and family to add whatever patch we wanted as our memorial. Dee embroidered a phoenix from one of his paintings, and we stitched a kiss each, including Isaac and Joe. Amy was born fourteen months after Clifford died, so she never knew him. Where's his quilt folded now (with its tapestry cupid by Andrew), in what storeroom, stacked beside all the others?

I'm happy that protease inhibitor combination therapies and PrEP (pre-exposure prophylaxis) mean young people (or at least young people in the West) won't experience the epidemic in anything like the same way, but health and treat-ment inequalities remain. There were 29 million deaths from AIDS-related illnesses between 1970 and 2009, and 37 million people were living with the virus in 2014. It may have slipped off the headlines, but it hasn't gone away.

I think of the people lost to me while I was writing this book. My friend Ian, who helped me plan the route, killed himself nine months after my walk, lying down in 1996 with a sleeping bag and pillow in the hallway of his house. At his funeral his wife Helen asked me to read the lines from the end of 'Four Quartets' about history being 'now and England'. Andrew died suddenly, four days before his forty-third birthday in 2002, collapsing in Leicester market on his way home. My mother died from pneumonia in a nursing home in Wanstead in 2009. Helen, who'd been such a support to me on the night of my overdose, died four years ago from cancer in a Kettering nursing home. My father Alf died two years ago in a Hackney hospice. Each death led to me stepping away from these pages – being lost for words, my motivation punc-tured. I concentrated on writing poems about each of them instead, until I slowly picked up the threads again, as if writing this might become a tribute to my 'little company'. I worked out I've lived without Clifford for longer than our friendship lasted: twenty-three years with him, twenty-six years since he died. Will I find enough words to lay him to rest? Will finishing this mean letting him go?

Last December on World AIDS Day at Brighton's memorial in New Steine gardens, Clifford and Andrew's names were spoken into a muffled microphone. Two hundred or more names were read into the cold night air, with all of us standing there to witness and honour, our candles blowing out in the black wind, but in the meantime they warmed our palms, cupped around each flame to protect them from the weather. After the crowd had left and I stood by the statue of two entwined men, candles extinguished below me in trays of sand, a drunk guy in his thirties with a lager can in his hand asked if it was my brother. I said it was two friends. He said he'd lost his best friend to AIDS and couldn't get over it. His friend took all the tablets he should, but it still got him. He asked if he could kiss my cheek and I said, 'Of course.'

What happened to Clifford and Andrew feels too personal, too raw, to be dismissed as history, although if history is now – the present moment – in England and elsewhere, I can live with that.

This morning I left two yellow roses on the grass outside the closed gate of Clare's cottage in Northborough – one for Clare and one for Dee, wishing her well in the ways her life is changing. Dee carried yellow roses at our wedding, so when I found them this morning at the garage I knew those were the flowers I needed to buy.

Ten minutes ago, I left two more roses beside Clare's grave in St Botolph's churchyard in Helpston in the spring sun – one for Clare and one for Clifford. They're my thank you to a poet who's captivated and eluded me for years. It's the least he deserves for bringing me this far, from the tormented man who first walked to find him, to the more contented one who's discovered a way to complete *A Length of Road* at last, while my children grow into their adult lives.

A smart new pillar at the head of his mottled stone reads 'HERE Rest the HOPES And Ashes of JOHN CLARE', an epitaph he wrote for himself after the first buzz of his success, forty years before he died. A plucked daisy lies limp on the lichen, which nibbles at his grave's old name.

This morning I said 'Thank you' aloud when a heron landed like a feathered messenger twenty yards away, beside the dyke at the beginning of Paradise Lane. I thought of Clifford again, although often when I think of him now all I grasp is a sense of him gone, the gap he's made in the day. Absence and presence: Keith sits beside me in the car, absorbed in checking the map. I was moving towards him without even knowing it. I've met my good companion. The story continues.

When I finish writing these lines to myself, I'll start the car again and we'll drive home.

Afterword 1861

Widow Clare

*Within a few years Patty even became known as 'Widow Clare',
so sure were the local gossips that her husband was 'put away'
for good and would never be seen again.*
  Edward Storey from *A Right to Song: The Life of John Clare*

Words went out with the candle at night.
We're a wedding of skin:
the smell of him dug in my fingernails,
his cough at my shoulder again
if I shut my eyes.

He's written into me, this man I picked
bruised as an apple from wet grass.
He was my fire in a sooty corner
while the children slept.
I try making do with drizzle now I've tasted rain.

A Length of Road

I blame words, worming inside his forehead
loosening his tongue: unspeakable things
scaring the children, until I gave him up
to the doctors. It takes a slow breath to say
it's twenty years since I've seen him.

I used to hope he'd walk home after winter,
stroke the new lines above my eyebrow
without looking for another woman behind my back.
He'd give his name to the air beside my name,
as if he knows where I stand at last and who I am.

What more do you want to hear?
how he held a buttercup at my throat,
made me believe its tiny halo
caught the sun under my chin
that first morning.

Acknowledgements

M y thanks to Johnathon Clifford and the National Poetry Foundation (GB) for encouragement with a grant to buy equipment for my walk. Thanks also to the late Peter Moyse of the John Clare Society for kind advice on Clare's route. Following the invaluable research in Hall and Somekh's *Love's Cold Returning* (details in Bibliography) it appears that the route I chose in 1995 differed at several points from Clare's route. I would recommend *Love's Cold Returning* to readers interested in Clare's route.

I am grateful for a Fellowship at Hawthornden Castle for an amazing month to devote to early drafts. The poems were published as *Heading North* by Flarestack in 2007, with thanks to Charles Johnson.

I am grateful to Kate Craigie, my editor at John Murray, for her tremendous encouragement and insights, and to the Future Bookshelf at Hachette UK for its dedication to under-represented writers. Thanks also to the staff at Hachette for their support and attention to detail, including Martin Bryant and Will Speed.

I've always been lucky in my friends. I'm indebted to Gillie Bolton and Marian McCraith who have been there throughout. Your support to me and your dedication to writing have lit my path. Thank you to Catherine Byron and Mahendra Solanki for encouragement and patience with my early drafts and the poems. Advice on poems was gratefully received from John Forth, Mark Goodwin, Pam Thompson and Michael Tolkien. Thanks also for unstinting support from Joan Poulson and Jackie Wills: your perceptions kept me going. Heartfelt gratitude to Inkskippers Hugh Dunkerley, Naomi Foyle and Joanna Lowry who kickstarted the final push after my five-year hiatus and gave helpful signposts for the best route. I've been very fortunate with the generous support of my family for the publication of this book, and I thank them.

My gratitude always of course to my husband, Keith Rainger, for warm guidance and seeing me through every line, every draft and every year.

Note on the cover

The cover illustration is a portrait by Clifford Haseldine (1956–1991) of his partner Andrew Copus (1959–2002). It was painted in Leicester, at a time when Clifford was painting and drawing a wide range of works, virtually on a daily basis, before the effects of his illness made painting impossible. Andrew was a willing and patient model, often posing either for life studies or portraits. Andrew liked the painting. I remember he displayed it in his flat after Clifford died, and it came to me after Andrew died. I feel sure that Andrew would be proud to be on the cover of this book.

Notes

Dedication

v *And every sound*: John Clare: *Selected Poetry*, Geoffrey Summerfield (ed.), p.49.

Preface

xii *that little personal pronoun*: to Eliza Emmerson, March–April 1830, *The Letters of John Clare*, Mark Storey (ed.), p.504.

First Day

5 'gardens, pleasure grounds': *John Clare: A Biography*, Jonathan Bate, p.424.

6 *the green variety*: John Clare: *Selected Poetry*, Geoffrey Summerfield (ed.), p.86.

6 *my escape from the madhouse*: *The Prose of John Clare*, J.W. and Anne Tibble (ed.), p.244.

6 *the greatest annoyance*: to Matthew Allen, after 27 August 1841, *The Letters of John Clare*, Mark Storey (ed.), p.650.

6 *very melancholly*: *The Prose of John Clare*, J.W. and Anne Tibble (ed.), p.244.

6 *did not seem so willing*: ibid.

6 *an old wide-awake hat*: ibid.

7 'when Clare lent Miss Fish': *The Letters of John Clare*, p.651, fn 5.

7 *madhouse traps*: *John Clare: Selected Poems*, Bate, p.245.

10 *my first feelings*: *John Clare: By Himself*, Eric Robinson and David Powell (eds.), p.29.

11 'the cruellest month': *T. S. Eliot: Collected Poems 1909–1962*, p.63.

11 *The fairest child*: *John Clare: The Shepherd's Calendar*, Eric Robinson and Geoffrey Summerfield (eds.), p.41.

11 *hid in a palace green*: *John Clare: A Critical Edition of the Major Works*, Eric Robinson and David Powell (eds.), p.284.

14 *real simple soul-moving poetry*: *The Prose of John Clare*, J.W. and Anne Tibble (eds.), p.45.

I made but few: *John Clare:By Himself*, Eric Robinson and David Powell (eds.), p.49.

14 *I often try'd*: ibid., pp.16–17.

14 'It cost Mrs Clare': *A Right to Song: The Life of John Clare*, Edward Storey, p.48.

14 *chilling damp with fear*: *By Himself*, Robinson and Powell (eds.) p.18.

17 *The squirrel sputters*: *Selected Poetry*, Summerfield, p.48.

17 *over head and ears*: *By Himself*, Robinson and Powell (eds.), p.21.

18 *Reconnitred the route*: *The Prose of John Clare*, J.W. and Anne Tibble (eds.) , p.244.

19 'one of the wonders': Iain Sinclair, *Edge of the Orison: In the traces of John Clare's 'Journey out of Essex'*, p.10.

19 'one of the great English journeys', ibid., p.123.

19 *I missed the lane*: *The Prose of John Clare*, J.W. and Anne Tibble (eds.), pp.244.

20 *my own old home*: *The Major Works*, p.250.

20 *lost roads leading*: ibid., p.5.

20 *Each hated track*: ibid.

21 *my happy spot*: *Selected Poems*, Bate, p.47.

21 *while the fond parent*: *ibid*.

29 *seeing when I was younger*: *By Himself*, p.18.

29 *wandering about the fields*: ibid., p.37.

29 *playing at marbles*: ibid., pp.39–40.

29 *the different greens*: *The Prose of John Clare*, Tibble (eds.)., p.25.

29 *the little ups and downs*: *By Himself*, p.39.

31 *voice of freedom*: to Matthew Allen, after 27 August 1841, *The Letters of John Clare*, p.650.

31 *most of them*: *The Prose of John Clare* , p.66.

33 *bye and bye*: ibid. , p.244.

34 *a Scotchman*: *By Himself*, p.2.

39 *And aye so different*: *Selected Poems*, Bate, pp.127–8.

40 *The more I listened*: ibid., p.127.

40 'Images from Nature': *John Clare: A Biography*, Jonathan Bate, p.189.

40 *his descriptions*: to Herbert Marsh, January–October 1830, *The Letters of John Clare*, p.519.

42 *I love to see*: *John Clare: Selected Poetry and Prose*, Merryn and Raymond Williams (eds.), p.154.

42 *thou humble flower*: ibid.

42 *waste of shining blossoms*: ibid.

43 'One must learn': to T. D. D, 7 July 1914, *D. H. Lawrence: Selected Letters* (selected by Richard Aldington), p.74.

44 *as she had made her bed*: The Prose of John Clare , p.64.

44: *I was in love*: ibid., p.55.

44 *And brush the weaving*: Selected Poems, Bate, p. 23.

44 *I was little fit*: By Himself, p.28.

45 *I held out*: The Prose of John Clare , p.65.

45 *I think (Patty)*: to James Hessey, 4 July 1820, *The Letters of John Clare*, p.82.

45 'When John came': *John Clare: A Biography*, Bate, p.87.

46 *homeless at home*: Selected Poems, Bate, p.264.

47 'My home is my self ': Robert Hamberger, *Warpaint Angel*, p.19.

49 'you must go on': Samuel Beckett, *Molloy, Malone Dies, The Unnamable*, p.418.

51 *meeting no enemy*: The Prose of John Clare , p.244.

52 *being careless*: ibid.

53 *The timid hares*: John Clare: Poems Selected by Paul Farley, p.75.

First Day 1841

57 *July 18 1841*: The Prose of John Clare , p.244.

58 *On friday*: ibid.

59 *July 19*: ibid.

60 *July 20*: ibid.

61 *to my good luck*: ibid., p.245.

62 *I lay down*: ibid.

Second Day

64 *whistles like a cricket*: *The Major Works*, p.248.

65 *I slept soundly* : *The Prose of John Clare* , p.245.

65 *That form from boyhood–* *The Major Works*, p.290.

66 'The Lord is my shepherd': Psalms 23, Verses 1–3.

67 *what happy discourses*: *The Prose of John Clare* , p.42.

69 'I bet that District Nurse': *Warpaint Angel*, Robert Hamberger, p.50.

74 *Over three-quarters*: *John Clare: A Biography*, Bate; see pages xvii and 507.

74 *I felt that I'd a right*: *Selected Poems*, Bate, p.122.

74 'A "peasant-poet"': *A Right to Song: The Life of John Clare*, Edward Storey, p.24.

74 'unwilling to play': *John Clare: A Biography*, Bate, p.167.

75 *ploughing and ditching*: *By Himself*, p.134.

75 *while I was lolling*: *The Prose of John Clare*, p.79. .

75 *it was less*: ibid., p.80.

75 *pathways on the street*: ibid., p.138.

76 *Fame blazed*: *The Major Works*. p.291.

76 *I kept one for years*: *The Prose of John Clare*, p.264.

76 'Clare refused to co-operate': 'John Clare's Prog' from *The Redress of Poetry*, Seamus Heaney, p.64.

77 *I think to please*: to James Hessey, ?10 July 1820, *The Letters of John Clare*, p.84.

77 *Though laurel wreaths*: *Selected Poems*, Bate, p.253.

78 *all I wish*: to Eliza Emmerson, 13 November 1832, *The Letters of John Clare*, p.604.

78 *Thy green memorials*: – *The Major Works*, p.108.

80 *I dreaded walking*: *Selected Poems*, Bate, p.230.

81 'a labourer might have been': *Green Shadows: The Life of John Clare*, June Wilson, p.19.

81 'In 1809, when Clare was sixteen': *The Independent Spirit: John Clare and the Self-Taught Tradition*, John Goodridge (ed.) 'An exercise in nostalgia?: John Clare and enclosure' by Judith Rowbotham, p.164.

81 'more than half of Northamptonshire's acres': *Green Shadows*, p.39.

81 *On paths to freedom*: *Selected Poems*, Bate, p.91.

81 *lawless law's enclosure*: ibid.

82 *Poetry was for a season*: *The Prose of John Clare* , p.34.

82 *Fence now meets fence*: *Selected Poems*, Bate, p.90.

82 'In 1816 Hunger Riots': *John Clare: Nature, Criticism and History*, Simon Kövesi, p.231.

82 'nineteen protestors being transported': *A Right to Song: The Life of John Clare*, Edward Storey, p.91.

82 *walking where there was no path*: *Selected Poems,* (Bate), p.230.

82 'a trespasser in the poetic': 'John Clare's Exposure' in *On Flirtation*, Adam Phillips, p.212.

82 'the evil of incompetent': *John Clare: A Biography*, Bate, p.230.

83 *are looked upon*: to Allan Cunningham, 9 September 1824, *The Letters of John Clare*, p.303.

83 'radical slang': *John Clare: A Biography*, Bate, p.219.

83 'a sum comfortably': ibid, p.175.

83 *damn that canting*: to John Taylor, 16 May 1820, *The Letters of John Clare*, p.69.

83 *the pruning hook*: ibid., to John Taylor, 10 July 1821, p.204.

84 *I had one of the proofs*: *The Prose of John Clare* , p.138.

84 'sold 425 copies': *John Clare: A Biography*, Bate, p.308.

84 *I feel very disappointed*: to John Taylor, 20 August 1827, *The Letters of John Clare*, p.394.

84 *when the cow*: ibid., to Allan Cunningham, 10 November 1832, p.601.

84 'for £40': *Green Shadows*, Wilson, p.219.

84 *I thank you*: to John Taylor, 27 August 1835, *The Letters of John Clare*, pp.627–8.

85 *everything . . . Appeared so beautiful*: – Selected Poems, (Bate,).p.230

85 *I've often thought*: ibid.

86 'Let us trespass': from 'The Leaning Tower' (1940) in *Street Haunting and Other Essays*, Virginia Woof, pp.206–7.

87 . . . *the old heron*: Selected Poems, Bate, p.136.

88 *this tormented mind . . . poor Jackself . . . let be . . . as skies*: Poems and Prose, Gerard Manley Hopkins, p.63.

91 *Daylight was looking in* : *The Prose of John Clare* , p.245.

92 *being night*: ibid.

93 *higher pailings*: ibid.

95 'an essay in civilisation': 'The changing face of Stevenage', *Guardian*, 4 September 1996.

98 'our persistent yet mysterious': journal entry April 1920, *The Letters and Journals of Katherine Mansfield: A Selection*, p.173.

99 *Heart bursting*: Selected Poetry, Summerfield, p.136.

99 *life's realitys*: ibid., p.135.

99 *And Mary*: ibid., p.138.

99 *The self-same voice*: ibid.

99 *her favourite*: ibid., p.139.

100 *'Tis youth*: ibid., p.141.

100 *would part*: ibid.

100 *When her small waist*: ibid.

103 *On searching*: *By Himself*, note, p.260.
104 *The dancing Cowslips*: from chapter 'Room enough to walk and search for flowers' in *Four Forest Years*, Pete Relph.
104 *hurry from the world*: ibid.
106 *on the left hand*: *By Himself* , p.258.
106 *I remember passing*: ibid., p.149.
107 *I have a feeling*: to Thomas Pringle, after 8 February 1832, *The Letters of John Clare*, p.572.
112 *Somewhere on the London side*: *The Prose of John Clare* , p.245.
112 *'here's another . . .'*: ibid.
112 *to get a half-pint*: ibid.
114 *dogs and men*: *Selected Poems*, Bate, p.226.
114 *The badger grunting*: ibid.
114 *a host of dogs*: ibid.
114 *and everyone's a foe*: ibid., p.227.
114 *He falls as dead*: ibid.
115 *Through well known*: *Poems Selected*, Farley, p.75.
116 *my legs were nearly*: *The Prose of John Clare* , p.245.

Second Day 1841

119 *I slept soundly*: ibid.
120 *on the left hand*: *By Himself,* p.258 .
122 *a Man passed me*: *The Prose of John Clare* , p.245.
123 *I sat down*: ibid., p.246.
124 *I called in*: *By Himself,* p.260.
125 *I then suddenly*: ibid., pp.261–2.

Third Day

127 *an odd house*: The Prose of John Clare , p.248.

129 *It now began*: ibid., p.247.

129 *Ariff, bumbarrel*: Selected Poetry, Summerfield, pp.378–89 and *Poems Selected*, Farley, pp.125–7.

134 *When shall I see*: Selected Poems, Bate, p.298.

134 *In early spring*: ibid.

137 'the profound experience': *Silences*, Tillie Olsen, p.43 (footnote).

140 *And little wren*: Poems Selected, Farley, p.48.

143 *I then went through*: The Prose of John Clare , p.246.

144 *for a shilling*: ibid., p.247.

144 *late evening*: ibid., p.246.

149 *Potton in Bedfordshire*: ibid.

149 *in a house*: By Himself,p.260.

150 *It heard me*: John Clare's Birds, Robinson and Fitter, p.14.

150 *It cannot sing*: ibid., p.15.

151 *a kind talking*: The Prose of John Clare , p.246-7.

151 *suddenly recolecting*: ibid., p.247.

151 *lay down by a shed*: ibid.

151 *the road was*: ibid .

152 *Skim and dip*: John Clare's Birds, Robinson and Fitter, p.61.

153 'cant and humbug': *Green Shadows*, Wilson, p.137.

153 *religion of the fields*: The Prose of John Clare , p.32.

153 *truth & . . . the Mystery*: to John Taylor, after 3 April 1824, The Letters of John Clare, p.292.

153 *I awoke*: to John Taylor, 7 March 1831, The Letters of John Clare, p.537.

153 *As to religion*: ibid., to James Hessey, after 15 September 1830, p.515.

154 *My creed*: *The Prose of John Clare*, p.220.

157 *Sweet gem*: *Selected Poems*, Bate, p.40.

157 *wake my fears*: ibid.

157 *God help thee*: ibid.

157 *the frowns*: ibid.

157 *itch at rhymes*: ibid., p.41.

157 *Lord help thee*: ibid.

158 *May thou*: ibid.

158 *I would advise*: to Charles Clare, 26 February 1848, *The Letters of John Clare*, pp.655–6.

158 *Lord knows*: *Selected Poems*, Bate, p.41.

160 *a lamp shining*: *The Prose of John Clare* p.248.

160 *the man came out*: ibid.

160 *having no fear*: ibid.

161 *Many are poets*: *The Major Works*, p.279. There is some debate about the ordering of stanzas and songs that Clare may have intended for any 'definitive' version of 'Child Harold'. I use the version as published in Robinson and Powell's edition of *The Major Works*.

162 *Summer morning*: ibid.

162 'Prison Amusements': *Selected Poetry*, Summerfield, p.372.

162 *Mary thou ace*: *The Major Works*, p.281.

163 *chain of contradictions*: ibid., p.283.

163 *angel Mary*: ibid.

163 *My life hath been*: ibid.

163 *I sigh for one*: ibid., p.284.

163 *I have had many*: ibid., p.285.

163 *Sweet Susan*: ibid.

164 *Night finds me*: ibid., p.286.

164 *England my country*, ibid., p.287.

164 *Icelands snows*: ibid., p.288.

164 *solitude in citys*: ibid., p.304.

164 *Quicksands And Gulphs*: ibid., p.308.

164 *Lapland Snows*: ibid., p.313.

164 *fire and iceberg*: ibid., p.315.

164 *the giddy mast*: ibid., p.314.

165 *Where solitude*: ibid., pp.317–8.

166 *My home*: *Selected Poems*, Bate, pp.292–3.

167 *within a mile*: *By Himself*, p.262 and note p.338.

168 *England my country*: *The Major Works*. p.287.

169 'gypsy-like': *A Right to Song: The Life of John Clare*, Edward Storey, p.40.

170 . . . – *a picture*: *Selected Poems*, Bate, p.237.

170 *the Smiths gang*: *By Himself*, p.82.

170 *the Boswell Crew*: *The Prose of John Clare* , p.35.

170 *I usd to spend*: ibid., p.35-6.

170 *a young fellow*: ibid., p.36.

170 'This atrosious tribe': *By Himself* , p.83.

170 *I usd to dislike*: *The Prose of John Clare* , p.36.

171 *fell in*: ibid. , p.244.

171 the basic map of the journey: *By Himself*, p.260.

171 *the shutters*: *The Prose of John Clare* , p.247.

173 *chimney sweeps*: *Selected Poems*, Bate, p.290.

173 *the sooty crew*: ibid.

173 *I love*: ibid.

173 *How peaceable*: ibid.

174 *I had no money*: *The Prose of John Clare* , p.247.

175 'Straying maps the path': *Ten Poems to Change Your Life*, Roger Housden, p.101.

176 *could not help*: *The Prose of John Clare* , p.248.

176 *The man whose daughter*: *By Himself*; Clare's note on p.338.

177 *a young woman*: *The Prose of John Clare* , p.246.

177 *She cautioned me*: ibid.
177 *old wide-awake hat*: ibid., p.244.
178 *she pointed*: ibid., p.246.
178 *be able to find*: ibid..

Third Day 1841

181 *I blest*: ibid. , p.248.
183 *I saw a tall Gipsey*: ibid., p.246.
184 *I then entered*: ibid., p.248.
185 *The Coach did pass me*: *By Himself*; Clare's note, p.339.
186 *on the third day*: *The Prose of John Clare* , p.248.
187 *one night I lay*: *By Himself*, p.263.

Fourth Day

191 *The pleasant leaves*: *The Major Works*, p.278.
191 *called . . .'Ladies of the Lake'*: ibid.
191 *white and yellow*: ibid.
192 He that has: *King Lear*, William Shakespeare, Act 3 Scene
    2 Lines 74–7; Arden Edition, 1974, p.104..
194 *I then got up*: *The Prose of John Clare* , p.248.
195 *a length of road*: ibid., p.249.
195 *As my doubts*: ibid., p.248.
195 *caught a cold*: ibid., p.151.
195 'Death's untimely frost': Robert *Burns: The Classic Poems*,
    George Davidson (ed.), Arcturus Publishing, 2010, p.73.
197 *before I got*: *The Prose of John Clare*, p.249.
198 *they clubbed together*: ibid.

198 *two half pints*: ibid.

199 *'Poets are born'*: *The Major Works*, p.318.

199 'The Sale of Old Wigs and Sundries': *Selected Poetry*, Summerfield, p.370.

200 *So reader now*: *The Major Works*, p.326.

200 *Milton sung Eden*: ibid., p.318.

200 'the idealisation of the woman': *The Haunting of Sylvia Plath*, Jacqueline Rose, p.151.

201 *driveling hoax*: *The Major Works*, p.319.

201 *that patched broken*: ibid., p.325.

201 *state prisons*: ibid., p.324.

201 *I really cant*: ibid., p.320.

201 *Lord Byron poh*: ibid., p.325.

202 *Eliza now*: ibid., p.322.

202 *A hell incarnate*: ibid., p.319.

202 'spoke of his loneliness': *John Clare: A Biography*, Bate, pp.438–9.

202 *Docter Bottle*: *The Major Works*. p.324.

203 *Where men*: ibid.

203 *I have two wives*: ibid., p.326.

203 *I wish*: ibid., pp.319–21.

203 *But I cannot*: *The Prose of John Clare*, p.239.

204 *Bessey, when memory*: *Selected Poems*, Bate, p.5.

204 'Platonic quest': *John Clare: A Biography*, Bate, p.505.

204 'O she said . . .': ibid., p.473.

204 *I am growing*: to Eliza Emmerson, March–April 1830, *The Letters of John Clare* p.504.

205 *If both are honest*: *The Major Works*, p.326

205 *It would be dishonest*: *The Prose of John Clare* , p.239.

207 *compleatly foot-foundered*: ibid. , p.249.

207 *a gravel causeway*: ibid.

207 'poor creature': ibid.

207 another of the broken-down: ibid., p.245.

208 I looked & asked: Northborough Sonnets, Eric Robinson, David Powell and P. M. S. Dawson (eds.), p.87.

209 Guardian spirit: The Prose of John Clare , p.231.

209 a lovely creature: ibid.

209 my guardian genius: ibid., p.233.

209 when I had not: ibid., p.231.

209 an immense crowd: ibid.

209 soldiers on horseback: ibid.

209 ladies in splendid: ibid.

209 you are the only: ibid.

209 a booksellers shop: ibid., p.232.

209 on a shelf: ibid.

209 she smiled: ibid.

209 a woman deity: ibid.

209 the lady divinity: ibid., p.233.

210 'The big strip tease': Ariel, Sylvia Plath, p.17.

211 Loaded wi'mockery: The Shepherd's Calendar, p.49.

211 'discipline of the eyes': Gerard Manley Hopkins: A Very Private Life, Robert Bernard Martin, p.58.

211 'The person undertaking': ibid., p.196.

212 most of us Boys & Girls together: to Charles Clare, 1 June 1849, The Letters of John Clare, p.663.

222 'the audacity of claiming': What is Found There: Notebooks on Poetry and Politics, Adrienne Rich, p.172.

222 'an old Latin tag': The English Path, Kim Taplin, p.103.

223 The Coach: By Himself, Clare's note, p.339.

224 It would be: to ?Richard Newcomb, early 1819, The Letters of John Clare, p.4.

224 Thou tiney loiterer: The Major Works, p.189.

227 *as soon as*: *By Himself*, p.264.

230 'Where have all': Hanif Kureishi, *Intimacy*, pp.106–7.

231 'work of love': Adrienne Rich, *Of Woman Born: Motherhood as Experience and Institution*, p.216.

231 'In learning': ibid., p.215.

232 *at a small*: *By Himself*, p.264.

233 *an immense crowd*: *The Prose of John Clare* , p.231-2.

237 'bright, grass-coloured coat': *Green Shadows*, Wilson, p.123.

237 *my two favourite*: to John Taylor, 7 March 1821, *The Letters of John Clare*, p.161.

238 *The bawks*: – *The Major Works*, pp.21–2.

239 *The bees fly*: *Poems Selected*, Farley, pp.86–7.

240 *homeless at home*: *The Prose of John Clare* , p.250.

241 *a cart met me*: *By Himself*, p.264. .

245 'On the manuscript': *John Clare: A Biography*, Bate, p.366.

245 'he had a right': Carolyn G. Heilbrun, *Writing a Woman's Life*, p.12.

245 'usurped her narrative': ibid.

245 'the daughter': *A Right to Song: The Life of John Clare*, Storey, p.53.

245 'infirm of body': 'Life Stories: The Coroner's Report on the Death of Mary Joyce', Sarah Houghton-Walker, *John Clare Society Journal Number 37, June 2018*, p.69.

249 *The cloud that* passes: *The Major Works*, pp.290–1.

249 'all my little': from 'Texts for Nothing' in *No's Knife: Collected Shorter Prose 1945–1966*, Samuel Beckett, p.74.

250 'then our Lord': *Revelations of Divine Love*, Julian of Norwich (translated by Elizabeth Spearing), pp.33–4.

251 *The wild duck*: *Northborough Sonnets*, Eric Robinson, David Powell and P. M. S. Dawson (eds.), p.69.

251 'could well have been': *A Right to Song*, Storey, p.250.

251 'an Acre of Orchard and Garden': *John Clare: A Biography*, Bate, p.361.

251 *there is no spot*: to ?Marianne Marsh, early 1832, *The Letters of John Clare*, Storey, p.576.

252 *I had imagind*: By Himself, p.40.

252 *I got out*: ibid.

252 *Ive left my own*: – The Major Works, p.250.

252 *The sun e'en seems*: ibid., p.251.

252 *Strange scenes*: ibid., p.252.

255 *The weary rooks*: Northborough Sonnets, Eric Robinson, David Powell and P. M. S. Dawson (eds.), p.69.

255 *I wandered out*: ibid., p.84.

255 *When somthing bolted*: ibid.

255 *my heart jumpt*: ibid.

255 *lined with moss*: ibid.

255 *I sluthered*: ibid.

255 *highest glee*: ibid.

257 'asked that the house': *A Right to Song*, Storey, p.229.

258 'Only slowly': Eavan Boland, *Object Lessons: The Life of the Woman and the Poet in Our Time*, p.220.

258 *my Childern*: to Henry Behnes, 30 December 1827, *The Letters of John Clare*, p.410.

258 *homeless at home*: The Prose of John Clare , p.250.

260 *My dear wife*: By Himself , p.265.

261 *Who am I*: Tim Chilcott (ed.), *John Clare: The Living Year 1841*, p.59.

261 *I was in prison*: ibid., p.93.

261 *surely every man*: The Prose of John Clare , p.239.

261 *fish leaping up*: The Living Year 1841, Chilcott, p.162.

261 *the people*: to Matthew Allen, after 27 August 1841, *The Letters of John Clare*, p.650.

261 *having neither*: ibid., pp.650–1.

262 'the want of restraint': *John Clare: A Biography*, Bate, p.465.

262 'thought him so much better': ibid., p.459.

262 'nature and causes': ibid., p.466.

262 'Widow Clare': *A Right to Song*, Storey, p.284.

263 'writing occasional love poems': *John Clare: A Biography*, Bate, p.474.

263 'over eight hundred': *The Major Works*, p.494; notes for pp.338–427.

263 *I am – yet what I am*: *Selected Poems*, Bate, p.282.

263 *I am the self-consumer*: ibid.

263 *in love-frenzied*: ibid.

263 *nothingness . . . waking dreams*: ibid.

263 *Where there is neither*: ibid.

264 *Even the dearest*: ibid.

264 *I long for scenes*: ibid.

264 *the Land of Sodom*: to Patty Clare, 19 July 1848, *The Letters of John Clare*, p.657.

265 *Dear Sir*: ibid., to James Hipkins, 8 March 1860, p.683.

265 'Why they have': *John Clare: A Biography*, Bate, p.524.

265 'a photo of him': ibid., illustration 31.

266 'It's all the same': ibid., pp.474–5.

267 'Still. Bless me': *Angels in America*, Part 2: Act 5, Scene 5, by Tony Kushner, p.266.

267 *you must go on*: Samuel Beckett, *Molloy, Malone Dies, The Unnamable*, p.418.

Fourth Day 1841

269 *I don't reccolect*: *The Prose of John Clare* , p.249.
271 *a young woman*: ibid., pp.249.
273 *a man & woman*: ibid.
274 *I could scarcely*: *By Himself*, p.264.
275 *when nearing me*: ibid.
276 *Mary was not there*: *The Prose of John Clare* , p.250.
277 *July 24 1841*: ibid., p.244.

Afterword

282 '29 million deaths': 'Here was a plague', Tom Crewe, *London Review of Books*, Volume 40, Number 18, 27 September 2018, p.16.
282 'now and England': *Collected Poems 1909–1962* (from 'Little Gidding'), T. S. Eliot, p.222.
282 'little company' from 'Texts for Nothing' in *No's Knife: Collected Shorter Prose 1945-1966*, Samuel Beckett, p.74.
283 'an epitaph he wrote': *By Himself*, p.246.

Afterword 1861

285 'Within a few years': *A Right to Song*, Storey, p.284.

Bibliography

By John Clare

Clare, John, *The Prose of John Clare*, edited by J. W. and Anne Tibble (Routledge and Kegan Paul Ltd, London), 1951

——, *The Shepherd's Calendar*, edited by Eric Robinson and Geoffrey Summerfield (Oxford University Press, London), 1973

——, *Selected Poems and Prose*, edited by Eric Robinson and Geoffrey Summerfield (Oxford University Press, Oxford), 1978

——, *John Clare's Birds*, edited by Eric Robinson and Richard Fitter (Oxford University Press, Oxford), 1982

——, *The Rural Muse*, edited by R. K. R. Thornton (The Mid Northumberland Arts Group, Ashington and Carcanet Press, Manchester), 1982

——, *John Clare's Autobiographical Writings*, edited by Eric Robinson (Oxford University Press, Oxford), 1983

——, *A Critical Edition of the Major Works*, edited by Eric Robinson and David Powell (Oxford University Press, Oxford), 1984

——, *The Letters of John Clare*, edited by Mark Storey (Oxford University Press, Oxford), 1985

——, *Selected Poetry and Prose*, edited by Merryn and Raymond Williams (Methuen, London), 1986

——, *Selected Poetry*, edited with an Introduction and Notes by Geoffrey Summerfield (Penguin Books, London), 1990

——, *Northborough Sonnets*, edited by Eric Robinson, David Powell and P. M. S. Dawson (The Mid Northumberland Arts Group, Ashington and Carcanet Press, Manchester), 1995

——, *The Works of John Clare*, with an introduction by John Goodridge (Wordsworth Editions, Hertfordshire), 1995

——, *By Himself*, edited by Eric Robinson and David Powell (The Mid Northumberland Arts Group and Carcanet Press, Northumberland and Manchester), 1996

——, *The Living Year 1841*, edited by Tim Chilcott (Trent Editions, Nottingham), 1999

——, *Selected Poems*, edited by Jonathan Bate (Faber and Faber, London), 2004

——, *Poems Selected by Paul Farley* (Faber and Faber, London), 2007

About Clare

Allnatt, Judith, *The Poet's Wife* (Transworld Publishers, London), 2011

Al-Wasiti, Salman, *A Reconstruction of Clare's 'Child Harold'*, from *The John Clare Society Journal*, Number 20, July 2001

Ashbery, John, *Other Traditions: The Charles Eliot Norton Lectures* (Harvard University Press, London), 2001

Bate, Jonathan, *John Clare: A Biography* (Picador, London), 2003

——, *The Rights of Nature*, from *The John Clare Society Journal*, Number 14, July 1995

Blythe, Ronald, *At Helpston – Meetings with John Clare* (Black Dog Books, Norfolk), 2011

Bond, Edward, *The Fool: Scenes of Bread and Love* (Eyre Methuen, London), 1976

Drabble, Margaret, *A Writer's Britain* (Thames and Hudson, London), 2009

Foulds, Adam, *The Quickening Maze* (Jonathan Cape, London), 2009

Gallas, John, *Mad John's Walk* (Five Leaves Bookshop, Nottingham), 2017

Goodridge, John (ed.), *The Independent Spirit: John Clare and the Self-Taught Tradition* (The John Clare Society and the Margaret Grainger Memorial Trust, Tyne and Wear), 1994

Goodridge, John and R. K. R. Thornton, *John Clare, the Trespasser* (Five Leaves Publications, Nottingham), 2016

Goodridge, John and Kövesi, Simon (eds.), *John Clare: New Approaches* (The John Clare Society, Helpston), 2000

Gorji, Mina, *John Clare and the Place of Poetry* (Liverpool University Press, Liverpool), 2008

Hall, Ellis and Somekh, Bridget, – *Love's Cold Returning: John Clare's 1841 Odyssey from Essex to Northamptonshire* (Thirteen Eighty One Press, Cambridge), 2019.

Haughton, Hugh, Phillips, Adam and Summerfield, Geoffrey (eds.), – *John Clare in Context* (Cambridge University Press, Cambridge), 1994.

Heaney, Seamus, *The Redress of Poetry* (Faber and Faber, London), 1995

Houghton-Walker, Sarah, *Life Stories: The Coroner's Report on the Death of Mary Joyce*, from *The John Clare Society Journal*, Oxford, Number 37, June 2018

Kötting, Andrew, *By Our Selves* (film) (Soda Pictures), 2015
—— (ed.), *By Our Selves* (book) (Badbloodandsibyl), 2015
Kövesi, Simon and McEathron, Scott (eds.), *New Essays on John Clare: Poetry, Culture and Community* (Cambridge University Press, Cambridge), 2015
Kövesi, Simon and Lafford, Erin (eds.), *Palgrave Advances in John Clare Studies* (Palgrave Macmillan, Springer Nature, Switzerland), 2020
Kövesi, Simon, *John Clare: Nature, Criticism and History* (Palgrave Macmillan, London), 2017
Lupton, Hugh, *The Ballad of John Clare* (Dedalus Limited, Sawtry, Cambs), 2010
Lynes, Jeanette, *Bedlam Cowslip: The John Clare Poems* (Buckrider Books, Ontario, Canada), 2015
MacKenna, John, *Clare: A Novel* (Blackstaff Press, Belfast), 1993
Morley, David, *The Gypsy and the Poet* (Carcanet Press, Manchester), 2013
Paulin, Tom, 'John Clare: A Bicentennial Celebration', from *John Clare: A Bicentenary Celebration*, Richard Foulkes (ed.) (Department of Adult Education, University of Leicester, Northampton), 1994
——, *Crusoe's Secret: The Aesthetics of Dissent* (Faber and Faber, London), 2005
Pearce, Lynne, 'John Clare's Child Harold: The Road Not Taken', from *Feminist Criticism: Theory and Practice*, ed. Susan Sellers (Harvester Wheatsheaf, Herts), 1991
Phillips, Adam, *On Flirtation* (Faber and Faber, London), 1994
Rae, Simon, *Grass* (Top Edge Press, Oxon), 2003
Relph, Pete, *Four Forest Years* (P. R. Books, Loughton, Essex), 2006
Rowe, Roger, *The Descending Spiral: John Clare*, The Arbour

Chapbook Series Number 9 (Arbour Editions, Ottery St Mary), 2020

Schmidt, Michael, *Lives of the Poets* (Orion Books, London), 1999

Sinclair, Iain, *Edge of the Orison: In the Traces of John Clare's Journey out of Essex* (Hamish Hamilton, London), 2005

Storey, Edward, *A Right to Song: The Life of John Clare* (Methuen, London), 1982

Taplin, Kim, *The English Path* (The Boydell Press, Ipswich), 1979

Wilson, June, *Green Shadows: The Life of John Clare* (Hodder and Stoughton, London), 1951

Others:

Arenas, Reinaldo, *Before Night Falls* (Serpent's Tail, London), 2001

Athill, Diana, *Somewhere Towards the End* (Granta Publications, London), 2008

Baldwin, James, *The Fire Next Time* (Penguin Books, Middlesex), 1964

Beckett, Samuel, *Molloy: Malone Dies: The Unnamable* (Calder and Boyars, London), 1966

——, *No's Knife: Collected Shorter Prose 1945–1966* (Calder and Boyars, London), 1967

Best, Clare, *The Missing List* (Linen Press, London), 2018

Boland, Eavan, *Object Lessons: The Life of the Woman and the Poet in Our Time* (Carcanet Press, Manchester), 1995

Burns, Robert, *The Classic Poems*, edited by George Davidson (Arcturus Publishing, London), 2010

Burnside, John, *A Lie About My Father* (Vintage, London), 2007

——, *I Put a Spell On You: Several Digressions on Love and Glamour* (Jonathan Cape, London), 2014

Byron, Catherine, *Out of Step: Pursuing Seamus Heaney to Purgatory* (Loxwood Stoneleigh, Bristol), 1992

Cole, Henri, *Orphic Paris* (New York Review of Books, New York), 2018

Crumley, Jim, *The Company of Swans* (Harvill Press, London), 1997

Cusk, Rachel, *Aftermath: On Marriage and Separation* (Faber and Faber, London), 2012

Didion, Joan, *The Year of Magical Thinking* (Harper Perennial, London), 2006

——, *Blue Nights* (Alfred A. Knopf, New York), 2011

Doty, Mark, *Heaven's Coast: A Memoir* (Jonathan Cape, London), 1996

——, *Firebird: A Memoir* (Jonathan Cape, London), 2000

——, *Dog Years: A Memoir* (HarperCollins, New York), 2007

Dyer, Geoff, *Out of Sheer Rage: In the Shadow of D. H. Lawrence* (Canongate Books), Edinburgh, 2012

Eliot, T. S., *Collected Poems 1909–1962* (Faber and Faber, London), 1963

Fitzmaurice, Ruth, *I Found My Tribe* (Vintage, Random House, London), 2017

French, Sean (ed.), *Fatherhood* (Virago Press, London), 1993

Gibran, Kahlil, *The Prophet* (Mandarin Paperbacks, London), 1991; originally published 1926

Gunn, Kirsty, *My Katherine Mansfield Project* (Notting Hill Editions, Honiton, Devon), 2015

Hall, Jill, *The Reluctant Adult: A Study of Choice* (Prism Press, Bridport, Dorset), 1993

Hearn, Jeff, *The Gender of Oppression: Men, Masculinity, and the Critique of Marxism* (Wheatsheaf Books, Brighton, Sussex), 1987

Heilbrun, Carolyn G., *Writing a Woman's Life* (The Women's Press, London), 1989

Herzog, Werner, *Of Walking in Ice: Munich–Paris, 23 November–14 December, 1974* (Vintage, London), 2014

Hopkins, Gerard Manley, *Poems and Prose of Gerard Manley Hopkins*, selected with an introduction and notes by W. H. Gardner (Penguin Books, London), 1985

Hornby, Nick, *Fever Pitch* (Indigo, London), 1996

Housden, Roger, *Ten Poems to Change Your Life* (Hodder and Stoughton, London), 2003

Julian of Norwich, *Revelations of Divine Love*, translated by Elizabeth Spearing (Penguin Books, London), 1998

Kay, Jackie, *Red Dust Road* (Picador, London), 2010

Kerouac, Jack, *On the Road* (Penguin Books, Middlesex), 1972

Kushner, Tony, *Angels in America* (Theatre Communications Group, New York), 2003.

Kureishi, Hanif, *Intimacy* (Faber and Faber, London), 1998.

——, *My Ear at His Heart: Reading My Father* (Faber and Faber, London), 2004

Laing, Olivia, *To the River* (Canongate Books, Edinburgh), 2012

Lawrence, D. H., *Selected Letters*, selected by Richard Aldington (Penguin Books, Middlesex), 1950

Levy, Deborah, *Things I Don't Want to Know* (Penguin Random House, London), 2014

——, *The Cost of Living* (Penguin Random House, London), 2018

Liptrot, Amy, *The Outrun* (Canongate Books, Edinburgh), 2016

Litvinoff, Emanuel, *Journey Through a Small Planet* (Penguin Books, Middlesex), 1976

Lorde, Audre, *Your Silence Will Not Protect You* (Silver Press, UK), 2017

Louis, Édouard – *Who Killed My Father* (Harvill Secker, London), 2019.

Macdonald, Helen, *H is for Hawk* (Jonathan Cape, London), 2014

Mansfield, Katherine, *The Letters and Journals of Katherine Mansfield: A Selection*, edited by C. K. Stead (Penguin Books, Middlesex), 1977

Maran, Meredith (ed.), *Why We Write About Ourselves* (Penguin Random House, New York), 2016

Martin, Bernard, *Gerard Manley Hopkins: A Very Private Life* (Harper Collins, London), 1992

Maupin, Armistead, *Logical Family: A Memoir* (Transworld Publishers, London), 2018

Miller, Sue, *The Story of My Father* (Bloomsbury, London), 2003

Montefiore, Jan, *Feminism and Poetry: Language, Experience, Identity in Women's Writing* (Pandora, London), 1987

Morris, Jan, *Conundrum* (Penguin Books, Middlesex), 1987

Morrison, Blake, *And When Did You Last See Your Father?* (Granta Books, London), 1993

Morrison, Toni, *Playing In The Dark: Whiteness and the Literary Imagination.* (Vintage Books, New York), 1993.

Nelson, Maggie, *The Argonauts* (Melville House UK, London), 2016

Olsen, Tillie, *Silences* (Virago Press, London), 1980

Owen, Ursula (ed.), *Fathers: Reflections by Daughters* (Virago Press, London), 1983

Plath, Sylvia, *Ariel* (Faber and Faber, London), 1965

Rich, Adrienne, *Of Woman Born: Motherhood as Experience and Institution* (Virago, London), 1976

——, *On Lies, Secrets and Silence (Selected Prose 1966–1978)* (Virago Limited, London), 1980

——, *Blood, Bread and Poetry (Selected Prose 1979–1985)* (Virago Limited, London), 1987

——, *What is Found There: Notebooks on Poetry and Politics* (W. W. Norton, London), 1993

——, *Your Native Land, Your Life* (W. W. Norton, London), 1986

Rose, Jacqueline, *The Haunting of Sylvia Plath* (Virago Press, London), 1992

Sarton, May, *Journal of a Solitude* (W. W. Norton, London), 1977

Sebald, W. G., *The Rings of Saturn* (Vintage, London), 2002

Shakespeare, William, *King Lear*, edited by Kenneth Muir (The Arden Edition, Methuen, London), 1972

Shepherd, Nan, *The Living Mountain: A Celebration of the Cairngorm Mountains of Scotland* (Canongate Books, Edinburgh), 2011

Smith, Patti, *Just Kids* (Bloomsbury Publishing), London, 2010

——, *M Train* (Bloomsbury Publishing, London), 2015

Solnit, Rebecca, *The Faraway Nearby* (Granta Publications, London), 2013

——, *Wanderlust: A History of Walking* (Granta Publications, London), 2014

Steinberg, David, *Fatherjournal: Five Years of Awakening to Fatherhood* (Times Change Press, Albion California), 1977

Strayed, Cheryl, *Wild: A Journey from Lost to Found* (Atlantic Books, London), 2012

Walker, Alice, *In Search of Our Mothers' Gardens: Womanist Prose* (The Women's Press, London), 1984

——, *Living by the Word: Selected Writings 1973–1987* (The Women's Press, London), 1988

Wicks, Susan, *Driving My Father* (Faber and Faber, London), 1995

Winterson, Jeanette, *Art Objects: Essays on Ecstasy and Effrontery* (Vintage, London), 1996

——, *Why Be Happy When You Could Be Normal?* (Jonathan Cape, London), 2011

Woolf, Virginia, *Street Haunting and Other Essays* (Vintage Books, London), 2014

ⓂRIGINALS

NEW WRITING FROM
BRITAIN'S OLDEST PUBLISHER

2020
Toto Among the Murderers | Sally J Morgan
An atmospheric debut novel set in 1970s Leeds and Sheffield
when attacks on women punctuated the news.

'An exhilarating novel'   Susan Barker

Self-Portrait in Black and White | Thomas Chatterton Williams
An interrogation of race and identity from one of America's
most brilliant cultural critics.

'An extraordinarily thought-provoking memoir'
                                                 Sunday Times

2019
Asghar and Zahra | Sameer Rahim
A tragicomic account of a doomed marriage.

'Funny and wise, and beautifully written'
                                    Colm Tóibín, *New Statesman*

Nobber | Oisín Fagan
A wildly inventive and audacious fourteenth-century Irish Plague novel.

'Vigorously, writhingly itself'   *Observer*, Books of the Year

2018
A Kind of Freedom | Margaret Wilkerson Sexton
A fascinating exploration of the long-lasting and enduring divisive legacy of slavery.

'A writer of uncommon nerve and talent'   *New York Times*

Jott | Sam Thompson
A story about friendship, madness and modernism.

'A complex, nuanced literary novel of extraordinary perception'   *Herald*

Game Theory | Thomas Jones
A comedy about friendship, sex and parenting, and about the games people play.

'Well observed and ruthlessly truthful'   *Daily Mail*

2017
Elmet | Fiona Mozley
An atmospheric Gothic fable about a family living on land that isn't theirs.

'A quiet explosion of a book, exquisite and unforgettable'
The Economist